THE MANY FACES OF CHRIST

THE MANY FACES OF CHRIST

*The Thousand-Year Story of the
Survival and Influence of the Lost Gospels*

Philip Jenkins

BASIC BOOKS

A Member of the Perseus Books Group

New York

Designed by Pauline Brown
Typeset in 11.5 point Adobe Caslon Pro

Library of Congress Cataloging-in-Publication Data

Jenkins, Philip, 1952– author.
    The many faces of Christ : the thousand-year story of the survival and influence of the lost gospels / Philip Jenkins.
        ages cm
    Includes bibliographical references and index.
    ISBN 978-0-465-06692-6 (hardback)—ISBN 978-0-465-06161-7 (e-book) 1. Apocryphal Gospels. 2. Christianity—Origin. I. Title.
    BS2851.J464 2015
    229'.8—dc23

                                                                2015028753

10 9 8 7 6 5 4 3 2 1

To Byron Johnson
With thanks and appreciation

CONTENTS

NOTE ON TERMINOLOGY

Historians vary in their presentation of dates. The traditional system of BC/AD has a Christian bias, as it explicitly refers not just to Christ but "the Lord," and many writers prefer the term "Common Era," CE, instead of AD. Yet the basis for Common Era dating is still the supposed date for Christ's birth. As it is still the most familiar usage, this book will use BC and AD.

Also problematic is the term "Old Testament," the Christian term for what Jews call simply the Bible or the Tanakh. Although a neutral term should properly be used, none is easily available. "Hebrew Bible" is unsatisfactory because of the importance of some Greek versions of particular books. In this work, there are special reasons for using the "Old Testament" label, because I will often refer to alternative scriptures attributed to patriarchs and prophets such as Enoch and Ezra. Most modern scholars classify such works under the title "Old Testament pseudepigrapha." With due awareness of the issues, then, I use "Old Testament" throughout.

There is one other unwieldy term for which it is difficult to find an alternative. Throughout Christian history, there have been multiple churches, some of which rejected the Christian credentials of others. I often mention the mainstream institution of the ancient and medieval world that was allied with the Roman Empire and had its great centers at Rome and Constantinople. When I refer to that church before the later split between the Eastern and Western traditions, I call it "Orthodox/Catholic."

1

Gospel Truths

The Myth of the Lost Gospels

What all disciples of heresy and of the heretics and schismatics, whose names we have scarcely preserved, have taught or compiled, we acknowledge is to be not merely rejected but eliminated from the whole Roman Catholic and Apostolic Church, and with their authors, and the followers of its authors, to be damned in the inextricable shackles of anathema forever.

Gelasian Decree, sixth century

AROUND THE YEAR 380 IN THE DESERT OF SOUTHERN EGYPT, a small party carried a collection of precious contraband to a secret hiding place. The group took at least thirteen large books, or codices, and packed them in clay jars for safekeeping before burying them. The contents included dozens of scriptures, gospels, and other sacred writings. After this collection was rediscovered in 1945, the so-called Nag Hammadi library would have an immense impact on popular conceptions of early Christian history. For a world used to speaking of "gospel truth," what could be more enthralling than the rediscovery of ancient lost gospels?[1]

But why were these texts concealed in the first place? Presumably, the works deviated so sharply from what was then defined as

Christian orthodoxy that they had to be saved from destruction by angry fanatics. They were concealed until it was once again safe to explore such ideas. Just possibly, the people burying the documents were themselves members of a mystical or Gnostic sect that was now deemed heretical, the last pathetic adherents of a dying creed. More likely, they were Christian monks forced to come to terms with new restraints on what they could legitimately read and own. Whatever the reality, the fact that the texts remained hidden for 1,600 years means that the people who concealed them never felt that such a time of safety and tolerance arrived in their lifetimes.[2]

INTERPRETATIONS OF FAITH were in flux in the centuries immediately following Jesus's lifetime, with different schools drawing on their own scriptures. Christians used and produced a great many texts that were loosely called gospels—hundreds at least. Modern-day readers are fascinated by these alternative scriptures with their intoxicating and often bizarre ideas. They love to explore what a historian of esoteric thought once termed "Fragments of a Faith Forgotten."[3]

For some writers, these might-have-been texts have become an alternative canon that reflects the early Christian message at least as authentically as the "real" New Testament that we have known for centuries. They propose that these writings represent various roads not taken by the Christian movement, usually with the suggestion that those paths would have resulted in much better historical outcomes for the faith. We think of Elaine Pagels's influential 1979 book, *The Gnostic Gospels*, and subsequent work by Karen King, Marvin Meyer, and others. To borrow the title of a book by Bart Ehrman, these lost gospels provided a foundation for various "Lost Christianities." Millions who have no acquaintance with scholarly Christian history still know something about the concept from Dan Brown's novel *The Da Vinci Code*.[4]

Box 1.1   Some "Lost" Gospels

I present these texts in their very rough order of composition. Dating is difficult, especially as the individual texts have gone through multiple stages of composition and editing.

Gospel of the Hebrews (early second century?). **Known from citations in ancient writers; full text still not available.**

Not a Gnostic text, this gospel reflects the views of Jewish Christians who believed in observing the Mosaic Law. Other works in this tradition include the gospels of the Nazoreans and of the Ebionites.

Gospel of Thomas (c. 140?). **Full text found at Nag Hammadi.**

Presents Jesus as a mystical teacher who utters wise and perplexing sayings. The gospel offers no hint of the doctrines of the Crucifixion and Resurrection, or a Virgin Birth. For its advocates, Thomas may represent the closest approximation we are likely to find to Jesus's actual words and teachings.

Gospel of Truth (c. 160). **Found at Nag Hammadi.**

Description of the Gnostic mythological scheme. Despite its "gospel" name, the work contains nothing about Christ's earthly life or career. Probably by the Egyptian Gnostic Valentinus.

Gospel of Peter (mid-second century). **Found in Egypt in 1886.**

Narrative of Christ's life, allegedly in the words of Peter the apostle. Noted for its very different account of the Crucifixion and Resurrection, including words spoken by the cross itself.

Gnostic Apocalypse of Peter (second century). **Found at Nag Hammadi.**

An account of Christ's sayings and teachings during the time of his arrest and Crucifixion. However, the crucified figure is only a material Christ, not the true and living Jesus, who laughs through the whole process.

CONTINUES

Gospel of Mary (second or third century). Found in Egypt in 1896.
The Risen Jesus delivers a lengthy discourse on such issues as sin and the nature of matter. The work shows Jesus demonstrating a special preference for Mary—probably Mary Magdalene—over his male disciples.

Gospel of Judas (late second century). Probably found in Egypt in the 1970s.
Presents Judas Iscariot as one of the few who understood Jesus's secret inner teachings, which were missed by the other apostles. The role of Judas is the subject of lively controversy. Some scholars believe Judas followed Christ's order to betray him, while others think he played a demonic role.

Gospel of Philip (third century?). Found at Nag Hammadi.
A lengthy Gnostic theological meditation or collection of teachings, much of which refers to the idea of mystical marriage. The work is best known for its suggestion that Mary Magdalene was Christ's "companion" (or spouse) and that he kissed her on the mouth.

Pistis Sophia (third or early fourth century). Found in Egypt in 1773.
Elaborate mystical teachings delivered by Christ after his Resurrection to a group of disciples including his mother, Mary; Mary Magdalene; and Martha. Sophia, or Wisdom, is a divine feminine figure in the Gnostic mythological scheme.

Box 1.1 lists some of the best known of these "lost" texts and the ways in which they differed from the approved canonical works. But what happened to these early scriptures and the faith—or faiths—that they represented? If they existed in the early church but not in the Middle Ages, then presumably there must have been a moment of transition, of spiritual silencing and closure. Many see this occurring in the fourth century, when the church gained the political power to enforce its opinions. Under the Emperor Constantine in 313, the church made its historic alliance with the Roman Empire, and in 325, Constantine summoned the great Council of Nicea, which defined Christian orthodoxy for centuries to come. In 380, the empire established Christianity as its official religion.[5]

Since the 1970s, the fact of the lost gospels vanishing in Late Antiquity has become a basic component of an alternative history of Christianity. From that era onward, we are told, all Christians were required to believe in the complex doctrines of the Incarnation and the Trinity, and the church strictly mandated which scriptures were to be regarded as authoritative. In this vision, the earliest centuries of the faith (before Constantine) were marked by sprawling diversity and creativity, and many schools of thought contested freely. But the democratic, egalitarian, and Spirit-filled Jesus movement then atrophied into the repressive, bureaucratic Catholic Church of the Middle Ages. The narrow orthodoxies of a monolithic church replaced the effervescent "many Christianities" of the earliest centuries. How natural for such a body to require strict uniformity of scriptures: One Church, One Dogma, One Bible. The medieval church was built on the ashes of burnt books. Matters had once been very different: before the dark times, before the empire.

From the late fourth century, we hear, the church would officially recognize only four gospels—Matthew, Mark, Luke, and John— and certainly not such pretenders as, say, the Gospels of Thomas, Philip, Mary, or Judas. In the early sixth century, a church policy document credited to Pope Gelasius named some sixty books that the church should not accept, including nine gospels, four sets of apostolic Acts, and three revelations. This Gelasian Decree listed some thirty-five other authors and alleged heretics who between them would have been responsible for (at least) hundreds of miscellaneous texts, gospels, and pseudo-scriptures. Everything they had written must be utterly destroyed, lest it mislead and pervert future generations.[6]

The popular historical account suggests that Christian diversity now went underground, in more senses than one. Together with the lost scriptures were banished the ideas they preached. The alliance with imperial power was disastrous news for Jews as well as for the many free-thinking Christians who now attracted the lethally damning label of "heretic." The fact that the newly defined heretics so often venerated women leaders and explored radical ideas of sexuality meant that these ideas were shut out from the emerging

Catholic Church. According to this account, bigotry, intolerance, anti-Semitism, patriarchy, and authoritarianism progressed side by side.[7]

IMPLICIT IN THE STANDARD PICTURE of the "lost scriptures" is a questionable historical narrative, or rather a myth. In reality, the lost gospels were never lost. Rather, older scriptures were lost only in the sense that they dropped out of mainstream use for some churches, at some times, in certain parts of the world. Indeed, some texts did vanish for centuries, but it is wrong to suggest that all alternative scriptures ceased to exist. Nor did their ideas. Such an obliteration of texts would be a major task even with modern methods of repression and propaganda, and nothing comparable was available at the time.

Centuries after Constantine—indeed, right through early modern times—the Christian world retained a much broader range of scriptures than would be imaginable today. Literally dozens of gospels, revelations, Acts, and other scriptures remained in use, and that situation remained true for some 1,200 years. Concepts of the canon were still more expansive when we shift our focus from Europe to the churches that still thrived so mightily further afield, in Ethiopia, Egypt, and the Syriac-speaking Near East. Alternative scriptures continued to be popular across continents.[8]

Standard visions of medieval Christianity suggest an image of rigid orthodoxy, with a hierarchical and homogeneous institutional church ruthlessly enforcing its will. But far from being hermetically sealed, European Christendom was always part of a much wider world with many different structures and attitudes toward faith and scripture. Many Christians lacked the dubious benefits of living under a state intimately allied to church authority. Centralized church authority obviously did not extend to Christian populations within the vast Muslim world. The kind of intrusive church measures possible in, say, medieval France were out of the question for the flourishing Christian communities in Muslim-ruled Iraq or Egypt. For much of the Middle Ages and the early modern period, even large portions of southern and eastern Europe were under Islamic rule.

So strong is the evidence for the survival and continuity of the "lost scriptures" that it makes us realize just how improbable the familiar historical view actually is. This fact must radically alter our understanding of Christian history, of the definition of orthodoxy, and of the role of scriptural authority within the faith.

Box 1.2 HINTS AT THE DIVERSITY of the continuing traditions that persisted, offering a random selection of extracanonical stories and sayings involving Jesus drawn from outside approved Christian scriptures. All of these stories and sayings were used and read by a variety of groups in the millennium or so after 500, long after the era of the early church.

Box 1.2 Some Reported Words and Stories of Jesus

1. Jesus said, "I shall give you what you have not seen with the eye, have not heard with the ears, and have not touched with the hand."

GOSPEL OF THOMAS 17, C. 140

2. Jesus said, "It came to pass when I was about to come hither from the Father of all things, and passed through the heavens, then I put on the wisdom of the Father, and I put on the power of his might. I was in heaven, and I passed by the archangels and the angels in their likeness, as if I were one of them, among the princedoms and powers. I passed through them because I possessed the wisdom of him that had sent me. Now the chief captain of the angels, [is] Michael, and Gabriel and Uriel and Raphael followed me unto the fifth heaven, for they thought in their heart that I was one of them; such power was given me of my Father."

EPISTULA APOSTOLORUM / THE LETTER OF
THE APOSTLES, MID-SECOND CENTURY

CONTINUES

3. Then did the King of glory in his majesty trample upon death, and laid hold on Satan the prince and delivered him unto the power of Hell. . . . And the Lord stretched forth his hand and made the sign of the cross over Adam and over all his saints, and he took the right hand of Adam and went up out of hell, and all the saints followed him.

GOSPEL OF NICODEMUS, C. 400

4. Jesus said, "Rise, Peter, and take the body of Mary, and send it to the right hand side of the city towards the east, and thou wilt find there a new tomb, in which you will lay her, and wait until I come to you." And thus saying, the Lord delivered the soul of St. Mary to Michael, who was the ruler of paradise, and the prince of the nation of the Jews; and Gabriel went with them.

PSEUDO-MELITO, THE PASSING OF
BLESSED MARY, FIFTH CENTURY

5. As a toddler, Jesus made several clay pools, with water running through little passages and dams. Seeing this, another child broke the passages. Jesus cried, "Woe unto you, you son of death, you son of Satan! Do you destroy the works that I have wrought?" And immediately, the other boy was struck dead.

GOSPEL OF PSEUDO-MATTHEW,
SEVENTH CENTURY

6. Jesus said, "If people appoint you as their heads, be like tails."

ISLAMIC TRADITION, NINTH CENTURY

7. Jesus said, "The world is a bridge; cross this bridge but do not build upon it."

ISLAMIC TRADITION, NINTH CENTURY

8. The night before the Crucifixion, Pontius Pilate entertained Jesus at a friendly dinner. Wishing to save him at all costs, Pilate offered to give up his own son to death in Jesus's place. But Jesus declined, telling him, "If I wished, I would not come to this moment. Come, sit down and see that I am able to escape." Jesus then made himself invisible and incorporeal, causing Pilate to faint with astonishment. Laying his hand on him, Jesus brought him back to consciousness. He then said, "Have you understood that, if I wish, I can escape?" Pilate said, "Yes my Lord."

ON THE LIFE AND THE PASSION OF CHRIST,
ASCRIBED TO CYRIL OF JERUSALEM,
PROBABLY NINTH CENTURY

9. [Jesus] is corn-colored, his hair is black, coming down to his shoulders like bunches of grapes, his nose is prominent, he has beautiful eyes, his eyebrows are joined together, his cheeks are red like roses. He wears a grape colored tunic, he has two silver studded adornments on his side like a sword and a linen garment covers him so that he looks like a royal son.

ON THE LIFE AND THE PASSION OF CHRIST,
ASCRIBED TO CYRIL OF JERUSALEM,
PROBABLY NINTH CENTURY

10. And still I, John, questioned the Lord, saying, "Lord, how did man have spiritual origin in a carnal body?" And the Lord said to me: "By their fall, spirits of heaven entered the female body of clay and took on flesh from the lusts of the flesh and took on [spirit at the same time]. . . . Spirit is born of spirit and flesh of flesh; and thus the reign of Satan ceases not in this world."

INTERROGATIO JOHANNIS, ALSO KNOWN AS
THE SECRET SUPPER, C. 1100

11. Jesus said, "I, a man, dust and clay, that walk upon the earth, say to you: Do penance and know your sins. I say, brethren, that Satan, by means of the Roman soldiery, deceived you when you said that I was God."

GOSPEL OF BARNABAS,
FOURTEENTH CENTURY

Sources: Parthian fragment of Thomas found at Turfan in modern China, in Hans-Joachim Klimkeit, "Apocryphal Gospels in Central and East Asia," in Manfred Heuser and Hans-Joachim Klimkeit, eds., *Studies in Manichaean Literature and Art* (Leiden: Brill, 1998), 189–211; *Epistula Apostolorum*, or Letter of the Apostles, in Montague Rhodes James, *The Apocryphal New Testament* (Oxford: Clarendon Press, 1924), 489; Gospel of Nicodemus, in James, *Apocryphal New Testament*, 139; Pseudo-Melito, *The Passing of Blessed Mary*, The Tertullian Project, www.tertullian.org/fathers2/ANF-08/anf08-112.htm; Gospel of Pseudo-Matthew, New Advent, www.newadvent.org/fathers/0848.htm; Tarif Khalidi, ed., *The Muslim Jesus* (Cambridge, MA: Harvard University Press, 2001), 101, 106; Roelof van den Broek, *Pseudo-Cyril of Jerusalem on the Life and the Passion of Christ* (Leiden: Brill, 2013); *Interrogatio Johannis*, also known as the Secret Supper, The Gnosis Archive, http://gnosis.org/library/Interrogatio_Johannis.html; Gospel of Barnabas, chap. 128, Answering Christianity, www.answering-christianity.com/barnabas.htm.

These texts present a very wide range of images and theologies, some truly bizarre. They represent the full range of motifs and settings that we might have expected in early alternative gospels—from

isolated sayings of Jesus to post-Resurrection appearances and dialogues. In terms of date of composition, they cover a huge time span
from the second century onward, with the verse from the Gospel of
Thomas being the oldest.[9]

But all survived long after Constantine's era. References to
Thomas surfaced sporadically across the wider Christian world; the
verse quoted in Box 1.2 is from a Parthian fragment found at Turfan
in the far west of modern China, probably dating from the ninth
century. Some of these texts, like Thomas itself, continued to be
read in limited regions of the Christian world, whereas others, such
as Nicodemus, Pseudo-Matthew, and Pseudo-Melito, were favorites across transnational Christendom. Both the Secret Supper and
the Gospel of Barnabas were actually produced afresh during the
medieval centuries, though they were grounded in older traditions.

In terms of chronology, the most remarkable example might be
number 2, from the Letter of the Apostles, originally composed
about 160. Not only has this work always remained in the library
of the Ethiopian church, as part of the Book of the Covenant
(*Mäshafä Kidan*), but it still forms part of that church's New Testament canon. In Ethiopia, at least, many of the ancient scriptures
never went away.[10]

Some of these texts remained in use for many centuries. Jesus's
saying that "The world is a bridge" is recorded in the ninth century,
but the Mughal Indian emperor Akbar inscribed it on a mosque
about 1600. As this example suggests, by no means did all these
texts circulate among Christians only. Muslims themselves included
plenty of references to Jesus and Mary in the Qur'an and in later
commentaries. So substantial were these passages in Muslim texts
that they constituted what some have called a Muslim Gospel,
which contained many sayings and stories lost to Christendom.
Jews had their own versions of the Jesus story, notably a bitterly
hostile "anti-gospel" called the Life of Jesus (*Toledot Yeshu*).[11]

Long after the supposed loss of the Gnostic gospels, Christians
(and Muslims) still knew a diverse set of images of Jesus, some
starkly at variance with the conventional stories we know today.
Through alternative scriptures, they continued to imagine one Jesus

who sounds like an arcane Zen mystic, and another who sounds like a cracker-barrel philosopher. They knew the Jesus who explicitly denied his divinity, the monstrous infant Jesus who demonstrated his divine nature by killing playmates who insulted him, and the conjuror Jesus, who made himself invisible at will to show how easily he could have escaped the crucifixion if he had so chosen.

FROM EARLY TIMES THE GREAT CHURCH had debated at length the contents of the New Testament canon, and achieved a fair unanimity by the fourth and fifth centuries. Already in 348, the church father Cyril of Jerusalem had declared that "Of the New Testament, there are only four Gospels. The others are falsely attributed [*pseudepigrapha*] and harmful." But official policy differed from regular practice, as clergy and laity at all levels made massive use of alternative scriptures.[12]

At least by the second century, faithful Christians were trying to fill in the gaps they saw in the stories of Jesus and his apostles left by the canonical Big Four gospels. These later writers added information about the birth and death of key characters, and for such central figures as Jesus and his mother, they offered luxuriant additional detail about their parentage and childhoods. To do so, they built on familiar genres, creating new Acts of various apostles as well as whole new gospels. These appeared over a lengthy period extending roughly from the second century through the sixth, just the time when the now-celebrated Gnostic texts were themselves being created and circulated.[13]

If the Gnostic Gospel of Mary (for instance) had disappeared by the fourth century, mainstream churches still cherished such "Authentic Apocrypha" as the Protevangelium, the Gospel of Pseudo-Matthew, the Infancy Gospel of Thomas, the Gospel of Nicodemus, the pseudo-Acts of multiple apostles, and a great many more writings. Nobody today takes seriously the alleged correspondence between Jesus and the Syrian king Abgar. In the Middle Ages, though, these reputed letters circulated widely, and copies exist in Greek, Syriac, Armenian, Latin, Arabic, Persian, Slavonic, and Coptic, not to mention several modern European languages. This range of languages in itself indicates a bestseller.[14]

Dozens of "non-lost" gospels persisted up to modern times in at least some major part of the Christian church. In many cases, these texts built upon each other over time and were issued in new and variant versions, which sometimes became known under separate names. Accordingly, they cannot be listed individually but must be grouped into cycles or families of traditions, such as Narratives of Jesus's Childhood, Narratives of Mary's Birth and Childhood, the Death or Passing of Mary, and the Adam pseudepigrapha. These cycles were often sizable. Some of these books were read in more or less complete and free-standing versions, others in extracts or in adapted form. Believers often encountered them in anthologies, such as the famous *Golden Legend*, which was the most popular book circulated and read in Western Europe between 1280 and 1530. Through such compilations, these ancient writings became the literary commonplaces of medieval and early modern Latin Europe. Christendom, in fact, was awash with gospels.[15]

Inevitably, reading these texts also meant absorbing the opinions they presented, although these might well have been judged heretical at particular times and places. Although medieval readers admired these ancient works as morally improving stories, many were deeply imbued with ancient heresies. These alternative scriptures gave medieval Christians continuing access to the unforgotten fringe worlds of the earliest church.[16]

A famous maxim declares *lex orandi, lex credendi*, or, roughly, "How we pray is what we believe." Whatever the official creeds and theological statements of a church might say, it is what happens in regular worship that reflects the real belief and doctrine of a religious community. By that standard, any account of the development of Christian doctrine should properly foreground the alternative gospels. For centuries, these noncanonical texts were admitted onto church premises, approved for liturgical reading, and cited as authoritative by some of the greatest scholars and theologians. They shaped the physical fabric of churches by supplying the legends and stories depicted in stained glass and paintings. They were what ordinary laypeople actually read for instruction and pleasure, and contrary to myth, by the thirteenth century Christian Europe had a sizable reading public, lay as well as clerical. If these works were not canonical, neither were they excluded or condemned.[17]

––––––––

THESE "OTHER" TEXTS PROVIDED the standard Christian narrative for the great majority of believers, certainly for the laity, and their influence lingers today. Although few nonspecialists think they know this apocryphal literature, they might be surprised to realize just how much of its features they have imbibed without realizing it.[18]

When modern believers celebrate Christmas, when we see the Christmas scene in the manger, we are witnessing the influence of the Protevangelium or Infancy Gospel of James, the so-called "First Gospel," written around 170. This was an alternative gospel composed before the controversial gospels of Judas and Mary, and one that never lost its audience. The text recounts the birth and childhood of the Virgin Mary and gives additional information about the birth of Jesus that is not included in the official gospels. The work was beloved in the Orthodox churches of the Eastern and Byzantine world, and its ideas circulated in the Latin West through derivative or plagiarized versions, including the Gospel of Pseudo-Matthew. It was one of the best-known and most esteemed Christian literary works—in different times and places, more so than most books of the canonical New Testament.[19]

Such gospels formed the Christian visual imagination. The Gospel of Nicodemus described Christ after his crucifixion raiding hell to free the souls of the righteous who had died before his time. As derived from Nicodemus, the Harrowing of Hell was not far behind the crucifixion as a theme in medieval Christian imagery, and its impact extended to art, drama, and literature. If the Protevangelium shaped popular images of Jesus's birth, then Nicodemus was the key text for understanding his Passion. For centuries, in European popular piety, the saying most closely associated with Jesus was neither "Do unto others" nor "Father, forgive them," but rather, "Lift up your heads, oh ye gates!"—the Savior's war-cry as he prepared to invade Satan's realm. So popular was the Harrowing story among Asian Christians that the image crossed over into Indian Buddhist scriptures, with Buddha himself taking the role of hell's conqueror. An image fundamental to mainstream Christian belief for over a thousand years was derived from an ancient alternative gospel.[20]

From the apocryphal gospels Christians found other mainstays of medieval art, such as the elderly Joseph marrying the young Mary. It was here that they found such familiar details of the Christmas story as the lowly animals that attended the infant Jesus. This scene, which today we attribute to the canonical gospels, is actually from Pseudo-Matthew:

> And on the third day after the birth of our Lord Jesus Christ, the most blessed Mary went forth out of the cave, and entering a stable, placed the child in the stall, and the ox and the ass adored Him.[21]

Many Western Christians know the story of the revolt that led Satan and his angels to forsake their obedience to God. They also know that Satan was led to this desperate step by his pride, which caused him to refuse to pay homage to God's new creation, mankind. Almost certainly, they take this story not from any scripture or pseudo-scripture, but from John Milton's *Paradise Lost*, which in turn draws on a sizable body of older lore. The story, though, does not stem from any biblical account, but from the Life of Adam and Eve, a widely distributed apocryphal work probably dating from the first century AD. This Life is the source of the scene in which Satan tells Adam his reason for envying and seeking to destroy him. The canonical Bible does not even identify the Serpent in Eden with Satan—another idea that we take from apocryphal writings.[22]

MAINSTREAM CHURCHES WERE quite accommodating to alternative texts, and marginal and sectarian groups were still more welcoming. However much mainstream churches might have wanted to believe that they held a monopoly on belief and doctrine, heretical movements proliferated. Throughout the Middle Ages, many diverse variants of Christianity coexisted, covering a spectrum of belief very much like the movements of the earliest church. Some of them constituted whole alternative churches, existing alongside the mainstream Catholic and Orthodox churches and operating in deadly rivalry with those bodies. Christianity never ceased evolving from the grass roots.[23]

The survival of ancient scriptures outside the church's European heartlands, in areas of Asia and the Middle East, has already been mentioned. But the fact that lost gospels survived in distant corners of the globe might have remained a fact of antiquarian interest if those documents had not constantly reinvaded Catholic/Orthodox territories by means of the great heretical movements. The Slavic Bogomils of the tenth century were Dualists who believed that the material world was the creation of a flawed and inferior god, and that Christ was the son of a higher deity of Light. Those were broadly the same views as the Gnostic/Dualist sects of antiquity, the groups that produced the original "lost gospels." In their medieval guise, groups like the Bogomils and their Western European affiliates continued to read and circulate ancient texts that the church had been trying to eliminate for centuries.[24]

We see this from the so-called Revelation (or Apocalypse) of Peter. A number of works circulated under this title, but the most notorious was the Gnostic Apocalypse of Peter, which was discovered at Nag Hammadi. It was Gnostic in the sense that the author believed that the material world was ruled by a defective lower God, while Christ was an emissary from the forces of Light. The Christ who appeared in Galilee was an immaterial spiritual being who laughed during the crucifixion:

He whom you saw on the tree, glad and laughing, this is the living Jesus. But this one into whose hands and feet they drive the nails is his fleshly part, which is the substitute being put to shame, the one who came into being in his likeness.

This bizarre depiction supplied the title for a pioneering 1976 book about the Gnostic gospels, *The Laughing Savior*. Clearly, according to the standards of the Catholic/Orthodox churches, that particular Peter taught monstrous heresy, and the book had to be suppressed—hence the burial at Nag Hammadi sometime about 380. And so, scholars believed, it was completely lost until it was rediscovered in 1945.[25]

But that chronology is wrong. In 1045, in Constantinople, the Orthodox monk Euthymius, denouncing the Bogomils, described the potent initiation rite in which the heretics read the words of a "Revelation (or Apocalypse) of Peter." Euthymius claimed that this "Satanic spell" exercised a stunning influence: "If the heretics get in first, reading this to a man, the devil makes his house in him and brings him to complete destruction. From then onwards, no arguments about knowledge of God enter his soul." Given the close harmony between Bogomil views and the Gnostic Apocalypse of Peter, it is very likely that this is the work Euthymius was referring to—some seven hundred years after the last known copy of the work supposedly vanished into the Egyptian desert.[26]

How on earth—where on earth?—had the book survived over all that time? Reputedly, the sect received it via Armenia, which does make historical sense, in that heresies tended to flourish in border territories rather than in the metropolitan cores of empire. In the seventh century, moreover, Armenia spawned a potent Dualistic heresy in the Paulicians, who are commonly seen as a major influence on the Bogomils. Somehow, this text found its way back to Europe, and the Bogomils smuggled it to Western Europe, where related heresies thrived into the fourteenth century.

This Apocalypse was by no means the only such widely traveled work. About 1100, a Balkan bishop named Theophylact of Ohrid condemned those who were introducing dangerous new doctrines of the Spirit. Sarcastically, he said that if the heretics could base their evidence on canonical scriptures, he would raise no objection, and would even praise his rivals as public benefactors. But as it was, they were no better than the *Manichaioi*, Manichaeans, with their heretical Gospel of Thomas. No, he said, anyone who introduces a fifth gospel is thrice accursed! His words only make sense if he knows contemporaries who were not only using Thomas, but treating it as equal to the canonical evangelists. As he was writing in such a cauldron of Bogomil activism, it is reasonable to suggest that those are the "Manichaeans" he is describing. If so, might they even have been reading it in a Slavonic translation? And which other supposedly long-buried scriptures were they actually reading? So much for suppressed works being "damned in the inextricable shackles of anathema forever."[27]

Meanwhile, new scriptures and gospels continued to be written afresh. Some were the work of mainstream clergy and scholars; others were produced by fringe groups and heretics. In many and various forms, medieval Europeans were familiar with genres and settings that would have been familiar to Gnostics of the first two or three centuries following Jesus: discourses attributed to Jesus after his Resurrection, revelations and apocalypses, heavenly visions, encounters with Mary Magdalene, the Virgin Mary, and the apostles. Were any Christianities truly lost?

———————————

THE PERSISTENCE OF THE OLD SCRIPTURES tells us much about the limitations of how history is written. Historians naturally focus on documents that survive, and when records are rare, they give disproportionate weight to the ones that happen to have been preserved. When we look at debates over the church's canon, we hear a great deal about a few well-preserved documents and famous councils, as if they settled the matter once and for all, always and everywhere. Repeatedly, we read commands that such and such a book is prohibited forever, and all copies must be destroyed forthwith. But theory and practice diverged, often widely. To say that a given church council declared that book X was acceptable or not need not have decided the issue outside a particular community—or indeed, even within that community.[28]

Then, as now, institutions claimed to wield more real power than they actually possessed, and official prohibitions of a particular book did not necessarily have much impact on the ground. Even the much-quoted Gelasian Decree may not have had much influence beyond a particular region of Gaul (France). Ironically, given this tract's concern with suspicious and falsely ascribed pseudo-gospels, we have no precise knowledge of who actually wrote the decree, or when, or where. Its very name suggests a false connection with the historical Pope Gelasius. It is a pseudo-decree.

We see a kind of self-fulfilling prophecy. Most scholars working on alternative scriptures focus on the "early church," roughly the first four centuries. As they pay little attention to the post-400 era, not much current literature is available on those later eras, and that absence leads other writers to assume that the Other Gospels must either have disappeared or faded into insignificance. If not a blank slate, the issue of alternative scriptures between the fifth and the sixteenth centuries AD has been covered sparsely.[29]

WE HAVE BEEN DISCUSSING alternative "gospels," but that last word needs some elaboration. What exactly is a gospel, and can we legitimately apply the term to the texts that circulated through the Middle Ages and beyond? After all, with a text like the Gospel of Thomas, scholars might at least claim that it belongs to the early church, and therefore fits into the same chronological category as the canonical gospels. That point is obviously not true of texts written several centuries after Jesus's time, such as the Gospel of Nicodemus. So are these really gospels, or should we consign such later works to the suspect realm of mere apocrypha? In fact, the definition of gospel is broad enough to accommodate those later productions.

"Gospel" is a translation of the Greek word *evangelion*, εὐαγγέλιον, "good news," a word that St. Paul used frequently, and which originally implied an oral proclamation. The term was then applied to the written accounts of Christ that proliferated in the early centuries. Texts were credited to individuals—not just the famous Big Four, but to other disciples as well, such as Peter or Thomas—or to groups, such as the Egyptians, Ebionites, or Hebrews.[30]

The gospel title did not of itself imply any kind of official approval. From early times, church leaders enthusiastically denounced rival gospels, but they usually did not challenge their claim to bear that name, whether on grounds of chronology or alleged claims of inspiration. The Gelasian Decree proclaims as canonical the four chief gospels, described, for instance, as *Secundum Marcum* (According to Mark). The decree then catalogs apocryphal and unapproved books, such as *Evangelium Nomine Barnabae* (Gospel in the Name of Barnabas), or *Evangelium Nomine Petri Apostoli* (Gospel in the Name of the Apostle Peter). But the Gelasian text does not describe these unapproved texts with a term like *pseudo*-gospels, or "so-called gospels," as it easily could have done. The document notes one gospel "that Lucianus forged" (*quae falsavit Lucianus*), but adds no such qualification to the gospels attributed to Thomas or Bartholomew. Nor do we find such a demeaning label in the later Stichometry of Nicephorus (from the seventh century?), a list of scriptures that consigns to the apocrypha one *evangelion* according to Thomas, and another according to the Hebrews. The implication is that such works are indeed gospels, but they are unacceptable because of their source or bogus attribution. They really *are* gospels, just bad or inadequate ones.[31]

Nor need the work follow the exact format or genre of the canonical gospels. The Nag Hammadi library includes four self-described gospels, none of which vaguely resemble the familiar biographical format of, say, Luke. The so-called Gospel of Thomas is introduced as a collection of Jesus's sayings, some of which have short narratives attached to them. If you did not know the canonical gospels, Thomas would allow you to reconstruct only a tiny portion of the larger story. The Gospel of Philip and the Gospel of Truth are both extended theological meditations; if it were not for the latter's opening words ("The Gospel of Truth is joy"), a modern scholar would have never thought to label it a gospel. The Gospel of the Egyptians is a cosmogony, an account of the origin of the spiritual universe produced by the Sethians—Gnostic followers who venerated Adam's son Seth. To use a circular definition, they were gospels because at least some people thought of them as gospels.[32]

No less diverse are the alternative texts that were so popular throughout the Middle Ages, but which are also commonly labeled as "gospels." Although deciding the exact criteria for that term is not straightforward, some rough principles can be identified. Usually, such works place themselves within the established gospel genre that we know from the New Testament, and they commonly borrow or imitate features of the canonical gospels. A would-be gospel should use a narrative or biographical format, although not necessarily covering the whole span of Christ's life. After all, neither the canonical gospels of Mark nor John say anything about Jesus's whole career, or mention his birth or childhood. Many ancient Gnostic gospels focus entirely on Christ's pronouncements after his bodily death. The work should also claim a contemporary quality, affecting to report events at first hand. That means reporting Christ's deeds or words from the standpoint of an observer or participant, usually named, and commonly identified with someone in the biblical narrative.

Normally, the text should focus chiefly or wholly on Christ himself, but the extensive writings about the Virgin Mary do raise problems for this criterion. At least from the second century, Christians were writing works about her life that followed precisely the model of Christ's life in the canonical gospels, and which look very much like gospels in their own right. We might rather say that many "gospels" place Christ's life and deeds in a deep biographical or historical context. That allows us to include the gospels of the Virgin, in which Christ's life is an assumed fact, and the action leads up to that event and follows from it. Christ also appears personally as a character in the narrative. We would also include works with a notional Old Testament setting, like the Syriac Cave of Treasures, in which the narrative of the patriarchs from Adam onward is placed in a wholly Christian context, with many passages pointing toward a culmination in Christ's life and career.

Provided that a candidate text meets the other criteria, its date of composition is irrelevant, as is its claim to historical authority. There is no reason why "gospels" should not continue to be written and read, even today, although that comment says nothing about treating modern-day works as authoritative in any sense.

With these criteria in mind, we should not hesitate to say that the Protevangelium and the Gospel of Nicodemus qualify as gospels, at least as much as the ancient texts to which we usually give that title. And although these texts are "apocryphal," that label should not diminish their significance. Ever since scholars started studying such works three centuries ago, they have used the term New Testament Apocrypha to suggest that the texts in question represent almost a parallel version of the canon, a dark shadow of the authentic work. From that perspective, they are at best also-rans, failed candidates for inclusion in the real Bible. Even if it is used in a technical or academic sense, the term "apocryphal" suggests something inferior and probably spurious, gossip rather than serious information. That label also suggests that the texts should have been written in roughly the same era that the New Testament canon was under debate—before 400 or so—leaving later works in the category of hagiography, religious speculation, or historical fiction.[33]

The canon/apocrypha distinction works well as long as we are dealing with a textual canon that is clear and universally recognized, with only a few outliers to be categorized. The quantity of known alternative texts has expanded enormously in modern times, though, and the more it expands, the harder it is to see clear demarcations between approved and apocryphal writings. Some books that are canonical in one Christian tradition are apocryphal or excluded in another.[34]

FOR WELL OVER HALF OF CHRISTIAN HISTORY, believers relied on a body of written and visual materials going well beyond the strictly defined Bible as we know it today. A strict Protestant might tell that story in terms of a millennium of betrayal, the long Catholic night, when the true Bible was all but abandoned. A better view would be to stress the different sources of faith in any religion, even those that most firmly declare their reliance on scripture alone. In its lived experience, religious practice never draws wholly and exclusively on a precise body of scriptural texts. How could it, when those texts were composed in a particular time and place, and must be applied to other quite different contexts? Religions naturally tend to develop other bases of faith, including alternative scriptures and devotions, until, periodically, these are swept away by puritanical reform movements claiming to take believers back to the basics. That is the cyclical story of all scripture-based religions.

Any picture of a religion has to take account of those incidentals, those ancillary ideas and motifs that, for most believers, are anything but incidental. Yes, Christianity has its Bible, but it also has the expansions and elucidations of the book. That means all the commentaries, sermons, and meditations on the text, as well as visual and aural representations, such as paintings and carvings, church murals, and manuscript illuminations, all the liturgies, hymns, and carols, and the dramatic representations. At first sight, most modern Christians seem to have rid themselves of this dependence on ancillary sources of faith. That is natural enough, given the widespread rise of literacy and the technological changes that have made printed and now electronic materials so freely available. Yet it would not be difficult to construct a modern equivalent of what has been termed the expanded "Whole Gospel," which, for Protestants, would include the hymns that are such a rich source for teaching and doctrine.[35]

THROUGHOUT HISTORY, believers have *always* felt the need to justify their ideas and practices by scriptures, so that the generation of new would-be gospels is an inevitable and even healthy part of evolving belief. Just from the past two centuries, multiple examples

have appeared in the English language alone—including the Book
of Mormon, the *Aquarian Gospel of Jesus the Christ*, and the alleged
revelations of Jesus's doings in India—but the production of such
works has been a steady process over two millennia. Apocrypha in
any tradition can be defined simply as "stories people want."[36]

Writers have regularly used stories and pseudo-gospels as a means
of teaching the core truths of the faith. As a vehicle for exploring
and explaining abstract concepts, narrative has no equal, especially
if the reader can follow the tale through particular well-known individuals. Central to the Christian message is the doctrine that Christ
died for all humanity, a theme that St. Paul's theological system
epitomized by using Adam as a universal human symbol. Adam's
Fall brought sin and death into the world, and as his descendants
and heirs, we share those burdens until Christ redeems us. Probably in the sixth century, the Syriac author of the *Cave of Treasures*
carried this process of personalization much further by telling the
elaborate tale of Adam and his descendants and linking it at every
point to Christ's mission. Adam is buried in a cross-shaped grave,
and the site of his skull becomes Golgotha, where Christ would be
crucified. The cross itself grows from a tree sprung from that grave:

> And when the Wood [the cross] was fixed upon it, and Christ
> was smitten with the spear, and blood and water flowed down
> from His side, they ran down into the mouth of Adam, and
> they became a baptism to him, and he was baptized.

The image of Adam's skull in that final sentence makes the theological lesson unforgettably clear.[37]

As popular needs and concerns changed over time, so particular
scriptures were produced to meet the new cultural demand, and
some won a significant following. Often, they arose from natural
curiosity, as when readers found what they felt to be gaps or con-
tradictions in the approved biblical narrative. The Bible says that
Christ died on a Friday afternoon and rose again on Sunday morning. So what had he been doing in the interim? We hear that Christ
spoke to his apostles for forty days after his Resurrection, but the

Bible gives us no specifics of his teaching during those discourses. What spiritual pearls might he have shared? From earliest times, writers tried to fill these narrative holes. Often, texts arose (or were rediscovered) to give scriptural weight to theological arguments, or to justify new forms of devotion, such as the cult of the Virgin Mary. Alternative scriptures became a vehicle for the discussion of sensitive, even explosive, theological ideas. People wanted to believe in certain doctrines, and sought out the scriptures that upheld them, and one way or another, they were going to find supportive texts.[38]

Although Christian anti-Semitism was so rife during the Middle Ages, the church's attitude to scripture had much in common with that of Judaism. Jewish scholars agreed wholly on restricting the biblical canon, and in fact defined it more narrowly than Christians did. But they also felt free to make editorial comments and additions to these scriptures in the light of later concerns, perhaps for legal or instructional ends. Such explanations and elucidations were called *midrash*, from a root implying study or inquiry, and they often constituted fine storytelling in their own right. Later readers were so struck by the additional nuances and stories that the interpreters had added that they assumed these must have been part of the original narrative. A common Jewish legend records that Abraham was the son of the idol-maker Terah, and that one of the young man's first deeds was smashing those images. Often assumed to be part of the canonical Bible, the idol-smashing story actually derives from later interpretive writings. Christians, too, venerated texts that elaborated the canonical scriptures on very much the same lines as Jewish midrash.[39]

REDISCOVERING THE LOST SCRIPTURES forces us to rethink much of Christian history. Our chronology of that story often reflects what was originally a Protestant mythology of the decline and betrayal of the original Christian message, a mythology that has subsequently been adapted by liberal and progressive Christians. So much popular writing pays close attention to the early church, but then slides over the next thousand years or so to the Reformation. Any kind of authentic Christianity seems to go missing in action from roughly 400 through 1500, the "long middle" of Christian history.

In contrast to that pseudo-history, this book stresses the very strong continuities that unite the Middle Ages with the earliest Christian world and the apostolic era. As we will see in Chapters 2 and 3, it is simply wrong to suggest that older scriptures were suppressed outright. Those ancient texts continued to flourish in different parts of the Christian world—not only in African and Asian churches, but also in such bastions of the Catholic faith as Britain and Ireland. Books that were burned in one region remained popular elsewhere.

But in no sense is this book a description of the distant peripheries of Christianity, whether we take that word in a cultural or a geographic sense. Chapters 4 and 5 demonstrate the immense and continuing influence of noncanonical early gospels even in the heart of Catholic Western Europe, through the Gospel of Nicodemus, the Infancy Gospels, and the scriptures devoted to the Virgin Mary. Although many church historians acknowledge the popularity of those alternative books, they rarely note the huge significance of Old Testament pseudepigrapha (such as the Adam literature) in shaping mainstream Christian thought. That substantial body of literature forms the theme of Chapter 6.

Nor are we dealing with scriptures in isolation, as the ideas they carried also survived, and had their impact on the churches and the culture. In Chapter 7, we trace the role of supposedly "lost" scriptures in spawning the heretical movements that the medieval church saw as such a deadly danger. When we take such movements into account, the post-Nicene Christian experience looks just as diverse and creative, just as radical and boundary-breaking, as the world of the earliest church. Medieval Christianity was complex and polychromatic, generating many different forms of faith. The Holy Spirit did not take a 1,200-year vacation after the Council of Nicea.

Very similar texts also had their impact on the Islamic world, which, geographically, coincided so neatly with the major centers of early Christianity. Chapter 8 describes the different concepts of Jesus that Muslims and Jews found in the alternative gospels.

Although the Reformation era witnessed a widespread suppression of alternative scriptures, the upsurge of learning and literacy generated many new approaches to Christian faith, including multiple new churches and denominations. Chapter 9 traces the growing elite hostility to noncanonical texts and how this attitude led to their marginalization. It also describes what the Reformers would have found a bitter irony, namely, that the same skepticism that ousted the alternative gospels ultimately challenged the canonical scriptures as well.

The popular view of Christian history is a myth, in the sense of a tale recounted to create or justify a particular kind of faith. It tells a romantic tale of the tragic loss of Truth, which remains for later generations to rediscover. Even if they reject orthodoxy, critical scholars even today accord a special authority to the earliest Christian centuries as being closer to Jesus himself. They try to mold the earliest centuries as much as possible in the image that they would like to find—a world of questing diversity, of the rejection of hierarchy and patriarchy—ideally supported by lost scriptures. In order to support this vision, it is rhetorically necessary to make the later centuries look as dark and authoritarian as possible. As we have seen, though, the contrast of eras is wildly exaggerated.

––––––––––

NOBODY DOUBTS THE CENTRAL ROLE of Christianity in the history of the West, nor of the Bible in Western culture and art. But for over a millennium, that biblical world was imagined very differently from anything we would recognize today, and was approached by means of other scriptures. However dismissive the names we give them, those apocryphal and alternative writings are essential to any attempt to understand the history of the Christian faith. To trace their history, we often have to look beyond the limits of "the West" as we traditionally define it.

2

Christ's Many Faces

The Survival of the Old Gospels
in a Wider Christian World

All possible care must be taken, that we hold that faith
which has been believed everywhere, always, by all.

Vincent of Lérins, AD 434

BORN IN WHAT WE WOULD NOW CALL UZBEKISTAN, THE MUSLIM
scholar Abu Rayhan al-Biruni (973–1048) was one of the greatest
minds of his era, at once a scientist, historian, and linguist. He
traveled extensively in Central Asia and India, endlessly beguiled
by the world's religious diversity, its breadth of texts and traditions.

Al-Biruni's descriptions of Christianity must startle anyone who
believes that the church's early heresies were long extinct by the
end of the first millennium. Those movements may have been dead
in European Christendom, but they were not in Asia, and neither were their gospels. After citing the canonical gospels that he
had read and knew well, al-Biruni reports that "every one of the
sects of Marcion, and of Bardesanes, has a special gospel, which
in some parts differs from the gospels we have mentioned." These
are familiar names in Christian history, or rather, they had been

centuries before. In the second century, Marcion had taught that the good God of the New Testament had sent his Son, Jesus, to confront the Jewish God of the old dispensation. Around 200, the Syrian Bardesanes (Bar-Daisan) was a deadly critic of Marcion, but he led a school influenced by Gnostic views. In the West at least, neither movement attracted much notice after the fourth century, but al-Biruni suggests that both groups still existed in about 1000, with their own gospels. Continued survival is also reported by the tenth-century Baghdad author al-Nadim, who knew of Marcionite communities worshiping openly in Khurasan (roughly modern Turkmenistan), as well as Bardesanites in Khurasan and China. Both authors described the transcontinental Manichaean religion of their time, based on the ideas of the third-century Mesopotamian thinker Mani, who drew on Jewish, Christian, Buddhist, and Zoroastrian ideas, and who taught a radical Dualist message. Manichaean groups also had their distinctive gospels.[1]

We do not exactly know how long these various groups, Christian and Manichaean, had access to the full panoply of texts suggested by al-Biruni. It is reasonable to assume, though, that these works really were "lost" closer to the fourteenth century than the fourth. In the intervening centuries, they may have been lost in Europe, but they were not in China or Turkestan.

When we tell the Christian story in any era on only a European scale—rather, with a West European, Catholic focus—we miss a very large part of the story. Throughout the Middle Ages, Christian churches thrived across Asia and Africa, and had quite different attitudes as to which texts might legitimately be received within the church. Yes, old gospels continued to be read around the Mediterranean, but they also persisted in churches across the transcontinental Christian world. Even when scriptures actually did drop from view, the process of "losing" them was drawn out over a thousand years. The story forces us to think about the nature of censoring or suppressing texts in early and medieval times, and even more, about the huge diversity of the Christian world.

EARLY CHRISTIANITY WAS DEEPLY DIVIDED over issues of doctrine and belief, and the controversies shaped attitudes toward scripture. Although schools of thought proliferated, some major themes recurred frequently. As we trace the history of the hidden gospels, we will often be encountering these perennial ideas.

Central to debate was the proper Christian attitude toward Judaism and the Old Testament. Jewish Christians insisted that believers should follow much or all of the old Law, and their views were reflected in such early texts as the Gospels of the Hebrews and the Ebionites. Other early Christians, such as Marcion himself, demanded a stark break with the old Law.[2]

Some believers accepted forms of Dualism, the irreconcilable conflict between the worlds of matter and spirit. Many thinkers taught a complex system in which the material world was a dreadful blunder resulting from the forces of Light lapsing into ignorance and sin. In the Gnostic scheme, Christ comes down from the heavenly realms to liberate the sparks of Light that have been trapped in the darkness of the material world, and it is in that sense that he redeems his followers. (This is the message of the Gospel of Judas.) Dualist and Gnostic strands united in the Manichaean movement, which achieved the status of a global faith parallel to Christianity and Islam.[3]

These various sects and schools preached a version of Christ very different from the Incarnate God of the Orthodox/Catholic Great Church. Adoptionists found the notion of God Incarnate blasphemous and illogical, teaching instead that the spirit of Christ descended upon Jesus only at the moment of his baptism. Suspicious of the material world, Docetists likewise taught that the Christ who appeared in the world was a purely spiritual being, and his earthly body was an illusion rather than a material reality. Similarly rejecting the world, followers of Encratism condemned sexuality as well as the consumption of meat and wine.[4]

Such ideas were deeply rooted in Christianity, and only gradually were they marginalized under the title of "heresy." Already in the New Testament, we hear of groups who differed from the emerging Christian consensus: 2 John condemns the "many deceivers" who

denied that Jesus had come in the flesh; 2 Timothy denounces believers who held that the Resurrection had already come, framing
the event in a purely spiritual and nonmaterial sense. That Docetic
theme proved extraordinarily resilient, and it surfaced repeatedly in
movements judged heretical. As the Manichaean apologist Faustus
wrote about 400, "Do I believe the gospel? Certainly. Do I therefore
believe that Christ was born? Certainly not." Each of these schools
favored particular scriptures that presented images of Jesus at odds
with those of the canonical gospels.[5]

OVER TIME, the views that would become standard orthodoxy
gained widespread support, and church leaders tried to eliminate
rival texts from congregations. A famous story from about 190 tells
of the Syrian bishop Serapion allowing a congregation to read a
Gospel of Peter in its services, only to forbid it when he learned that
the work was Marcionite and Docetic. In his Paschal Letter of 367,
the great Alexandrian patriarch Athanasius warned against using
apocryphal scriptures, which he termed "an invention of heretics,
who write them when they choose, bestowing upon them their
approbation, and assigning to them a date, that so, using them as
ancient writings, they may find occasion to lead astray the simple."
This letter, incidentally, marks the first appearance of the term "canonized" (*kanonizomena*) in the context of Christian scripture. By
this point, the Christianized Roman Empire was becoming ever
harsher in its treatment of those groups the mainstream bishops
deemed heretical. Soon, patriarchs and bishops, including Athanasius himself, came to exercise civil functions over large sections of
the shrinking empire.[6]

But a sizable gulf separated merely rejecting certain scriptures
and extirpating them altogether, and the Athanasian letter just
quoted has become the basis of a contemporary myth. In her 2003
book, *Beyond Belief,* Elaine Pagels remarked that Athanasius "issued
an Easter letter in which he demanded that Egyptian monks destroy
all writings, except for those he specifically listed as 'acceptable,'

even 'canonical.'" The letter sounds astonishing in its far-reaching savagery, especially given the patriarch's near-imperial influence in much of the Christian East. Indeed, that letter is now commonly cited as the great charter for medieval intolerance of rival scriptures. But the Athanasian source quoted by Pagels includes no order for the destruction of any document, and certainly not for a mass purge. In reality, attempts at destruction were patchy and local, lacking any kind of systematic central effort.[7]

Undoubtedly, particular church authorities did seek out non-canonical texts with a view to eliminating them altogether. One ferocious champion of orthodoxy was the Egyptian monastic leader Shenoute, who about 380 wrote, "Who will say that there exists another gospel outside of the four gospels and not be rejected by the church as heretical? What did the apostles lack and all the saints? What is not in the scripture, through the Holy Spirit who speaks in them, that we shall look for apocrypha?" Shenoute's heterodox rivals at this point held to a canon of no fewer than twelve core gospels, besides multiple additional texts. Presumably, they assumed that twelve apostles deserved a gospel apiece.[8]

Shenoute's opinions mattered, because he commanded legions of monks who were anxious to seek out and destroy vestiges of paganism or heresy. Not coincidentally, his main base was located near sites where suspect scriptures were concealed at this very time, including Nag Hammadi itself. His monks were probably to blame for the concealment of these and other Gnostic texts that have turned up in the region in fairly modern times. These rediscovered texts include the priceless Berlin Codex, which contains such wonders as the Apocryphon of John and the Gospel of Mary. However much he would have loathed the idea, Shenoute's depredations are the principal reason for our firsthand access to most of the Gnostic texts we have today.[9]

Nor was Shenoute an isolated fanatic. In the fifth century, Pope Leo alerted a Spanish bishop to the errors of Priscillian, who had taught an ultra-rigorous form of Christian practice, and who in 385 had won the dubious honor of becoming the first heretic to be executed by a Christian state. Leo warned that

the apocryphal scriptures, which, under the names of Apostles, form a nursery-ground for many falsehoods, are not
only to be proscribed, but also taken away altogether and
burnt to ashes in the fire. Wherefore if any bishop has either
not forbidden the possession of apocryphal writings in men's
houses, or under the name of being canonical has suffered
those copies to be read in church which are vitiated with the
spurious alterations of Priscillian, let him know that he is to
be accounted heretic, since he who does not reclaim others
from error shows that he himself has gone astray.

Leo's letter, reinforced by many similar documents from church
leaders through the centuries, shows that book-burning is no myth.[10]

BUT THE IDEA THAT NONCANONICAL TEXTS were successfully suppressed is exaggerated. Nor was a disappearance necessarily a result
of any conscious policy by church authorities. The fact that a particular text is not familiar in the mainstream church tradition is
not in itself evidence of censorship. Some books just faded from use
when they lost their audiences, perhaps because they were felt to be
irrelevant or old-fashioned. Sometimes, a work became superfluous
when much of its content was absorbed into more substantial or
better-written works.

We have to be careful about retroactively applying modern standards to texts that to us seem highly significant. For many modern
scholars, the Gospel of Thomas is a critical work that may well
preserve the structure and content of the earliest written record of
Jesus, meaning it could be the predecessor of our canonical gospels. Some proclaim it a true fifth gospel, and it long continued
to be cited and denounced throughout the Eastern churches. In
Western church writings, though, its impact was close to nil, and
it rarely attracted comment or discussion. (Later Western scholars
who mention a Gospel of Thomas are often just recycling those
early citations at second or third hand.) That silence fell long before

any church hierarchy was sufficiently powerful to enforce censorship policies. In the Western world, at least, Thomas may never have circulated widely. As far as we know, nobody cared enough even to translate it into Latin.[11]

Other quite orthodox works vanished without any hint of active suppression. As an analogy to Thomas, look at the Didache, the Teaching of the Twelve Apostles, which today is regarded as a treasured remnant of the earliest church. Dating from around 100—roughly the time of the canonical Gospel of John—it includes by far the earliest Christian liturgy, and it was a serious candidate for inclusion in the New Testament. The early fathers demoted it to apocryphal status, but that need not have been fatal to its continued circulation. The Didache was not heretical or alarming in anything like the same way as the Gnostic texts. No church council or writer ever explicitly condemned it, and even Athanasius approved its use for pious reading. For whatever reason, though, it utterly dropped out of circulation and effectively disappeared. Only in modern times was a copy of the work rediscovered as part of an eleventh-century gospel codex. Even the canonical Gospel of Mark, which is today so highly valued, declined sharply in popularity and readership during the second and third centuries, and briefly ran the risk of similarly vanishing from common use.[12]

Some of the "lost" gospels never enjoyed more than a limited circulation. The great majority of alternative texts that were created between the second and fourth centuries were originally written in Greek, Syriac, or Coptic, and they circulated mainly in the eastern regions of the empire. They did not necessarily even appear in the increasingly confident churches of the Latin West, the ancestors of what would become the heart of later Western Christendom, so it is hardly surprising that they were not available to scholars in those regions. The mainstream Syriac-speaking churches produced plenty of alternative scriptures that never found their way to the West, but that was a result of language barriers rather than for doctrinal reasons.[13]

Even within the Catholic/Orthodox realms, it is far from clear that the churches utterly destroyed the offending books. One

puzzling piece of evidence comes from the writings of Nicephorus, the ninth-century patriarch of Constantinople. Appended to
one of his works is a stichometry, a list of scriptures known to the
church, although not necessarily approved. The fact that each is
listed together with its length suggests that the author had access
to complete physical manuscripts, presumably in a Constantinople
library. If that's true, then someone at the time of writing could
still lay hands on a Gospel of Thomas, a Gospel of the Hebrews, as
well as many other writings now included among the (orthodox and
non-Gnostic) apostolic fathers.[14]

The problem is that we don't know just when this section of the
manuscript was added. Most scholars believe that the stichometry
was written earlier than Nicephorus's time, perhaps in the seventh
century. But whatever the actual date, the document shows that
the "lost" gospels were still available long after they supposedly
vanished from circulation. Perhaps they survived on library shelves
right up to the sack of Constantinople in 1204, or even later.

PLENTY OF WORKS SURVIVED determined attempts at suppression.
We have already encountered the Gospel of Thomas, which church
fathers were criticizing and anathematizing from the third century
onward. But the sheer number of denunciations proves that the book
failed to just evaporate when it was banned. At least through the
twelfth century, Eastern Church writers referred to the work as if it
was still being used and read, usually in a heretical or Manichaean
context. Not surprisingly, given the importance of border territories,
the last probable reference comes from Armenia about 1285.[15]

But it's not clear how long Thomas circulated in a Catholic/
Orthodox context. One cryptic mid-sixth-century list falsely credited to Athanasius lists Thomas with other apocryphal works, noting, "By these, quite true and divinely inspired matters have been
selected and paraphrased. These are read [*anaginoskomena*]." In the
Eastern churches, that last word is applied to semi-approved texts
that are read for instruction or improvement, although they can't be

used to establish doctrine. Thomas is thus listed among the "disputed" books, *antilegomena*. Even so, it is mind-boggling to think that, somewhere in the Mediterranean world, some orthodox diocese was still happily recommending the Gospel of Thomas to its faithful as late as 550, and who knows how long afterward.[16]

Still more resilient was the Protevangelium, the Infancy Gospel of James, the second-century book that told the story of Mary's birth and childhood. The text circulated widely in Greek and other languages, but Western churches disliked some of its statements about Joseph and his family history. As a text, the Protevangelium largely disappeared from most of Western Europe, though it remained popular in Ireland. Probably in the seventh century, though, virtually the whole work was recycled as part of a new Latin text called the *De Infantia*, or Gospel of Pseudo-Matthew, which purged the offending theological passages. In this edited form, the Protevangelium was hugely influential in the Latin Catholic world.[17]

Technically, then, the Protevangelium is an example of a work that was censored and suppressed. In reality, that was true only in one portion of the Christian world, and the work remained easily available in only slightly altered form. The fact that the original version was barely known in the medieval Latin West does not indicate that the post-Nicene church had miraculously achieved a successful worldwide sweep of deviant texts.

FAR MORE CONTROVERSIAL in their content were the apocryphal Acts of the apostles, a much-beloved genre. Five works won particular acclaim, all dating from the period between roughly 150 and 250: these were the Acts of John, Paul, Thomas, Peter, and Andrew. Manichaeans treated the five as a canonical collection, which they substituted for the canonical Acts we know from the New Testament. St. Augustine probably referred to these works in the early fifth century when he complained that among "the apocryphal books of the Manichaeans there is a collection of fables, published by some unknown authors under the name of the apostles."[18]

Because of their heretical tendencies, these apocryphal Acts fell under church disfavor, and the Gelasian Decree condemned the Acts of Thomas, Peter, and Andrew. Even so, the process of suppression was very gradual and patchy. Even in the late ninth century, the patriarch of Constantinople, Photius, had read all five.

The Acts of John indicates the continuing power of these texts. Probably composed in the late second century, the book still entrances modern readers. In one section, John gives a surprising account of the Last Supper that features a kind of liturgical dance. Jesus says,

> Before I am delivered up unto them let us sing a hymn to the Father, and so go forth to that which lies before us. He [Jesus] bade us therefore make as it were a ring, holding one another's hands, and himself standing in the midst he said: Answer Amen unto me. He began, then, to sing an hymn and to say:
>
>> *Glory be to thee, Father.*
>> *And we, going about in a ring, answered him: Amen.*
>> *Glory be to thee, Word: Glory be to thee, Grace. Amen.*
>> *Glory be to thee, Spirit: Glory be to thee, Holy One:*
>> *Glory be to thy glory. Amen.*
>> *We praise thee, O Father; we give thanks to thee,*
>> *O Light, wherein darkness*
>> *dwelleth not. Amen.*

Also famous is the account of John's trial and condemnation by the Emperor Domitian. John is sentenced to death, but the poisoned cup from which he must drink does not harm him. It does, however, instantly kill another prisoner who is given the dregs, and John brings the man back to life.[19]

Church authorities became increasingly suspicious of the work, partly because it seemed tainted with Gnostic ideas. In particular, it recalled the thought of the second-century Egyptian Gnostic Valentinus. In 787, a second church council held at the historic venue of

Nicea finally condemned the Acts of John, ordering it "consigned to the fire." That decision caused the loss of many copies of the Acts, but the work existed in so many manuscripts, spread so widely, that much of it continued to be read and copied. Unlike modern printed books, those manuscripts differed from the original, however, and the differences grew over time. Latin manuscripts especially tended to purge anything that looked mystical or vaguely heretical, but many of the toxic portions survived in Greek copies. Around 70 percent of the original Acts of John survived, and the whole can be reconstructed with fair confidence.[20]

The best illustration of the work's continued popularity is the image of John holding the poisoned chalice, from which emerges a snake or dragon. This has been a mainstay of Christian art through the centuries, from the Middle Ages through the present day. If the Acts were no longer known in their entirety, core images and stories persisted.

No less enduring were the Acts of Thomas (no relation to the Gospel of Thomas). This second- or third-century Syriac work describes Thomas's missions in India and other distant lands. Early church leaders disliked it because it so often assumes Gnostic ideas and myths and was popular with various heretical groups, including Manichaeans, Priscillianists, and Encratites. Among other red flags for the strictly orthodox, the Acts demonstrate a deep hostility to sexuality, including acts between the newly married. These heretical associations made it far more incendiary than, say, the harmless Didache, which really did vanish from public use. At first sight, the Acts of Thomas would seem a prime candidate for suppression, and it was duly targeted by repeated councils and episcopal statements. As we have seen, the Gelasian Decree ordered its elimination.[21]

But as with John's Acts, the work was so widely read that it was bowdlerized, purged of at least some of its heretical statements, and then allowed to run loose across the wider Christian world. Apart from its early Greek and Syriac forms, the Acts of Thomas appeared in multiple translations, including Arabic, Coptic, Georgian, Latin, Armenian, and Ethiopic. In consequence, we can reconstruct the whole text.[22]

In some versions, the Acts of Thomas includes the Hymn of the Pearl (or Hymn of the Soul), a lovely vestige of the religious world of Late Antiquity. It survives in just two copies of the Acts, and many scholars think it originally circulated independently. Almost certainly a remnant of an early Gnostic movement, the hymn probably dates to the second or third century. It is a gospel, in the form of an allegory, in which a prince is sent to Egypt to retrieve a pearl from a serpent. However, the prince forgets his mission and even his identity, and is stripped of his royal garments:

> *I forgot that I was a King's son,*
> *And became a slave to their king.*
> *I forgot all concerning the Pearl*
> *For which my Parents had sent me;*
> *And from the weight of their victuals*
> *I sank down into a deep sleep.*

He has to be restored to his true self by another emissary from the King of Kings. Retrieving the pearl, he returns home. According to most readings, the story reflects a Gnostic worldview, probably that of Bardesanes, who was famous as the founder of the Syriac tradition of hymn-writing. The prince represents the soul trapped in the word of matter, the dark Egypt, from which Christ redeems him, while the pearl is salvation. Those themes of sleep and awakening, of being lost amid the world's snares, were central to Gnostic systems. They feature prominently in the Gospel of Judas.[23]

As a Gnostic text, the Hymn of the Pearl stood little chance of survival within the established church. Yet isolated copies did survive, at least into the tenth and eleventh centuries. One Syriac text was copied into the Acts of Thomas in 936, and other versions were known in Greek. Whether or not the hymn was the work of Bardesanes—and it probably was—it represents a remnant of the ancient Gnostic tradition.

WHILE UNAPPROVED ANCIENT TEXTS survived within the established Catholic/Orthodox church, other bodies outside its control or influence were still more enthusiastic about such documents. In the wider Christian world, very different scriptures were treated as holy or even canonical.

In the fifth century, theologian Vincent of Lérins defined Christian orthodoxy in terms of its universal presence and practice. The problem was that no authority, religious or civil, had the power to enforce any decisions over Christians "always and everywhere." At no point in Christian history have believers been united into one single united church. A century ago, Catholic author Hilaire Belloc made the spectacularly inaccurate claim that "Europe is the Faith, and the Faith is Europe." In historical terms, he was doubly wrong, particularly as he was referring to the Faith in its Catholic, papal form.[24]

From the fourteenth century at least, Western Europe was the demographic and cultural center of the Christian faith, and that dominance only grew over the following centuries. Obviously, then, later scholars tend to look at European circumstances and assume they were the historic Christian norm. But matters were very different in earlier eras. Christianity began not in Europe but in the Near East and the Mediterranean world, and the faith long retained that transcontinental identity.[25]

Throughout the Middle Ages, Christianity in its various forms reached far beyond Europe, extending deep into Africa and Asia. At its height, the Christian world stretched from Ireland to China, from southern India into Siberia, and from the borders of Kenya to the Arctic Circle. By some accounts, Europeans did not even make up a numerical majority of the Christian world until the tenth or eleventh centuries. Outside Europe, few Christians had much knowledge of either the pope or the increasingly expansive claims being made for that office, and they did not follow the orders of Rome.[26]

Besides the Catholic Church looking to Rome, there was also the great Orthodox Church with its spiritual center in New Rome, Constantinople, which since 1054 has not recognized Rome as part of the same communion. Technically, Rome and Constantinople are and have been in a state of schism, but other transnational churches also existed that were by Roman standards not just schismatic but outright heretical. These included the so-called Monophysite churches of Africa and Asia, namely the Copts, Ethiopians, Armenians, and others. (Monophysites supposedly held that Christ had one divine nature, rather than the united human and divine natures taught by mainstream orthodoxy. However, those Eastern churches reject the Monophysite label on the basis that it distorts their actual beliefs, and modern scholars prefer the more precise term "Miaphysite.") Also widespread was the Iraq-based Church of the East, which Rome and Constantinople condemned as Nestorian—that is, as teaching that Christ's human and divine natures were separate rather than fully united. This church mattered so much because at its medieval height, its adherents could be found across Asia, deep into India and China.[27]

If we take a broad definition of the Middle Ages as meaning between, say, 500 and 1500, there were never fewer than four overarching Christian communions: Catholic, Orthodox, Monophysite/ Miaphysite, and Nestorian.

FOR ALL THEIR DIVERSITY, these churches agreed on much. Each of the four was very much an heir of the fourth-century Council of Nicea and accepted doctrines of Trinity and Incarnation, however much they squabbled over the details of these matters. In practice, though, different churches varied greatly in terms of the particular texts that they used in their liturgies and the ones they accepted as authoritative.

Modern Protestants are used to a precisely defined Bible with contents that are entirely predictable, and any departure from it is deeply disturbing. But in fact, the content of the Bible has been different at various times and places, and we do not have to go too far back in history to find examples of that. Throughout the Middle Ages and well beyond, Christians accepted an Old Testament significantly larger than what might appear in standard modern translations like the New International Version.

The early church commonly used the Greek Bible translation, the Septuagint, while the Jewish community relied on the common Hebrew version. The latter might seem an obvious choice: Why use a translation when you can turn to the original text? However, matters are not so simple, because the Septuagint clearly includes some authentically ancient readings. Reliance on the Septuagint also helped determine which books were regarded as canonical. That translation included a number of books that were not found in the Hebrew, and which Jews increasingly marginalized and excluded from their canon. These books constituted the so-called Second Canon, the Deuterocanonical books such as Judith, Tobit, Wisdom, Sirach (Ecclesiasticus), 1 and 2 Maccabees, Baruch, and some additional passages in Daniel. From the early Christian centuries, churches accepted them.[28]

Occasionally, individual scholars would protest against their inclusion in the Christian canon. One very weighty voice in favor of a narrow canon was St. Jerome (347–420), the brilliant scholar and linguist who, among other achievements, undertook the Vulgate translation of the Bible, which would remain the standard Latin version until modern times. But such critics admitted that they were in a small minority, and the church's overwhelming consensus won out over time.[29]

Many Western Protestants have heard of these books and think of them under the general title of "apocrypha." For most non-Protestant churches around the world, though, they are not apocryphal but rather fully accredited components of the canon, still read in the liturgy. This is true of the Roman Catholic and Orthodox traditions as well as the Oriental Orthodox, Armenian, Coptic, and Ethiopian churches. Prior to the Reformation, the situation was quite unequivocal: all Christian churches accepted the Deuterocanon as an integral part of scripture. Once upon a time, these books were in all Bibles.

Beyond the Deuterocanonical works, different churches include in their standard canon works beyond what we know in the West.

Churches vary greatly, for example, in which particular works credited to Ezra or Baruch they accept in their biblical canons. (I will discuss these names in more detail in Chapter 6.) The canonicity of Maccabees is a matter of local option, as is the number of works included under this label in different times and places. The short Psalm 151 is canonical for the Syriac Orthodox, Armenian, Assyrian, and Ethiopian churches, and even for the Eastern Orthodox.[30]

Even in the Western Catholic church, one text in particular has proved controversial. Throughout Christian history, readers have studied the fourteen epistles attributed with more or less probability to St. Paul. (The Epistle to the Hebrews is certainly not Pauline, but at least some scholars are prepared to credit him with some or all of the others.) At least from the sixth century through the sixteenth, though, Paul's oeuvre was commonly cited as *fifteen* epistles, the additional one being a Latin text called the Epistle to the Laodiceans. This was a short, pedestrian document cut and pasted from canonical writings. St. Jerome, in the fourth century, summarily dismissed it, pronouncing Laodiceans "rejected by everyone," which it assuredly was not. Although no formal church council over the next millennium actually approved the forged text, even medieval writers sternly opposed to apocryphal scriptures had no difficulty in acknowledging it as authentic. If heretics like the Albigensians and Paulicians treasured it, so did mainstream Catholics, and it appears in many standard editions of the Bible. In the words of celebrated English Bible critic J. B. Lightfoot, "For more than nine centuries, this forged epistle hovered about the doors of the sacred Canon, without either finding admission or being peremptorily excluded."[31]

DIFFERENT CHURCHES APPLIED DIFFERENT CANONS, and some wandered further from the consensus than others. In terms of its divergent biblical canon, the most egregious example is the venerable church of Ethiopia—or, to give it its proper name, the Ethiopian Orthodox Tewahedo [Oneness] Church. This community traces its roots to the early fourth century, and today it claims an impressive

40 million followers, making it about as numerous as all the Baptist denominations in the United States combined. The church still recalls its ancient connections with the Monophysite Syriac and Coptic churches to which it owes its foundation. In its selection of scriptures, it retains tastes and preferences that were once far more widespread.

Ethiopians speak of both a Broad and a Narrow Biblical Canon, but even the latter is much more expansive than any Western counterpart. It contains, in all, eighty-one books, compared to the standard North American Protestant count of sixty-six. The Ethiopian canon includes most of the Deuterocanonical works as well as the books of Jubilees and Enoch, once-celebrated Jewish pseudo-scriptures that largely died out in the West. Jubilees (or Lesser Genesis) grows out of a thought world dominated by angels and apparitions. It is founded on a rigorous Jewish legalism that makes it a curious candidate for inclusion in a Christian canon. Moreover, the writer of Jubilees probably denied that Gentiles could obtain salvation—so do three Books of Maccabees (Meqabyan) that are only vaguely related to the texts of that name known in the West.[32]

Westerners would be surprised to see several additional texts in Ethiopia's New Testament as well, including a book attributed to the early Pope Clement, a disciple of the apostle Peter. After the Book of Revelation that concludes standard Western Bibles, Ethiopians proceed with eight "Books of Church Order": *Sirate Tsion* (the Book of Order), *Tizaz* (the Book of Herald), the books of *Gitsew*, *Abtilis*, 1 and 2 Covenant (Dominos), Clement, and the Didascalia. The Didascalia (Teaching) is a book on church life and order that is related to other similarly titled works that circulated in the third and fourth centuries.[33]

Also in the Ethiopian New Testament is the Book of the Covenant (*Mäshafä Kidan*), a discourse supposedly delivered by Christ after his Resurrection in a format that closely recalls the old Gnostic gospels. This text is sometimes called the *Epistula Apostolorum*, the Letter of the Apostles; it also survives in Coptic and is very old indeed, dating to a time when the author still felt the need to denounce such "false apostles" as Simon and Cerinthus, who belonged to the early second century. It includes some ideas that are surprising, if not shocking. Christ, for instance, tells how, at the Annunciation, he begat himself on his mother Mary:

> Jesus asked the apostles, "You know that the angel Gabriel came to bring the message to Mary?"
>
> "Yes Lord," we said.
>
> He answered and said, "Don't you remember that I once told you that I became an angel among the angels, that I was like an angel?"
>
> "Yes Lord," we said.
>
> He told us: "Then, under the appearance of the archangel Gabriel, I myself appeared to the Virgin Mary and spoke with her, her heart agreed, she believed and she laughed. I, the Word, I entered into her and became flesh, and that is how I myself became a minister to myself, and it was under the appearance of an angel that I did that."

Outside Ethiopia itself, most of these texts remain unknown except to a small group of experts.[34]

Although it is an extreme case, the Ethiopian story shows that enormous variations existed within the large communions, and also recalls the diversity of earlier times. The openness to works like Jubilees recalls a distant age when other churches, too, ranged much wider in their choice of canonical works. As we will see, Enoch was once widely popular. Indeed, some European churches once looked more like present-day Ethiopia in their attitudes to canon.

RELIGIOUS THOUGHT AND EXPERIMENT were never as closely supervised as churches affected to believe, but the power of orthodoxy was particularly weak on the fringes of the Christian empires. Enforcement ceased to function altogether beyond the frontiers. These border areas in the Middle East and in eastern and southeastern Europe served as laboratories of faith. From here, ideas and movements could be freely imported into the core territories of Christian Europe.

Geographical factors explain how, in one particular region, ancient Gnosticism survived as a living faith long after its supposed obliteration within the Roman Empire. In the nineteenth century, Western travelers encountered the Mandaean people, who lived in the remote marshes of southern Iraq. The Mandaeans followed (and still follow) a complex Dualist religious system intimately related to ancient Gnosticism that featured strong astrological themes. Their beliefs are supported by a sizable corpus of venerated scriptures, some of which date back to the first or second centuries. Like many early Gnostics and medieval Dualists, the Mandaeans venerate Old Testament figures such as Adam and Seth while rejecting Abraham and Moses, and they scorn the lying prophet, Jesus. What allowed the near-complete preservation of a system destroyed elsewhere by Christian states was the Mandaeans' location, altogether beyond the reach of Christian clergy and only barely regulated by Muslim authorities. Mandaean legend reports how the group had fled from Palestine in the early Christian period and settled safely in Iraq. Incredibly, some 60,000 Mandaeans still practice a faith that was so long ago condemned by Roman patriarchs and emperors.[35]

Many Christians likewise lived outside the rule of a Catholic/ Orthodox state. Some were subject to Islamic rule; others lived in border states beyond the power of either Rome or Constantinople. For much of the first millennium, Rome confronted hostile empires to the east, first the Persian state, and later the Muslim caliphate. Imperial rivalry meant that the Great Powers were forced to tolerate a network of smaller kingdoms between their borders. These served usefully as buffer states, leaning from one side to another as conditions changed. As successive wars and persecutions swept Rome and Persia, so refugees and dissidents fled beyond the frontiers, making such small states hothouses of religious development. Suspect texts may not have survived in regions where the writ of Constantinople ran, but they did in Armenia and Georgia and in such European lands as Bulgaria.[36]

The existence of such border states permitted alternative Christian texts to be preserved from ancient times to the present. Often, we find ancient scriptures that were certainly composed in one of the great scholarly languages of the Near East, such as Greek, Hebrew, or Syriac, but today exist only in translated versions, in Armenian, Ethiopian, or Slavonic. The reason is not hard to find. At one time, a work may have circulated within the Christian Roman Empire, but then it ran afoul of church authorities, who ordered its destruction. By that point, the work had been carried to other neighboring states, where it was copied and preserved. Once manuscripts were translated, they acquired a life of their own. Like the Acts of Thomas and the Protevangelium, many alternative scriptures survive in a diverse range of languages, including Syriac, Coptic, Armenian, Georgian, Ethiopic, Arabic, and Persian, over and above various European tongues.

SOME OF THE BEST EVIDENCE for the survival of ancient gospels comes from the Silk Route, which ran from Syria through Central Asia and into China. Not a road in any recognizable modern sense, this was rather a sequence of familiar routes and tracks, and in its day it was the central artery of transcontinental commerce. Besides its economic importance, the Silk Route was a highway of ideas and faiths that was used extensively by Muslims, Buddhists, Manichaeans, and Christians. From the fifth century through the thirteenth, this was the great missionary road used by the "Nestorian" Church of the East, which operated major centers at Merv, Kashgar, Samarkand, and Herat (Afghanistan). Some ancient waystations on the Silk Route have preserved amazing fragments of documents long thought lost, including old gospels. The oasis site of Turfan, in present-day China, has produced many such finds, mainly from between the eighth and tenth centuries.[37]

Many of the most intriguing texts belong to Manichaeans, followers of the prophet whose life was too incredible for a historical novelist ever to have invented. Mani was born in what is now Iraq about 216, and he joined a Jewish-Christian baptismal sect closely related to the Mandaeans. Deeply interested in the religious currents of his day, he traveled through Persia to India and gained firsthand knowledge of Zoroastrianism, Hinduism, and Buddhism. Drawing on these roots, he developed a complex faith based on a war between the forces of Light and Darkness. He saw himself as a messianic figure, an alternative Christ. As he claimed in his Shabuhragan, the book that he wrote for the Persian king Shapur:

> From aeon to aeon the apostles of God did not cease to bring here the Wisdom and the Works. Thus in one age, their coming was into the countries of India through the apostle that was the Buddha; in another age, into the land of Persia through Zoroaster; in another, into the land of the West through Jesus. After that, in this last age, this revelation came down and this prophethood arrived through myself, Mani, the apostle of the true God, into the land of Babylon.

The Persian regime persecuted his followers, and Mani himself died in prison, although his followers claimed he was crucified. Although Mani drew on many religious ideas, his own faith was, above all, heir to early Eastern Christianity, especially in its Gnostic forms. Manichaeans claimed to be the only true Christians.[38]

From the fourth century well into the High Middle Ages, the Manichaean faith was followed by millions across the Middle East and deep into Asia. In various forms, Manichaeanism lingered on into the seventeenth century in China.[39]

Manichaeans had always possessed quite a collection of gospels. In the fifth century, Pope Leo complained that the sect had "[forged] for themselves under the Apostles' names and under the words of the Savior Himself many volumes of falsehood, whereby to fortify their lying errors and instill deadly poison into the minds of those to be deceived." According to Leo, the Manichaeans had doctored canonical gospels in order to remove traces of Christ's Incarnation and material existence and to deny the reality of the Crucifixion and Resurrection. But such a statement is misleading, as the sect was in fact using many authentically early gospels in which these orthodox doctrines were underplayed or wholly absent. Instead of alleging that the Manichaeans had censored the orthodox passages in such texts, we might rather suggest that the original works had never included these doctrines in the first place.[40]

Just what books the Manichaeans might have deployed is open to debate, but "many volumes" suggests a sizable library. Among their canonical scriptures were several of the old Gnostic writings, including the Gospel of Thomas, not to mention Thomas's Psalms and Acts.

When early church fathers referred to the Gospel of Thomas, it was usually in this Manichaean context. In the sixth century, the Gelasian Decree condemned "the Gospel in the name of Thomas which the Manichaeans use." So close did the association become that orthodox writers regularly denounced "Thomas, the disciple of Mani." Scholars debate whether a disciple of that name ever existed, presumably during the third century, or whether those writers were just misdating the original apostolic "Thomas" credited with writing the gospel. About 870, the anti-Dualist writer Peter of Sicily warned that no one should read the Gospel of Thomas, "for it is not from one of the twelve disciples, but from one of the twelve evil disciples of the Antichrist Mani." You only forbid someone from reading a book if it is actually available, and if people are tempted to venture into it.[41]

Some scholars also question whether the gospel used by the sect was identical with the famous version found from Nag Hammadi. Yet finds from Silk Route sites like Turfan show clear quotations from that same text in eighth- or ninth-century fragments in Parthian and Sogdian. One Parthian fragment includes Thomas's saying 23, "I shall choose you, one out of a thousand, and two out of ten thousand, and they shall stand as a single one."[42]

Manichaeans also claimed a mysterious gospel credited to the twelve apostles. In the eighth century, the orthodox Christian bishop Theodore Abu Qurrah of Harran (in modern Turkey) quoted Manichaean evangelists who urged their hearers: "You must attach yourself to the true Christians, and give heed to the word of their

Gospel. For the true gospel is in our possession, which the twelve apostles have written, and there is no religion other than that which we possess, and there are no Christians apart from us. No one understands the interpretation of that gospel save Mani our lord."[43]

The traveler al-Biruni lived around 1000, at a time when Manichaeanism still flourished in Asia. In fact, he thought that the Manichaean faith in his day claimed the loyalty of most of the Eastern Turks, besides many believers in China, Tibet, and India. Even at this late date, al-Biruni still knew of complete texts of Mani's Living Gospel (written c. 260) and the Shabuhragan, as well as other key Manichaean texts, such as the Treasure of Life, the Book of Giants, and others.[44]

Al-Biruni also refers to a rich library of gospels and early Christian texts in these Central Asian contexts. After describing a Manichaean gospel, he writes, "Of this gospel there is a copy, called The Gospel of the Seventy, which is attributed to one Balamis [or possibly Iklamis]. [I]t is not acknowledged by Christians and others." Much scholarly ink has been spilled over this passage. Might Iklamis refer to the first-century Pope Clement, whose authority was often claimed for heretical writings? (We have already seen the Ethiopian veneration of one of his alleged works.) How does this reported gospel relate to other works with similar titles cited by early Christian authors, even the Gospel of the Twelve Apostles? Some scholars believe that this Gospel of the Seventy actually survives in fragmentary form in some of the scattered Christian manuscripts found at or near Turfan.[45]

Manichaeans also used gospel harmonies, works that combined and synthesized individual texts into more substantial connected narratives. One of these harmonies combined several "lost gospels," including the Gospel of Peter, the Acts of Pilate, and the Gospel of Nicodemus. They probably knew gospels credited to Eve, Bartholomew, Peter, and Philip, a Gospel of the Twelve Apostles, and an Acts of Philip. In this Central Asian context, too, we find evocative sayings, or *logia*, of Jesus.[46]

MUCH OF OUR KNOWLEDGE of these textual survivals comes from Central Asia, where the expanding Christian and Manichaean movements came into contact with Indian-derived Mahayana Buddhists. This was exactly the period when the Mahayana ideas, and their scriptures, were spreading throughout the vast Buddhist world. Relations between the faiths were remarkably close, to the extent that the Church of the East adopted a symbol that merged the Christian cross with the Buddhist lotus.[47]

In some instances, Buddhist scriptures borrowed heavily from ideas that were ultimately Christian, although we do not know whether these were transmitted by Manichaeans or by the Church of the East. The Buddhist *Karandavyuha Sutra*, best known as the source of the famous mantra *Om Mani Padme Hum*, is a core Buddhist text that shows signs of influence from Christian alternative gospels. In the sutra, the bodhisattva Avalokitesvara enters the Avici Hell to liberate the sentient beings trapped there, to the horror of the gods of death. This passage closely echoes Christ's Descent into Hell as reported in the Gospel of Nicodemus.[48]

Other examples point to the influence of alternative Christian scriptures on Buddhism. Buddhism has often taught a kind of pantheism, the idea that the sacred—the Buddha-nature—permeates all things. But similar ideas occur in early Christian scriptures. In a famous passage in the Gospel of Thomas, Jesus preaches pantheism, proclaiming,

> I am the light that is over all things. I am all: from me all came forth, and to me all attained. Split a piece of wood; I am there. Lift up the stone, and you will find me there.

Such words have raised the question of possible Asian or Buddhist influence on early Christianity. When we look at the dates of the respective scriptures, however, it is far more likely that Buddhists were drawing on Western concepts than the other way around. Particularly in those Central Asian regions that were exposed to the Christian gospels, Buddhists taught that "the essence of the Buddha Vairocana is everything: earth, mountains, stones, sand, the water of streams and rivers, all ponds, brooks and lakes, all plants and trees, all living beings and men." A Turkish Buddhist text from Turfan declares that "the essence of the Buddha Vairocana is everything."[49]

The two bodies of scripture show other parallels as well. Some Indian sutras use the idea of Buddhas giving their lives to ransom other beings, a strictly Christian (and non-Buddhist) concept. In the *Maitreya-Samiti* we hear, oddly, of "the jewel of the law that the divine Buddha preached by giving his life for sale." The idea might have come via the Gospel of Philip. Popular accounts of the Buddha's precocious childhood strongly recall the Infancy Gospels that were such a centerpiece of early and medieval Christianity.[50]

Not only did the ancient gospels survive, then, far beyond the boundaries of the Roman Empire, but they exercised a potent influence deep into southern and eastern Asia. In religious matters, at least, globalization is nothing like as new as we think.

MANY CONTROVERSIAL BOOKS survived attempts at suppression. Even when books themselves did vanish, that did not mean that their ideas disappeared altogether, and in some cases, they continue to resonate up to the present day. We see this in the so-called Revelation of Peter, a very early apocalyptic text that was once popular in the church, but faded from view by the fourth century. (This is not to be confused with the Gnostic Apocalypse of Peter mentioned in Chapter 1.)

The Revelation of Peter was originally written in the early second century, probably in Egypt, and perhaps near the time of the disastrous Jewish rising against Rome in the 130s. The scripture is "revealed" by the risen Christ, who describes the wonders of heaven and the atrocities of hell. It draws heavily on Jewish apocalyptic writings, particularly 1 Enoch.

The work seems to have been wholly forgotten for over a thousand years. Only in the 1880s was a Greek text discovered in a ninth-century grave at Akhmim in Egypt, ancient Panopolis. Portions of several books were laid alongside the dead man—perhaps a monk. They were chosen either because they were his particular favorites or because their themes of heaven, hell, and judgment were so appropriate to his passing from this world. This was, after all, Egypt, where for thousands of years pharaohs had been buried with manuscripts instructing them about how to navigate the afterlife. Besides the Revelation of Peter, these buried fragments included portions of the Gospel of Peter and 1 Enoch. The Revelation of Peter was also well known in Ethiopia, and modern scholars base much of their knowledge of the text from an earlier and much fuller version found in Ethiopia. Outside Ethiopia, the actual text of Peter's Revelation vanished between the ninth century and the nineteenth, but its ideas had an amazing subterranean existence.[51]

What was new about Peter's Revelation was its very sensory conceptualization of heaven and hell, which cried out for the attention of painters and poets. Here is the portrait of heaven:

> And the Lord showed me a very great region outside this world exceeding bright with light, and the air of that place illuminated with the beams of the sun, and the earth of itself flowering with blossoms that fade not, and full of spices and plants, fair-flowering and incorruptible, and bearing blessed fruit. And so great was the blossom that the odor thereof was borne thence even unto us.

The portrait of hell is much more substantial. Although the canonical New Testament mentions the torments of the damned (eternal flames and the worm that dies not), these are not described at any length. Peter, in contrast, supplies excruciating details of the appropriate punishments inflicted for sins committed during life:

> And some there were there hanging by their tongues; and these were they that blasphemed the way of righteousness, and under them was laid fire flaming and tormenting them. And there was a great lake full of flaming mire, wherein were certain men that turned away from righteousness; and angels,

tormentors, were set over them. And there were also others, women, hanged by their hair above that mire which boiled up; and these were they that adorned themselves for adultery. And the men that were joined with them in the defilement of adultery were hanging by their feet, and had their heads hidden in the mire, and said: "We believed not that we should come unto this place."

Women who aborted their children sit up to their necks in a lake of excrement under the accusing gaze of the weeping children whose lives had been cut short.[52]

The work was hugely popular in Christian churches around the Mediterranean world, and especially in Egypt and Palestine. For centuries, the two Revelations of Peter and John were both debatable candidates for inclusion in the New Testament canon and in church liturgies. One of the first attempts to define the limits of the official New Testament was the Muratori Canon of the late second century, and this document cited both Revelations as approved texts, although it noted that some contemporaries wanted to purge Peter's version. Although the work attributed to Peter gradually dropped from mainstream use, it was widely cited for several centuries. It influenced many other long popular Christian texts written from the second century onward, including the Acts of Perpetua and the Sibylline Oracles, and especially the vision of heaven and hell found in the Apocalypse of Paul (*Visio Pauli*). Even in the mid-fifth century, church historian Sozomen wrote that "the so-called Revelation of Peter, which was esteemed as entirely spurious by the ancients, we have discovered to be read in certain churches of Palestine up to the present day, once a year, on the day of preparation, during which the people most religiously fast in commemoration of the Savior's Passion [Good Friday]." As we know from the Egyptian discovery just noted, the Revelation was still cherished in Egypt until at least 800, and the Armenian scholar Mechitar had a text to copy as late as the thirteenth century. What probably drove Peter's Revelation out of general circulation was not that it taught some particularly dreadful heresy, or even that it was "spurious," but that its ideas just became so commonplace and familiar from so many other sources.[53]

The fact that the text itself was eventually lost did not mean that its influence disappeared. Through the works that it inspired and which quoted from it, this "lost" apocalypse contributed mightily to shaping the imagination of medieval and early modern Europe, and that impact lingers today.

This is apparent from the work's pictures of heaven and, even more, of hell. Little in "Peter's" account of the afterlife would surprise anyone who knows Dante's *Divine Comedy*, or the history of Christian art more generally, with all its images of demons and postmortem tortures. But that in itself is a remarkable statement. If these medieval artists did not know Peter's Revelation directly, why do they echo it so faithfully? As we have seen, Peter's Revelation inspired other writings, and the work was alluded to indirectly. Dante himself was well read in apocryphal scriptures, including the *Visio Pauli*, and he tapped into these sources. The more we know of that ancient apocalyptic current, the more familiar Dante becomes.[54]

However completely a text seems to have disappeared, its words and images often survived and were accepted, provided they met a powerful popular need. Demand trumped censorship. And however much institutions might have wished to annihilate texts and the ideas they carried, few, in fact, could implement such policies convincingly.

3

The Isles of the West

How Irish and British Churches
Kept Ancient Christian Cultures Alive

Here begins the reading from the Gospel according to James, son of Alphaeus.

Irish sacramentary, c. 800

ABOUT THE YEAR 1000, AN UNKNOWN EUROPEAN MONASTERY compiled a manuscript of the Roman writer Sallust, using for the cover some discarded parchment. That trash proved to be a fragment of an older Irish missal or sacramentary showing appropriate readings for different feasts and special occasions. At the Mass of the Circumcision, the text for the day came from James's gospel, following the exact format that would have been used to introduce a passage from canonical Mark or John. There was no indication that this text held a status any different from those fully credentialed gospels.[1]

From the text quoted, a brief account of Jesus's circumcision, it is impossible to know just what else might have been in this gospel, but it bore a weighty name. In the sixth century, the Western church had already known (and rejected) a gospel under the name of James the Less, the son of Alphaeus. What is most surprising about the story is not that an Irish church owned a copy of such a text some centuries later, but the totally unremarkable way in which it was approved for liturgical use.[2]

As we have seen, church authorities were limited in their power to restrict access to ancient alternative scriptures. Surprisingly, even European churches that were firmly within the Catholic/Orthodox mainstream were often highly independent, including in the scriptural texts they read. Merely accepting papal headship did not mean slavishly following Roman direction in every aspect of spiritual and intellectual life. Nor did it mean scrupulously obeying some distant bureaucratic center as to which particular writings could or could not be used. Over time, the papacy certainly extended its control of church life, but that was not achieved overnight.

This was nowhere more so than in the British Isles, which played a critical role in preserving and circulating ancient scriptures and lost gospels that had all but vanished elsewhere. Most remarkable of all, perhaps, are the mysterious Jewish-Christian gospels that take us back to the earliest apostolic times. Tracing the history of these texts offers surprising evidence of continuities from the older Christianity of the Mediterranean world to the newly converted territories of Western Europe, from the core to the distant margins.

IRELAND WAS A STAGGERINGLY RICH TREASURY for alternative gospels and scriptures. This would be so important because of the role that Irish monks played in the conversion of England and Scotland in the sixth and seventh centuries and their activity through much of Western Europe over the next two hundred years. Medieval Christianity owed an immense debt to these Insular (Irish and British) influences.[3]

Ireland's conversion to Christianity began in the fifth century, although the process probably took a century or more to complete. The country held a curious position in the Christian world. Lacking any record of Roman occupation, it had none of the political structures that shaped the church elsewhere. Without cities, bishops could have nothing like the same central role, and the church's life depended on monasteries. Only with the English Conquest of 1170 was the Irish church fully integrated into the standard Catholic structure and hierarchy. Yet, if earlier Ireland existed outside the Roman political realm, its church was unequivocally part of the wider Western communion that acknowledged the popes as the heirs of Peter. Contrary to some modern wishful thinking, we are not dealing with a fringe "Celtic" entity soaked in New Agey mysticism. This was definitely a *Catholic* church. Although Irish churches had their disagreements with Rome, chiefly over issues of keeping the calendar, they never lost that sense of fealty to Peter.[4]

From the time of its conversion, Ireland was closely connected to the wider world of Gaul, and beyond that, to the Mediterranean. Well-known routes of trade and communication united Ireland and western Britain with Spain and western Gaul, and beyond that with North Africa and the Levant. Time and again, scholars of Irish art and literature trace literary sources or artistic motifs directly to Visigothic Spain and to Christian North Africa. If we ever wonder where the vibrant cultural life of Christian North Africa went after the land was devastated by Vandals, Byzantines, and Arabs, we have our answer. The Irish even had some knowledge of the Greek language, at a time when this was a very rare accomplishment in most of Western Europe.[5]

Egyptian influences were strong both in Ireland itself and in the English territory of Northumbria that was closely linked to the Irish church. We can trace a traffic in books and manuscripts, as well as literary and artistic motifs, pointing to what scholar William Dalrymple has termed an "Egyptian Connection." In the seventh and eighth centuries, Insular gospel books were bound and prepared with specifically Coptic techniques, and the image of the Virgin and Child in the famous Book of Kells closely resembles Egyptian precedents (which in turn imitated pictures of the goddess Isis suckling the child Horus). As Dalrymple remarks, "The Irish wheel cross, the symbol of Celtic Christianity, has recently been shown to have been a Coptic invention, depicted on a Coptic burial pall of the fifth century, three centuries before the design first appears in Scotland and Ireland."[6]

One material sign of this connection is the so-called Faddan More psalter, which was recovered from a peat bog in Ireland's County Tipperary in 2006. As an intact book from the early Middle Ages, the psalter is an amazing enough find in its own right. But its story became even stranger when archaeologists reported finding eighth-century Egyptian papyrus in its binding.[7]

In the late seventh century, the brilliant monk Adomnán headed the island monastery of Iona, off the western coast of Scotland. Here he wrote a popular Life of St. Colmcille (Columba), the abbey's founder, and about 680 he published a detailed and largely accurate account of the Holy Places in Palestine, *De Locis Sanctis*. He obtained his information from a Gallic bishop named Arculf, who had visited Palestine, Egypt, and Constantinople and was shipwrecked at Iona on his return. Around 820, another Irish scholar, named Dicuil, gave a good description of the Pyramids, based on what he had been told by a group of Irish monks who had seen them as they were sailing up the Nile. (They thought they had visited the granaries that Joseph had built for Pharaoh many centuries before.)[8]

Not just from Egypt, goods and books from the Mediterranean region circulated widely in the British Isles and were avidly imitated by local craftsmen. This helps us understand how literary and artistic Christian influences from distant Palestine, Syria, and Egypt made their way to the far West, to manifest themselves in manuscripts, paintings, and carvings. In the furthest West, Christians never forgot they were part of a world rooted in Jerusalem.

IRISH MONASTERIES HELD IMPRESSIVE COLLECTIONS of manuscripts that could have come from any of these ancient Christian territories, and they had been acquired anywhere from the fifth century to the tenth or eleventh. These included distinguished collections of apocrypha and alternative Christian texts. Modern scholars have painstakingly collected these records, enumerating over a hundred titles known in Ireland. Many are poetic elaborations of well-known stories, but we also find a full spectrum of widely known alternative texts. Some texts survive in the vernacular, in Irish Gaelic.[9]

Tantalizing hints suggest some of the gems that might have been available to the Irish church, including early gospels. Irish churches were certainly familiar with such Old Testament apocryphal texts as the Life of Adam and Eve, the Apocalypse of Moses, and Jubilees. From the New Testament Apocrypha, they knew versions of the Gospel of Nicodemus along with the Descent into Hell, the Letters to Abgar, Pseudo-Matthew, the Infancy Gospel of Thomas, Paul's Epistle to the Laodiceans, and all the standard alternative Lives of the apostles.[10]

Surprisingly, Irish clerics had direct knowledge of the Protevangelium, the pseudo-gospel on the early life of the Virgin Mary. This work was very well known in the Greek- and Syriac-speaking Eastern world, but far less so in the Latin West. Most of Western Europe, in fact, adapted the material into the gospel known as Pseudo-Matthew. Ireland, though, knew this Eastern text firsthand.[11]

Not only did the Irish know such texts, but they incorporated them fully into their vernacular literature. Irish writers were so at home with such works that they freely adapted them in their storytelling. Writing of the Magi who sought the baby Jesus, one medieval book records the range of different pseudo-gospels that shed light on the event. This is what "James of the Knees says in his Gospel of the Children," or "what Matthew son of Alphaeus said in this Gospel, and in *Libro de Infancia Mariae*, that is in the book in which is narrated the Birth of Mary." The wonderful name "James of the Knees" refers to Jesus's brother, who was reputedly so devout in prayer that his knees were as callused as the skin of a camel.[12]

In one Irish story, St. Joseph sees the Magi approaching the scene of Jesus's birth. Joseph calls his son Simeon, and they try to make sense of the odd behavior they witness: "I fancy, my son, that it is the omen art of the druids, and it is soothsaying they are practicing, for they take not a single step without looking up, and they are discussing and communing one with another among themselves."

Joseph is in fact describing the Three Wise Druids—or rather the Seven, as Irish sages counted them.[13]

Successive invasions and waves of destruction have uprooted much of Ireland's early Christian culture, especially from its most glorious age, which ran from about 550 through 800. Enough, though, remains to suggest that Ireland in these years must have retained a library of alternative Christian texts that would have surprised mainstream church authorities in Rome or Constantinople.

———————

ENGLAND, TOO, produces many surprises in terms of the books that were read and respected. What makes England so important for scholars is that the surviving texts allow us to pin down exactly what was used at particular times in ways that we cannot do elsewhere. We know that alternative texts circulated broadly in the Christian world; the number of manuscripts in different languages gives some idea of their popularity. Yet we often do not know the exact point of time in which they were used. In Armenia, for instance, a host of apocryphal texts survived, but in fairly late copies, from the sixteenth century or afterwards. It is a reasonable assumption that these were read much earlier, but we can't be entirely sure.[14]

In England, though, historical circumstances give us reliable limits for dating. Anglo-Saxon England was converted in the century or so after 597, and in the following centuries it became one of the liveliest cultural heartlands of Western Europe. Scandinavian invasions caused massive damage in the ninth century, but Anglo-Saxon culture and literature continued to thrive until the Norman Conquest of 1066. Within a couple of generations after that cataclysm, the Anglo-Saxon language ceased to matter as a learned tongue. When we find a text associated with the Anglo-Saxon church, then, we can say confidently that it was used somewhere between 600 and 1066 or so, and is unlikely to have been much earlier or later.[15]

The English drew from very diverse cultural and spiritual influences. Partly, they were avid disciples of Irish learning. In the century after 550, the Irish church launched a great missionary endeavor into Scotland and Northumbria (northern England), in the process creating some of the greatest cultural and artistic centers of the contemporary Christian world. Northumbria, in turn, became a prolific sender of missions throughout Western Europe, as well as a source of books and written materials.[16]

But England also received Mediterranean influences directly. Although it seems difficult to think of texts circulating freely around the premodern world, cultural and commercial ties could extend very far, even in the darkest of Dark Ages. In the 770s, the English king Offa decided to mint some splendid coins, which are among the oldest surviving examples of their kind in the Anglo-Saxon world. On the coin's back there is what the designer obviously thought was fancy decorative work on the original he copied from, which was an Arab dinar from Spain or North Africa. And that is why the pioneering coin of this strictly Christian king bears the Islamic declaration of faith—"There is no God but Allah"—in Arabic Kufic script.[17]

From the earliest mission in 597, the Anglo-Saxons maintained a special relationship with the popes and with Italy, to the point that the English were among the earliest advocates of universal papal power. In 668, the pope revived the stagnant English mission by sending two towering figures—the Syrian/Byzantine Theodore of Tarsus, archbishop of Canterbury, and the North African abbot Hadrian. This mission brought a new dawn to the English church. The eighth-century Northumbrian historian Bede tells us that Theodore and Hadrian were "well read both in sacred and in secular literature." He continued: "They gathered a crowd of disciples, and there daily flowed from them rivers of knowledge to water the hearts of their hearers; and, together with the books of holy writ, they also taught them the arts of ecclesiastical poetry, astronomy, and arithmetic. There are still living at this day some of their scholars, who are as well versed in the Greek and Latin tongues as in their own, in which they were born." Native English Christians like the abbot Benedict Biscop shuttled back and forth between England and Italy to find manuscripts and liturgical materials.[18]

By the eighth century, England and Ireland were being exposed to Mediterranean influences of all sorts, and this contact manifested in the legendary artwork of the gospel books of Lindisfarne and Kells. Mediterranean-looking vine-scroll decoration appears on Anglo-Saxon stone crosses in remote corners of England and Scotland. We see similar influences in religious writing and devotion. It was through the influence of Theodore the Syrian that the Anglo-Saxons acquired their deep devotion to the apostle Thomas, a saint cherished by Syrians. Thomas was celebrated in multiple apocryphal works that circulated in the British Isles.[19]

THE ENGLISH CHRISTIAN BOOKSHELF included all of the then-standard books of the Bible, including such Deuterocanonical works as Judith, Tobit, and Wisdom. But English clergy also knew and read a sizable body of Old Testament pseudepigrapha, "falsely titled" writings attributed to the great patriarchs and prophets. They knew the Assumption of Moses, Psalm 151, and many writings purporting to describe the career of Adam and his immediate family. They even used the obscure Irish text *De Plasmatione Adam*, which was added to the older Life of Adam and Eve. And when writers used such texts, they did not draw any serious distinctions between those books and what we today think of as the mainstream Old Testament. The medieval English church—a paragon of Catholic orthodoxy and papal loyalty—was reading a package of scriptures very different from any modern Western concept of the Bible.[20]

Among New Testament apocrypha, few English readers of the time doubted the authenticity of Paul's Letter to the Laodiceans or the Gospel of Nicodemus. In Northumbria, Hexham's eighth-century bishop Acca built up what Bede calls "a very full and distinguished collection" of the Lives and Passions of the apostles and martyrs, among many other ecclesiastical books. Anything dealing with apocalyptic or the end times commanded special interest, including the *Visio Pauli*, the Apocalypse of Paul, which we encountered in Chapter 2. The English knew and loved the Christian sections of the Sibylline Oracles (*Versus Sibyllae de Iudicio*), in which an ancient pagan seer reputedly foretold the career of Christ and the Christian apocalypse (to be described further in Chapter 6). A legendarily strong English devotion to the Virgin Mary meant that scriptures and pseudo-gospels concerning her life or career circulated widely.[21]

Also esteemed in the British Isles was the so-called Sunday Letter, the Carta Dominica, one of the odder apocryphal pieces. Supposedly penned by Jesus himself, the letter allegedly fell to earth at some great Christian shrine some years after the crucifixion, and it urged strict observance of Sabbath laws. First appearing in the sixth century, it circulated in various forms, often responding to recent events and controversies, and sometimes incorporating the correspondence between Christ and the legendary Syrian king Abgar. It scarcely seems adequate to describe this text as tenacious, as it still resurfaced in pamphlets and posters in Victorian England.[22]

Anglo-Saxon readers were by no means uncritical in their acceptance of these alternative texts. In the eighth century, the great historian Bede acknowledged doubts about authenticity but still advocated reading them. Clearly suspect, for instance, was 1 Enoch, "because that book which is presented under his name is considered not truly written by him, but edited by some other one under the title of his name." Yet it still deserved reading, especially because it was cited as scriptural in the New Testament epistle of Jude.[23]

Other scholars were more dubious and denounced particular alternative texts as spurious. The eighth-century scholar Aldhelm condemned the *Visio Pauli*. So did the later writer Aelfric, who would have favored a wholesale national purge of apocryphal manuscripts if that had been vaguely feasible. In fact, he consigned many to a damning category of *lease gesetnysse*, "false [or lying] compositions," a much more hostile term than merely "apocryphal." Yet even Aelfric himself cited apocryphal accounts of the Virgin's birth and parentage as authoritative. He also cited the *fifteen* letters of Paul, including Laodiceans. Lacking the resources of later scholarship, just how was it possible even for such a skeptical and widely read churchman to tell what was canonical and what not?[24]

QUITE APART FROM SURVIVING MANUSCRIPTS and contemporary references, we see the influence of these alternative scriptures in art and poetry.[25]

One strange survival involves the Book of 1 Enoch, a once-influential scripture from the third and second centuries BC that we will explore in more detail in Chapter 6. For centuries, the book's most intriguing section was the so-called Book of the Watchers, Chapters 1 to 36. To read Enoch is to plunge into an esoteric world of angels and secret revelations, the phantasmagoric universe of "the Watchers, the children of heaven." Vastly elaborating a cryptic tale in Genesis, Enoch tells how the Watchers mated with human women, leaving as issue terrifying giants, the Nephilim. Very popular in the early church, 1 Enoch faded from mainstream use from the fourth century, and in much of the West it was relegated to the status of yet another lost scripture. In recent times, the Watchers story entered popular culture through its use in the 2014 film *Noah*.[26]

Oddly, though, 1 Enoch strongly influenced the great English poem *Beowulf*. Probably composed in the eighth century, *Beowulf* tells of a village besieged by a terrifying monster called Grendel. The mighty hero Beowulf defeats Grendel only to find that he must then combat a still more alarming enemy, Grendel's mother. Although the poem seems to stem from a heroic pagan past, the characters' names show that its origins are in part biblical.

"Grendel" makes sense in terms of a thing that grinds, that crushes with its ferocious teeth, but if it was strictly Anglo-Saxon, the name would be something like "Grendr." So the "-el" part is mysterious. As literary scholars have long recognized, though, whoever composed *Beowulf* knew 1 Enoch. In Enoch, the Nephilim become cannibals and giants, and they sound very much like Grendel's horrible family. Enoch also delights in listing those giants and angels, whose names usually end with the Hebrew "-el." So we have Ramiel, Danel, Asael, and so on. How natural then for a medieval writer to invent Grend-el. The poem must have been written by someone who had read Enoch, and in the context of the time, that must have been a bookish Christian cleric.[27]

IF WE LOOK AT ENGLAND'S THRIVING Christian culture in about 1000—roughly the halfway point of the Christian story to date—then "Holy Scripture" was still a flexible concept. It definitely included, say, the Gospel of John, but other books now largely forgotten also carried scriptural authority.[28]

This mattered because, far from being isolated at a distant corner of Christendom, the English church in its day was one of the world's great missionary bodies. The English, together with their Irish allies—both proud heirs of that Mediterranean/African/Asian tradition—launched themselves into Western Europe. Between the seventh and ninth centuries, these fervent Islanders converted pagan societies in Germany and the Netherlands as they revived moribund churches in France and Italy. Their inheritance survived in such crucial medieval monasteries as Bobbio (Italy), Luxeuil (France), St. Gall (Switzerland), and Fulda (Germany). And where those missionaries went, they took the Bibles they knew. Centuries later, these were the libraries and schools where Renaissance scholars rediscovered invaluable manuscripts containing otherwise lost remains of classical antiquity, as well as alternative Christian texts.[29]

At the end of the eighth century, the Emperor Charlemagne turned to these Irish and English scholars to give a new cultural birth to what he hoped would be a restored Roman Empire in the West. To his court, and that of his successors, flocked Insular scholars and book-lovers, mystics and artists, who together undertook the so-called Carolingian Renaissance. Charlemagne's main adviser in matters cultural and spiritual was the Northumbrian monk Alcuin, heir to those Irish and English pioneers, and beyond them, to their Mediterranean inspirations. Charlemagne's efforts laid the cultural foundations of medieval Europe.[30]

THROUGHOUT THE MIDDLE AGES, scholars across Western Europe made puzzling references to Jewish-Christian gospels otherwise thought lost. We can debate at length what exactly they might have been referring to, but often we can track their citations back to the influence of Ireland and to the Irish monasteries founded in Western Europe. If, indeed, the Irish church preserved these documents in any form, that would be an amazing fact.

Scholars see the Jewish-Christian gospels as priceless relics of the earliest Jesus movement in the decades before Christianity defined itself as a new faith. According to a common interpretation of Christian origins, most of Jesus's first followers saw themselves primarily as Jews, faithfully following Jewish ritual laws, including food laws and circumcision. Within a couple of decades, Gentiles were admitted without the need to accept these demands, and these newer believers gradually played an ever larger role in the church. Those who followed Jewish ways were marginalized, and even labeled as a heretical movement, the Ebionites, who lasted at least into the fourth century. From the second century onward, we hear of gospels that appealed particularly to this wing of the movement, gospels variously named after the Ebionites themselves, the Hebrews, or the Nazoreans, and some at least circulated in Semitic languages and script. None survive in anything like intact form; nor can we be sure just how many works were covered under these titles. Such scarce texts stood little chance of surviving into the Middle Ages, all the more so as their content was so radically contrary to emerging Christian orthodoxy. (As we will see, some of those gospels and their ideas may well have survived in Islamic tradition, and left traces in the Qur'an itself.)[31]

One in particular, though, the Gospel according to the Hebrews, retained a special aura. Even when they rejected it from the canon, early champions of orthodoxy refused to classify the work as simply bogus, and treated it almost as a fifth gospel. In the third century, the church father Origen quoted the Gospel of the Hebrews as his source for Jesus's saying that "even now did my mother the Holy Spirit take me by one of mine hairs, and carried me away unto the great mountain Tabor." The fourth-century father Jerome quoted extensively from that and other Jewish-Christian gospels. The Gospel of the Hebrews appears in very distinguished company in the canon list known as the Stichometry of Nicephorus, which lists four New Testament works as "disputed" rather than condemned outright. Besides the Gospel of the Hebrews, the list includes the Epistle of Barnabas, the Apocalypse of Peter, and the Revelation of John, which is, of course, a well-established component of the New Testament we know. This "Hebrews" would have had 2,200 lines, making it about the same size as canonical Matthew. Around 700, the English writer Bede still thought that "what is called the Gospel of the Hebrews [*evangelium iuxta Hebraeos*] is not among the apocrypha, but to be numbered among the church histories."[32]

But what happened to Hebrews and the other Jewish-Christian works? Although we find many later references to these books, most must be treated cautiously. Medieval authors did not cite or footnote the books they used as carefully as modern scholars would like. On occasion, a medieval writer will credit a quotation to the Gospel of the Hebrews or the Nazoreans, suggesting that he had a physical copy of that work in front of him, which he almost certainly did not. To take one example, about 1200, French cleric Petrus de Riga wrote his immensely popular *Aurora*, a verse commentary on the Bible. As people read and transcribed it, they expanded his commentary, glossing his glosses. One annotated copy survives in Cambridge's Fitzwilliam Museum, and some of the comments startle. Seemingly out of nowhere, the account of Christ driving the moneychangers from the Temple attracts the note, "In the books of the Gospels that the Nazarenes use, it is read that rays issued from [Christ's] eyes, whereby they were terrified and put to flight."[33]

Such references are tantalizing. Was the author *really* using the ancient Gospel of the Nazoreans? When we follow up such references, though, we almost always find that the author is quoting the passage from an earlier writer, and that is certainly what happened in this instance. By far the most common source is Jerome, who had actually used those Jewish-Christian texts firsthand back in the fourth century. We need to watch out for medieval readers showing off their learning by casually throwing out the names of books they know only by reputation. In reality, it is very difficult to find evidence of anyone after the sixth or seventh centuries actually using and quoting one of the Jewish-Christian gospels at first hand. Probably, even Bede had never actually handled a copy of the Gospel of the Hebrews personally, although we are not sure of the basis for his remark.

That said, we do have a few plausible indications of likely survival, and most point to Ireland, or to Irish-connected libraries overseas. From the eighth century at the latest, Irish scholars commenting on the canonical gospels cited alternative readings that they reputedly found in a work they called the Gospel According to the Hebrews, and such references continue to appear through the twelfth century. About 850, the text was quoted by Sedulius Scottus ("the Irishman"), the scholar who was so critical in transmitting Irish learning to Latin Europe in the years after Charlemagne. Almost casually, he refers to the apostle James swearing not to eat until after Christ had risen from the dead, "as we read in the Gospel according to the Hebrews." Such citations show that the gospel included stories from throughout Christ's life, including his infancy, his public career, and indeed the time after his Resurrection. Medieval writers applied generic names like "the Hebrew Gospel" to a wide variety of mysterious texts. In this case, though, the work that the Irish cited closely fits those ancient desriptions.[34]

Might the last copy of the gospel used by Jesus's stubborn Jewish followers have existed in medieval Ireland, a continent away from Palestine? And did that solitary volume perish in some war or disaster, perhaps a ninth-century Norse raid on some great monastery? Most intriguing, perhaps, might we someday expect a fragment to appear in the waste used to bind a book, like the pathetic remnant of the Gospel of James, son of Alphaeus, mentioned at the start of this chapter?

THE BRITISH ISLES also preserved another very early gospel, which also drew on the perplexing Jewish-Christian tradition. This was the Diatessaron, a harmony or synthesis of the four canonical gospels composed around 170. (The name means "Through Four.") Because the work was so convenient and accessible, it became immensely popular. Some church leaders disliked it, though, given the personal theological views of its Assyrian compiler, Tatian. He was a prominent Encratite, whose faith demanded the rejection of wine, meat, and sexual activity. From the fifth century, orthodox bishops replaced the work wherever possible in the churches under their control. So the Diatessaron was "suppressed," at least in the sense of being excluded from official church worship. And indeed, no full copy survives intact today.[35]

Yet although it was notionally abolished, copies certainly circulated long afterward. Distinguished scholars in the Syriac Church of the East were still using the work as authoritative through the thirteenth century. Manichaeans favored the work and carried copies deep into Central Asia.

Copies of the Diatessaron found their way to the West, where it continued to shape the New Testament readings of faithful Catholics throughout the Middle Ages. That was so important because Tatian had used the four gospels as they were known in his time, and the readings he knew often differed substantially from what would become the standard texts used in the mainstream churches. Through the Diatessaron, then, the medieval and early modern worlds had access to many readings that were usually associated with lost Jewish-Christian gospels. These works had, for instance, told of the light or fire that illuminated the river Jordan at the time of Jesus's baptism; they reported how Jesus, after the Resurrection, told his disciples that he was no "phantasm" (rather than the "spirit" of the canonical texts). Both of these readings appeared in the Diatessaron. In Matthew 8, Jesus heals a leper and tells him to go to a priest and offer the gift commanded by Moses. In many early texts, Jesus tells the healed man to go to a priest "and execute the Law," words that resonated with Jewish Christians. Again, this early tradition—which may have been the original reading—survived in the Diatessaron. Some modern scholars think that "Through Four" might actually have used material from another, fifth gospel, perhaps Hebrews itself.[36]

Curiously, then, a book composed in second-century Syria became very popular in medieval northern and western Europe, and
that fact tells us much about how manuscripts traveled in these
times. In the 540s, Bishop Victor of Capua (near Naples) discovered a Latin version of the work and ordered it copied, although he
was not entirely sure just what he was dealing with. By the eighth
century, that copy found its way to the English missionary Boniface
by means still unknown. We have already seen the Anglo-Italian
cultural axis of the seventh and eighth centuries. Boniface's book
might have traveled from Italy directly to England, or conceivably
could have been diverted via Ireland. However Boniface found it,
about 750 he gave it to the new German monastic house of Fulda,
which his disciples had founded. Repeatedly copied, this manuscript, Codex Fuldensis, became a major channel for spreading Di-
atessaronic readings in the Latin West. It certainly was not the only
channel, and other Latin versions existed, but the manuscript was
enormously important.

Although the book was technically "lost," scholars have been able
to reconstruct large sections of the Diatessaron because of the many
different fragments that still exist around the world. It gives some
idea of the work's vast influence when we realize that these odds
and ends exist in dozens of languages. Apart from Christianity's
ancient languages of Greek, Syriac, and Latin, the Diatessaron left
its inheritance in tongues as diverse as Armenian, Parthian, Old
Saxon, Arabic, Old English, Old High German, Middle Dutch,
Middle Italian, and Old French. It is in these languages that, all
through the Middle Ages, we find gospel accounts in which a great
light shines in the Jordan, or where Jesus tells the leper to go and
execute the Law. From the eighth century, traces of the Diatessaron
appear not just in copies of the scriptures but in the poems and epics
that mark the first stirrings of European vernacular literature. These
signs appear, for example, in the *Heliand* (Savior), the ninth-century
epic of Christ's life and work that stands at the beginning of German literary history.

From the thirteenth century, vernacular gospel harmonies drawn
directly from the Diatessaron became very common across Western

Europe. They supplied exactly the well-organized material that clergy needed to meet the needs of preaching to the lay faithful. These preachers would have been appalled to know that the "biblical" texts they were using had been condemned by the church as heretical, and moreover, that they preserved ancient Jewish-tinged readings.

However splendid the libraries available to the Irish and the English, the Island peoples were far from unique in their wide-ranging interest in alternative scriptures. Wherever we look among the European nations, Catholic or Orthodox, we find a similar fascination with alternative and apocryphal texts, some of which were in effect treated as canonical scripture. As we will see in the next chapter, alternative gospels persisted in the heart of European Christendom just as they did in the Isles of the West.

4

Old Gospels Never Die

Ancient Gospels That Gave the Medieval Church Its Best-Known Images of Christ

And the Lord set His cross in the midst of Hades, which is the sign of victory, and which will remain even to eternity.

Gospel of Nicodemus, c. 400

ABOUT 1270, AN ITALIAN PRELATE COMPOSED AN INTERNATIONAL bestseller. In the *Golden Legend* (*Legenda Aurea*), Dominican friar Giacomo de Voragine compiled a huge series of stories of the apostles, saints, and martyrs of Christian history structured around the church's liturgical year. In English translation, the whole work runs over half a million words.[1]

Like most bestsellers, it appealed to a large and unmet public demand, in this case the quest for detailed information about the church's heroes and their miraculous deeds. Unlike modern bestsellers, though, the *Legend* remained popular for centuries. It was translated into most of the languages of Western Europe, in multiple independent versions, and it survives in over a thousand manuscripts, far more than any other medieval work. That popularity continued after the arrival of printing in the late fifteenth century, when the *Legend* appeared in hundreds of editions, both in Latin and in various vernacular languages. Between 1470 and 1530, the *Golden Legend* was simply the book most often printed in Europe. When William Caxton began the English printing business in the 1480s, the *Legend* was naturally one of his first projects. As Caxton remarked, just as gold was treasured above all metals, so this *Legend* was held to be noble above all other works. For a contemporary publisher, this was the best of the best, gold among gold. It was a prime source for the stories and motifs depicted by late medieval artists in paintings and especially in illumination.[2]

We can read the *Legend* in different ways. Opening the book at random, it seems like a collection of miracle stories improbable even by the none-too-critical standards of the medieval church. After the Reformation, the *Legend* became a byword for extravagant and even ludicrous tales in which saints of dubious historicity perform superhero feats, such as fighting dragons or surviving decapitation.

Some stories are so outrageous that the modern reader suspects they must be deliberately intended as self-parody. To take one example out of hundreds, we read of Sicily's faithful St. Lucy, who staunchly refuses to sacrifice to Roman idols. The pagan consul orders her taken to a brothel, where she can be gang-raped. However, she remains so fixed in place that a group of men cannot move her, and neither can a gang of a thousand workmen, or even a thousand yoke of oxen. The consul orders her drenched in urine, as a means of combatting what he supposes to be sorcery, but to no avail. Eventually, boiling oil is poured over her as she is burned alive. In her final words, Lucy prays that her martyrdom may last as long as possible, so that believers may learn not to fear suffering (the consul himself is decapitated). Nothing in that account is excessive by the standards of the *Legend*. The Life of Saint James the Dismembered is exactly, and gruesomely, what the title promises.[3]

But the book offered many attractions to prospective readers, not least the large number of highly active and devout female characters. If we want to know what ordinary European Christians—including many sophisticated and educated laypeople—believed on the eve of the Reformation, then we must turn to the farrago of bizarre tales and miracles of the *Legend* and the apocryphal texts it reports. In its lavish superstition, it perfectly epitomized the old world that the sixteenth-century church Reformers were desperate to overthrow.[4]

Viewed another way, though, the *Golden Legend* was an anthology of alternative scriptures, much of it dating back to Late Antiquity. Much of its material was drawn from early Christian pseudo-gospels and apocryphal Acts, which in various forms had been circulating since the third and fourth centuries or before. Reading the *Legend* in 1500, say, a pious Christian could delve into stories drawn from the ancient (and fictitious) Acts of apostles like Thomas and John. In the story of the Resurrection, we find the account of Christ's appearance to Joseph of Arimathea, "as it is read in the Gospel of Nicodemus." A lengthy account of the Virgin's Assumption is credited to "a book sent to St. John the Evangelist, or else the book, which is said to be apocryphal, is ascribed to him."[5]

There was no sense that such reading was at all daring or subversive, that the book was offering clandestine or suppressed texts. Giacomo de Voragine was, after all, a Dominican, from the order formed to eradicate the heresies threatening European orthodoxy at this time. He went on to become archbishop of the critically important city of Genoa. Nor should we imagine him as an intrepid archaeologist retrieving lost texts from ancient caves. Rather, he was synthesizing and compiling the popular religious readings of his day. These were familiar fixtures of Catholic piety, endorsed by church authority.

EVEN ORTHODOX WRITERS who disliked the apocryphal texts recognized that in practice they had to be tolerated. In the late fourth century, Jerome himself denounced "the absurdities of the apocrypha" [*apocryphorum deliramenta*]. He tried to show once and for all that "only four gospels must be accepted, and . . . all the lullabies of the apocrypha [*apocryphorum nenias*] ought to be sung rather to dead heretics than to living ecclesiastics." He declared a simple principle: *Caveat omnia apocrypha!*, "Beware of all apocrypha!" But he knew this warning was not going to be followed too strictly. He contin-ued: "Let her [the church] avoid all apocryphal writings, and *if she is led to read such*, [my emphasis] not by the truth of the doctrines that they contain, but out of respect for the miracles contained in them. Let her understand that they are not really written by those to whom they are ascribed, that many faulty elements are introduced into them, and that it requires infinite discretion to look for gold in the midst of dirt [*aurum in luto quaerere*]."[6]

Just as skeptical was the widely read seventh-century Spanish scholar Isidore of Seville, who firmly rejected any claims that these works might have canonical authority. Yet even Isidore admitted that besides "much falsehood" (*multa falsa*), the apocrypha included some spiritual truths. That concession opened the door to reading the texts, ideally in a careful and critical way.[7]

The value of the apocrypha was hotly debated during the ninth century as the churchmen at the court of Charlemagne and his successors tried to purify and restructure the Western European churches. The best evidence of how entrenched these works had become is the determined attempt to exclude them once and for all. The reforming bishop Agobard (c. 820) shows just how commonly texts from these allegedly lying and heretical apocrypha were used in regular liturgies. He warned, "Let no one dare to meditate or say in the congregation responsories or antiphons taken not from canonical Scripture, which some are accustomed to sing at a mel-ody that they have composed at their pleasure." But it was a losing battle. A few years later, the Frankish scholar Notker opined that the apocryphal materials dealing with the apostles were "very near the truth, or even very true" (*uerisimillimam, seu certe ueracissimam*).[8]

Any would-be censors faced problems in classifying the texts. A work clearly labeled as a gospel posed a challenge to authority and might infuriate church leaders, especially if it could be asso-ciated with some heretical movement. But at no time did churches insist that the faithful confine their reading solely to the canonical scriptures, so that it was quite acceptable to enjoy such genres as hagiography, church history, or devotional works. However much the accounts of Mary's birth and Assumption looked like gospels

or scriptures, they could safely be categorized as hagiographical accounts of a cherished saint. What modern scholars call the Gospel
of Pseudo-Matthew in its time bore the innocuous title *Liber de
Infantia*, the Book of [Jesus's] Childhood; and only in the sixteenth
century did the Protevangelium acquire its modern name, with the
radical suggestion of being the "First Gospel." At times, writers did
slip into "gospel" terminology, as in the case of Nicodemus, but by
the early Middle Ages the works were so firmly established in the
wider culture that they seemed beyond challenge.[9]

There are two main reasons for the appeal of these stories. One
is simple curiosity about the elements of the holy narrative that
were left blank in the approved scriptures, or that lent themselves to
creative expansion. The other reason is both more subtle and more
pressing. Over the centuries, believers mulled over theological problems that the church did not confront or adequately explain, at least
in the version of faith accessible to thoughtful Christians. Believers
used narrative forms in order to explore these doctrines and formu-
late solutions. These were the things that Jesus (for example) should
have said or done, had he had the time to do so. The theological
need produced the appropriate scriptural texts.

Two potent apocryphal traditions fascinated Christians
through the centuries. Both involved aspects of Jesus's life that were
neglected in our canonical gospels, namely, his infancy and childhood and what he did immediately following his bodily death. Particularly persistent were gospels purporting to tell stories of Christ's
childhood. Apart from one scene in Luke, in which the young boy
confounds Jewish scholars with his erudition, the Big Four say
nothing of his life between his birth and the age of thirty or so.[10]

Jesus's infancy was the theme of several works, but most famously
the Infancy Gospel of Thomas, which for some 1,500 years was one
of the most popular of all Christian writings. It is an open question whether the collection of stories as we have it was the creative
work of one author or a compilation built upon folktales already in

circulation. But we do know it was circulating at a very early date, during the golden age for the production of pseudo-gospels in the century or so after 150. Already around 180, the orthodox controversialist Irenaeus was complaining about a Gnostic sect called the Marcosians:

> They adduce an unspeakable number of apocryphal and spurious writings, which they themselves have forged, to bewilder the minds of foolish men, and of such as are ignorant of the Scriptures of truth. Among other things, they bring forward that false and wicked story which relates that our Lord, when He was a boy learning His letters, on the teacher saying to Him, as is usual, Pronounce Alpha, replied, Alpha. But when, again, the teacher bade Him say, Beta, the Lord replied, First tell me what Alpha is, and then I will tell you what Beta is.

The Marcosians were thus using the Infancy Gospel of Thomas, in which that tale appears. Sometimes, when early lists of noncanonical scriptures cite a gospel according to Thomas, this is the work they are referring to, rather than the mystical sayings that have become so famous in recent years. The work would probably have been known at first as the *Paidika*, the "Childhood Deeds."[11]

The work long held a grip on the popular imagination. Translations survive in at least thirteen languages, including not only Syriac and Greek but also Slavonic, Georgian, Ethiopic, and Latin. In Western Europe, the content mainly became familiar because it was absorbed into Pseudo-Matthew, and as such, it circulated widely for many centuries.[12]

Infancy Thomas records many miracles attributed to the child Jesus. It takes its inspiration from Luke's story of the twelve-year-old Jesus in the Temple, but Thomas goes much further in presenting the child's superiority not just to other children, but to all human beings. The text shows how extraordinarily mighty Jesus was from his earliest years, using stories of that power to demonstrate his supernatural qualities and his divine origin. So lacking is Jesus in any human qualities as to flout any theological subtleties about the nature of Incarnation: Jesus is a divine being visiting Planet Earth. At no point, moreover, do stories of miracles and healings have any moral or theological content beyond the crude demonstration of divine might. There is no parallel, for instance, to the metaphorical use of the blindness theme in canonical miracle tales, where lack of sight symbolizes a failure of understanding. In its approach, Infancy Thomas is almost wholly free of any form of Christian (or indeed Jewish) doctrine or morality.

Most modern readers are likely to find the gospels' accounts perturbing and, at worst, repulsive. After a boy curses him, the young Jesus causes him to "dry up" and die. Woe betide the child who casually bumped into him:

> After that He was again passing through the village; and a boy ran up against Him, and struck His shoulder. And Jesus was angry, and said to him: You shall not go back the way you came. And immediately he fell down dead. And some who saw what had taken place, said: Whence was this child begotten, that every word of his is certainly accomplished? And the parents of the dead boy went away to Joseph, and blamed him, saying: Since you have such a child, it is impossible for you to live with us in the village; or else teach him to bless, and not to curse: for he is killing our children.[13]

Jesus retaliates by striking blind those who had complained about him. He mocks and humiliates a scholar who tries to teach him letters. In one instance, the boy Zeno dies in a fall. The neighbors gather, expecting that it was Jesus who had killed him—plausibly enough, given his recent track record of mayhem and slaughter. Jesus, though, resurrects Zeno so that he can testify to what really happened. The miracle occurs solely to score a point. If we imagine a hypothetical gospel of the early years of the Antichrist, it would not be too different.

Some of the gospel's stories are more attractive. When he is not killing people, the child Jesus is playful and carefree. In the most famous tale, the five-year-old boy is sitting by a river on the Sabbath.

He makes twelve birds out of the riverbed clay, to the horror of a pious Jew, who complains to Joseph. Joseph remonstrates with Jesus for his impiety, but the boy immediately conceals the evidence: "And Jesus clapped His hands, and cried out to the sparrows, and said to them: Off you go! And the sparrows flew, and went off crying." On other occasions, he heals local children who have suffered or died through accidents, resurrecting some from the dead. When his brother James gathers wood, and is bitten by a viper, Jesus cures the wound.[14]

Over the centuries, these stories permeated Christian popular culture. The story of the birds was one of the best-known tales of Jesus in the Middle East, and in the seventh century it was included in the Qur'an. It also entered vernacular literature. A seventeenth-century Irish manuscript includes the infancy tales in versified form, probably composed in the eighth century. In the bird story, for instance, we read:

> *Jesus clapped his two hands.*
> *His small voice resounded.*
> *Before their eyes—a wonder of sudden movement—*
> *He scared away the birds. . . .*
> *Someone reported to the people*
> *—it was an extraordinary tale—*
> *that the cries of the birds*
> *were heard as they flew.*[15]

To see just how mainstream these alternative texts became in the medieval churches, consider one image that pervades the religious thought of the era, namely, the Harrowing of Hell. The story tells how Christ, after the Resurrection, broke the gates of hell and rescued the souls of the righteous who had died before his time, including the great figures of the Old Testament narrative from Adam onward. To do this, he had to confront and defeat the evil spiritual powers represented by Satan and Hades.[16]

The direct source of the Harrowing was an apocryphal work called the Acts of Pilate. From early times, inquiring minds had wanted to believe that Pontius Pilate must have left some kind of written record of his interactions with Jesus, and authors duly invented the accounts they would have liked to have found. The "original" Acts of Pilate was in existence by the fourth century, but the legend kept on growing and morphing as it absorbed other traditions and folktales. One was the story of the woman Berenike, who wiped Jesus's face as he was on his way to crucifixion only to find an image of that face miraculously preserved on the cloth she had used. Throughout the Middle Ages, alleged relics of that cloth were widely venerated, as the woman's name was corrupted into Veronica. Another addition to the legend involved the Roman destruction of Jerusalem in AD 70, which came to be interpreted as vengeance for the Jewish betrayal and killing of Jesus. One popular Latin text presenting that point of view was the *Vindicta Salvatoris*, the Avenging of the Savior, which made the fall of Jerusalem the climax and conclusion of the larger gospel narrative. But the *Vindicta* was a very late production, dating from perhaps 700. Thus the Pilate narrative was composed over a period of at least four centuries, illustrating the very long historical development underlying apocryphal story cycles.[17]

The original Acts of Pilate had two main sections. The first purported to be a record of the events surrounding Christ's trial, death, and Resurrection as recounted by Nicodemus, the secret follower of Christ who is mentioned in the canonical Gospel of John. The second—and much more influential—part described the "Harrowing" in a detailed and dramatic section called *Descensus Christi ad Inferos*, "Christ's Descent to Hell."[18]

In their present form, both sections seem to date from the fifth century, but they include older stories about a descent to hell, some of which appeared in other gospels. In an alternative gospel credited to Bartholomew, Jesus reports how "when I vanished away from the cross, then went I down into Hades that I might bring up Adam and all them that were with him, according to the supplication of Michael the archangel." Over time, Nicodemus's gospel overwhelmed the earlier versions and became the standard account.[19]

It is not hard to understand why the story could have come into existence. Several canonical texts point to some such event, although they do not describe it explicitly. The Gospel of Matthew says that, immediately after the crucifixion, "the bodies of many holy people who had died were raised to life. They came out of the tombs after Jesus' resurrection and went into the holy city and appeared to many people": 1 Peter speaks of Christ preaching or proclaiming the gospel to the imprisoned spirits; and the Letter to the Ephesians reports that, "when he [Jesus] ascended on high, he led captives in his train and gave gifts to men." At the start of the fifth century, St. Augustine wrote that nobody but an unbeliever, an infidel, would deny that Christ had been in hell. He descended, said Augustine, to free Adam, the patriarchs, and the prophets consigned there on grounds of original sin.[20]

The *Descensus* illustrates a process very much like Jewish midrash. In both, later authors build substantially on hints in the canonical text. "Many holy people were raised to life"? So which ones? Well, the *Descensus* lists them: John the Baptist, Abraham, Isaiah, Adam, Seth, and the rest. And naturally, each prophet or patriarch describes the event that led to his deliverance.

If the story's existence is no mystery, its astounding appeal does need some explanation. Chiefly, it addressed theological questions that troubled believers at many different levels of learning, supplying a means of posthumously rescuing from hell the venerated and noble figures of pre-Christian times. This dilemma arose early in the church. As nascent Christianity increasingly broke from the Jewish parent stem, Christians had to address the relationship between the two traditions. All orthodox thinkers valued such prophets and patriarchs as Abraham, Moses, and Isaiah, but some, at least, questioned how people who died before the time of Christ's sacrifice could benefit from it and gain salvation retroactively. Matthew's gospel offered the hint by which this dilemma could be solved, and Nicodemus developed it floridly.

In this vision, Christ intervened directly and personally to save those who clamored for salvation, overwhelming the constraints of time and place. Although only certain individuals are mentioned as being liberated, there are no obvious limits to the list of those saved after death. That idea proved very convenient when Christian missionaries were trying to convert European pagans, but sought to avoid preaching that all their pagan ancestors were confined to hell forever. In eighth-century northwest Europe, some preachers used the lessons of Nicodemus so extensively as to slip into something like universalist heresy—the claim that all could or would be saved. In later centuries, the Harrowing story meshed perfectly with the growing idea that the dead could be assisted and ultimately liberated by the prayers and deeds of their living friends and relations as part of a cosmic chain of being. It was a wonderfully attractive vision of the limitless power of Grace. For many centuries, the doctrine also held something like canonical status for most Christians.[21]

Beyond solving the historical conundrum—How could salvation at a given moment in time echo back into previous history?—the crushing conquest of death held out hope for Christians living in any period. Although death was certain, they knew that Christ could and would rescue them, even from the depths of hell. This was important in the later Middle Ages, when ordinary laypeople became increasingly concerned about their chances of salvation after death, and ever more pessimistic about their chances of achieving it. If salvation depended on endless good works and pious deeds, how could one ever be sure that enough had been done? Not until the Reformation did a new view of Christian doctrine teach an absolute hope of salvation through faith in Christ alone. Until that point, troubled souls had to take refuge in the narrative of Christ's conquest of death and hell.[22]

ADDING VASTLY TO THE STORY'S APPEAL were its dramatic qualities. A simple narrative might have described Christ advancing on the infernal city, defeating Satan, and liberating captives. In fact, the *Descensus* is much more complex. It is framed as a reported narrative, introduced in a way that creates maximum anticipation and provides rich opportunities for dialogue and dramatic interaction. It also begins as a genuinely eerie ghost story. (The text exists in several versions: the one quoted here is from the Second Latin Form.) Initially, three pious rabbis testify of Christ's Ascension. They report meeting two men, Karinus and Leucius, newly raised from the dead, who are summoned before the skeptical priestly leaders, Annas and Caiaphas:

> Then Karinus and Leucius signed to them with their hands to give them a sheet of paper and ink. And this they did, because the Holy Spirit did not allow them to speak to them. And they gave each of them paper, and put them apart, the one from the other in separate cells. And they, making with their fingers the sign of the cross of Christ, began to write on the separate sheets; and after they had finished, as if out of one mouth from the separate cells, they cried out, Amen. And rising up, Karinus gave his paper to Annas, and Leucius to Caiaphas; and saluting each other, they went out, and returned to their sepulchres.

The papers they read describe the events of the Harrowing. The reader is present at the making of sacred history.[23]

The *Descensus* splits the main evil character in two, creating a villainous pair who can engage in dialogue about the situation, and traces the growing peril through overheard speech. Satan is Lord of Death, but Hades (originally a place for the dead) has become personified as another speaking character, a partner in ultimate evil. Satan orders his minions to defend the citadel while he himself flees to seek advice from his ally Hades. Satan clutches at straws of hope, but Hades fades in terror of one so powerful, whose mere word can defeat death. The two fall into vulgar quarrelling:

> Then Hades thus replied to Satan: If, then, you can do nothing else, behold, your destruction is at hand. I, in short, shall remain cast down and dishonored; you, however, will be tortured under my power.[24]

We then meet an all-star cast of the great prophets and patriarchs from Adam onward and witness their growing hopes. A climax follows, as Christ proclaims a castle-shattering biblical verse:

> And again there came the voice of the Son of the Father most high, as it were the voice of a great thunder, saying: Lift up your gates, you princes; and be lifted up, you everlasting gates, and the King of glory will come in! Then Satan and Hades cried out, saying: Who is the king of glory? And it was answered to them in the voice of the Lord: The Lord strong and mighty, the Lord mighty in battle. . . . And, behold, suddenly Hades trembled, and the gates of death and the bolts were shattered, and the iron bars were broken and fell to the ground, and everything was laid open.[25]

The story's setting is that of a siege as the villainous figures of Hades and Satan struggle desperately to defend their city and its gates against Christ's onslaught. These themes had a potent appeal for an audience in the later Middle Ages, roughly from 1200 through 1500. Visual depictions of the Harrowing in this era commonly portray hell as a walled city, just like the fortified strongholds that Crusaders encountered in the Middle East. Christ bears a banner with a cross, as did the contemporary Crusaders who struggled against the enemies of Christendom, originally in Palestine and Syria, and later in the Balkans and Eastern Europe. The Harrowing now came to be seen as a massive supernatural siege operation followed by an act of conquest and the liberation of hostages.[26]

But the *Descensus* is not intended only as a historical description of events that happened in the afterlife at some point in the past. Rather, it is meant to give hope and comfort to Christians in later generations, who can know that the victory over death is final and absolute. After the blessed leave hell, they

> asked the Lord to leave as a sign of victory the sign of His holy cross in the lower world, that its most impious officers

might not retain as an offender any one whom the Lord had absolved. And so it was done.

However terrifying the place had once appeared, hell is defeated and left desolate.[27]

THE NICODEMUS STORY SPREAD across Christendom. In the visual arts, the Harrowing story was portrayed in thousands of paintings and carvings, windows and wall-paintings, which reached a climax between 1380 and 1520, the years leading up to the Reformation. Major Renaissance artists who treated the theme included Andrea Mantegna, about 1470, and the German Albrecht Dürer, about 1510. In the Eastern church, the common ikon theme of the Anastasis (Resurrection) depicts the Harrowing and the liberation of the righteous dead.[28]

The Gospel of Nicodemus survives in five hundred manuscripts in various languages, a phenomenal number for a medieval text. The Harrowing was a central theme of the vernacular literatures that emerged across Europe from the twelfth century onward. It featured in every major language, in plays, sagas, chronicles, pious poems, and bloody epics. Apart from the obvious major languages, it was known in Catalan and Occitan, Dutch and Welsh. The Norse turned the story into a saga, the twelfth-century *Nidrstigningarsaga*, in which the Christ storming hell becomes a classic medieval warrior, a Crusader king on a white horse:

> His eyes were like burning flames. He had a crown on his head and many tokens of victory were visible. He had a blood-drenched banner wrapped around himself and on it were written these words: *Rex regum and dominus dominorum* [King of kings and lord of lords]. He was brighter than the sun. He led a great army and all those who accompanied him rode white horses and were clothed in white silk.

His enemy Satan is the classic World-Serpent of Viking mythology, the *Midgardsormr*, who was previously defeated by the pagan god Thor. Like Thor before him, Christ fights a Tolkienesque roster of evil foes, including giants, trolls, and dark champions.[29]

Each country developed its own Harrowing mythology. The story was sung in French verse, and it drew the attention of Europe's greatest medieval poet, Dante Alighieri. In the *Inferno*'s fourth canto, Virgil records how, as a newly arrived shade, he witnessed the arrival of *un possente con segno di vittoria coronato*, "a powerful One crowned with trophies of victory."

> *Hence he drew forth the shade of the First Parent [Adam],*
> *And that of his son Abel, and of Noah,*
> *Of Moses the lawgiver, and the obedient*
> *Abraham, patriarch, and David, king,*
> *Israel with his father and his children,*
> *And Rachel, for whose sake he did so much,*
> *And others many, and he made them blessed;*
> *And thou must know, that earlier than these*
> *Never were any human spirits saved.*

Dante's story of the entry into the hellish city of Dis assumes a knowledge of Christ's previous conquest of the place.[30]

Of course, the Harrowing features in the *Golden Legend*, too. In Caxton's English version, from around 1480, Carinus and Leucius report that

> when we were with our fathers in the place of obscurity and darkness, suddenly it was all so light and clear as the color of the sun. . . . And anon Adam the father of the human lineage began to enjoy, saying: This light is the light of the creator of the light sempiternal, which promised to send to us his light perpetual.

Liberation is at hand:

Anon as Jesu Christ descended into hell, the night began to wax clear. And anon the porter black and horrible among them in silence began to murmur, saying: Who is he that is so terrible and of clearness so shining? Our master received never none such into Hell, ne the world cast never none such into our cavern. This is an assailer, and not debtor, a breaker and destroyer, and no sinner but a despoiler, we see him a judge but no beseecher, he comes for to fight and not to be overcome, a caster-out and not here a dweller.[31]

The story even has a claim to rank as the origin of European drama. That is not surprising, given the theatrical character of the *Descensus* itself, with its extensive dialogues in scenes that cry out for dramatization. As early as the eighth century, the Anglo-Saxon collection known as the Book of Cerne included a dramatized version of the Harrowing. This may be the oldest Christian play ever designed for actual performance.[32]

The Harrowing featured in the "mystery" plays, a term that needs some explanation. Europe's Christians expressed their faith through many activities carried on outside the churches, through acts of devotion and pilgrimage. One popular form of public faith was the dramatic cycles prepared by the craft guilds of cities and towns, each of which was responsible for a particular topic—the glovers might tackle Cain and Abel, while the barbers reenacted Christ's baptism. As the crafts were also known as "mysteries," the presentations were called mystery plays. The French featured the Harrowing in their Mysteries of the Passion. Italians initially sang the story liturgically in praise hymns, *laudes*, which evolved into formal theatrical presentations.[33]

The mystery plays are well known in the English context. Although many such plays have been lost, records of some of the great English cycles survive, and they demonstrate which aspects of faith were thought to be most important and compelling at the time. The greatest and most complete series is the York Mystery Plays, a cycle of forty-eight presentations that traces the world's story from its Creation through the Last Judgment. Of the plays, eleven were drawn from the Old Testament, thirty-seven from the New. Among the latter, though, apocryphal sources were much in evidence. In some cases, these were incidental borrowings from sources such as the Life of Adam and Eve and the tales of Mary's life, but several whole plays were rooted entirely in alternative scriptures. The Harrowing was a standard fixture of the cycles. Far from fading in popularity over time, the Harrowing theme was actually reaching its greatest popularity in the years leading up to the Reformation.[34]

Probably a fifteenth-century production, York's Corpus Christi play closely follows the *Descensus*. (For whatever reason, this topic was given to the Saddlers' Guild.) We see a band of patriarchs and prophets awaiting liberation—Adam, Eve, Isaiah, Moses, John the Baptist. As the devils tremble before the approaching Savior, we finally hear Jesus's proclamation:

> *Attollite portas principes*
> *Open up, you princes of many pains!*
> *Et elevamini eternales*
> *Your endless [everlasting] gates that you have here.*

Jesus tells Satan that he is no mere man, but the Son of God. He commands his angel to bind Satan, which he duly does, ignoring the Devil's desperate appeal to his own ally, Mahounde, or Muhammad. (Mahounde also appears in another play as the god invoked by King Herod.) Satan is defeated and humiliated, his power smashed, as Michael leads the souls of the newly freed blessed to heaven.[35]

PROOF OF THE STORY'S DOMESTICATION in popular culture comes from William Langland's epic poem *Piers Plowman*, written about 1380. A sprawling vision of contemporary England, with a radical social and religious critique, *Piers Plowman* is a worthy rival to Chaucer's work in the English literary canon. It also demonstrates the Harrowing's lavish potential for elaboration even more fully and effectively than the contemporary mystery plays. Drawing on the mysteries, Langland reinterprets the *Descensus* through the eyes of a major poet and dramatist. Yet he is also a radical theologian who uses the story to present Christ's refusal to be bound by legalism. In the true Christian worldview, says Langland, mercy will always triumph.[36]

Langland's drama even offers important female roles. We first hear the dialogue of the women Truth and Mercy, as Truth reports the dreadful situation of the old patriarchs and prophets lying in hell. And how could someone be saved in such a place? When Mercy tries to interrupt, Truth rebukes her:

> *Never believe that yonder light will raise them up,*
> *Nor have them out of Hell—hold your tongue, Mercy!*
> *You are speaking nonsense. I, Truth, know the truth.*
> *That once something is in Hell, it never comes out.*

But Mercy will not be silenced: "Through experience, she said, I hope they will be saved." When Peace arrives, she agrees with Mercy. Although she had never hoped to see Adam, Eve, and the rest, now hope had come: "Mercy shall sing, and I shall dance thereto! Do thou so, sister." Just then, a distant voice cries *"Attolite portas"*—Lift up your gates![37]

Langland describes the conflict through the eyes of the lords of hell, who anxiously await the assault, until at last, Christ stands at their doors:

> *Again the light bade unlock and Lucifer answered,*
> *"Who is this? What lord art thou?"*
> *The Light soon said, "The King of Glory*
> *The lord of might and of main, and all manner of virtues*
> *The Lord of virtues.*
> *Dukes of this dim place, open these gates right now*
> *That Christ may come in, the son of Heaven's king!"*[38]

Satan protests that Jesus's raid violates divine Law. Sinful human beings had deserved hell, argues Satan, so how could he be blamed for carrying out that sentence? He was only obeying divine orders. Jesus, though, explains why he does not propose to be bound by theories of original sin. In the Garden of Eden, Satan entrapped humanity by deceit and trickery, and that fact voids any legal claim that he might propose. You robbed God of his proper possession, says Christ, and God will now return the favor.[39]

This message appealed to a medieval world structured according to precisely defined rights and obligations set down either in documents or customary form. Any party that breached a contract or treaty had to suffer the consequences without complaint. In Langland, those were the harshly clear words of Truth. Christ, though, preaches and practices the law of mercy, which towers above all other values. Langland's Christ is admirably unconcerned with the letter of law—even divine Law.

The vision of the Resurrection ends with angelic music, and Mercy and the others do get to dance:

> *Till the day dawned*
> *These damsels danced*
> *As men rung [bells] to the Resurrection.*

We recall that the ancient Acts of John featured a startling scene in which Jesus teaches his disciples while leading them in a ring dance. But as *Piers Plowman* shows us, the linkage between dance, prayer, and liturgy did not simply vanish with the early church.

Modern historians point out that Langland's critiques of legalism echo those of the proto-Protestant Lollard movement that was subverting church authority in the England of his time. If he was not himself a revolutionary, he was playing with deeply critical ideas. And where better to find those than in the texts that had grown up around the Bible, and that had become largely indistinguishable from it?[40]

APOCRYPHAL STORIES NOT ONLY SHAPED Christian life all around
the church building—in the streets and the churchyards—but also
penetrated thoroughly into the churches themselves, even into the
sanctuaries in which the divine liturgy was proclaimed. So heavily
did Catholic liturgies draw on alternative scriptures, especially the
apocryphal Acts of the apostles, that they became a major source of
apocryphal lore for ordinary believers.[41]

The centerpiece of the church's ritual year was Holy Week, which
began with Palm Sunday and ended with commemoration of the
Crucifixion and Resurrection. In Christian Europe, this was by
far the year's holiest season. Even so, medieval churches celebrated
Palm Sunday with an exchange that was best known through Nicodemus. Leading the procession, the priest would strike the church
door while proclaiming the words of Psalm 24, "Lift up your heads,
oh ye gates . . . and the King of glory shall enter in." Those in the
church responded by asking, "Who is this king of glory?" to which
the priest answered "The Lord of Virtues, he is the king of glory."[42]

The fifteenth-century English visionary Margery Kempe left no
doubt that this Palm Sunday ceremony combined Christ's entry
into Jerusalem with his postmortem conquest of hell. When she
saw the priest and people entering the church, she reported, "Then I
thought how God had spoken to the Devil and opened the gates of
Hell. How he had confounded him and all his army—what grace,
what goodness he has shown these people, to deliver their souls
from that everlasting prison!" That passage has no basis in the New
Testament: it is pure Nicodemus.[43]

———

JUST HOW ARTIFICIAL WAS THE LINE SEPARATING canonical and
apocryphal was noted long ago by Ernest Renan, a pioneering
scholar of early Christian history. Any history of modern Christianity notes the publication in 1863 of his epoch-making *Life
of Jesus*, but Renan also wrote a valuable *History of the Origins of
Christianity*, which makes some acute remarks about the apocryphal gospels.[44]

Renan was writing at a time when educated Europeans were deeply sensitive to issues of authenticity and fraudulence, and they often treated popular culture with supercilious contempt. As a historian, though, Renan had to admit the enormous power of the apocryphal gospels in capturing popular tastes and interests. "Although of humble origin," he said, "and tainted with an ignorance truly sordid, the apocryphal Gospels assumed very early an importance of the first order. . . . The canonical Gospels were too strong a literature for the people." Besides the widespread popular appeal of such "fraudulent" texts, clergy were delighted to have such rich ammunition for sermons, and artists exploited the wonderful opportunities for visual representations. Whether in the Eastern or Western churches, apocryphal stories were fundamental to Christian iconography.[45]

Paradoxically, the church's wars against heretical insurgencies in the later Middle Ages made the alternative scriptures *more* rather than less popular, and even more central to Christian consciousness. As society developed in wealth and sophistication from the twelfth century onward, an ever larger number of believers, clerical and lay, sought the right to read the Bible. The church reacted harshly, forbidding vernacular translations for fear that heretical doctrines might creep in. This prohibition caused intense conflict as independent-minded groups undertook translations for themselves, flouting church authority. Across Europe, we find such dissident predecessors of later Protestantism as the English Lollards, French Waldensians, and Bohemian Hussites. Meanwhile, more overtly deviant groups, like the Albigensians, also turned to the scriptures to justify their particular take on Christian truth. At its strictest, the church's ban on vernacular translations was enforced on pain of torture or death.[46]

That story is familiar enough. But the church's prohibition extended only to translating canonical texts, and not, for instance, to the Gospel of Nicodemus or the Infancy Gospel of Thomas. At a time when possessing a translated version of the canonical Gospel of Matthew could lead to a terrifying encounter with the Inquisition, no such problems arose with the spurious Pseudo-Matthew. Renan noted the paradox:

Not being a sacred Scripture, [apocryphal gospels] can be translated into the vulgar tongue. Whilst the Bible is in a manner put under lock and key, the apocryphas are in everybody's hands. The miniaturists were ardently attached to them; the rhymers seized upon them; the mystics represented them dramatically in the porches of the Churches. The first modern author of a Life of Jesus—Ludolphe le Chartreux— made them his principal document. *Without theological pretension, these popular Gospels succeeded in suppressing, in a certain measure, the canonical Gospels* [my emphasis].[47]

Renan was broadly describing the period from about 1200 to 1500, the era that witnessed the appearance and triumph of the *Golden Legend*. Ludolphe wrote in the fourteenth century, but like the *Legend*, his Life of Jesus enjoyed its greatest distribution with the coming of printing. Together with the *Legend*, this book, deeply rooted in the ancient pseudo-gospels, was for centuries a standard text of European devotion.

HAD A MEDIEVAL BISHOP EVER BEEN ASKED DIRECTLY, he would probably have known that the Gospel of Nicodemus and other apocryphal works were not approved scriptures in the same way as the Gospel of John. But what difference did that distinction make in practice? Apocryphal stories were painted on church walls, recited in the liturgy, and performed in the churchyards and the streets. Matters would not have been very different if a council had officially made such works canonical. That quasi-canonical status was especially true of the wildly popular gospels of the Virgin Mary, which came close to dominating medieval Christian devotion.

Two Marys

How Alternative Gospels Continued
to Present the Feminine Face of God

Scandit ad aethera	*She mounts to the skies*
Virgo puerpera	*The virgin mother*
Virgula Jesse	*The shoot of Jesse*
Non sine corpore	*Not without her body*
Sed sine tempore	*But outside of time*
Tendit adesse	*She goes to be present*

Liturgical chant, c. 1200, quoted in *Golden Legend*

ABOUT 375, THE CYPRUS BISHOP EPIPHANIUS WROTE HIS *Panarion*, an encyclopedic compendium of the heresies of his day. He aimed to provide a medicine chest, a panarion, from which readers could choose cures and preventives to ward off the most dangerous heresies of the age. As Epiphanius rarely allowed a sense of fairness or skepticism to interfere with the flow of a good polemic, modern historians have to be very careful in assessing his claims.[1]

One group that he denounced has attracted interest in modern times as an intriguing manifestation of underground early Christianity. According to Epiphanius, Arabia was home to the

Kollyridians, a female-led group that worshiped the Virgin Mary as divine (or virtually so), with seasonal rituals that involved eating consecrated bread rolls or cakes. The word for cake, *kolluris*, explains the sect's name. Epiphanius sputtered his horror at the group's monstrous opinions: "Now the body of Mary was indeed holy, but it was not God; the Virgin was indeed a virgin and revered, but she was not given to us for worship, but she herself worshiped him who was born in the flesh from her . . . even though Mary is most beautiful and holy and venerable, yet she is not to be worshiped." But what could you expect? After all, says Epiphanius, "women are unstable, prone to error, and mean-spirited."[2]

Over the centuries, the church drew sharp lines between the worship due alone to God and Christ and the lesser kinds of veneration accorded to Mary and the saints. Latter-day believers are left to wonder how the world might have been different if the church had kept that near-divine feminine figure—if it had in fact worshiped a woman. And what if the church had continued to cherish such early female-oriented texts as the Gospel of Mary, or the lengthy Gnostic tract we know as *Pistis Sophia* (Faith of Wisdom), both of which starred Mary Magdalene? Surely, the whole history of the West would have been quite different.[3]

In reality, though, not only did plenty of "Other" gospels actually survive, but many concerned a woman who was a source of awe and worship to generations of perfectly orthodox Christian believers. The heroine in question was not the Mary Magdalene of the Gnostic gospels, but rather the other Mary, Jesus's mother, who became the female face of the divine.

Historically, something is deeply wrong with the view of the Virgin as a kind of anti-Magdalene. However scholars extol the importance of the Gnostic gospels, they are chronologically much later than the canonical texts of the New Testament, in which the Virgin was already becoming a highly significant figure. None of the alternative gospel texts that give such a role to Mary Magdalene can be dated with any confidence before the mid-second century. In contrast, the Virgin Mary was well on her way to something like deification well before this time. We might ask whether popular mythology has the sequence wrong, so that Gnostic authors actually built up the mythological figure of the Magdalene as a counterpart to the Virgin who was already so pivotal to Christian devotion.[4]

Comparing the historical fates of the two Marys tells us much about the church's changing theologies and the creation of scriptures to meet these needs. It also suggests that, oddly, even the Kollyridians were not such a bizarre byway of Christian devotion as they sometimes seem.

As NOTED EARLIER, many modern scholars tell a highly loaded story of evolving church attitudes. In early times, we are told, the church venerated strong female figures like Mary Magdalene, who starred in alternative gospels that the churches then suppressed out of a fear of uppity women. The Magdalene has become the missing superstar of Christian history.[5]

Mary Magdalene was indeed the key figure in many noncanonical gospels. She dominates the *Pistis Sophia*, and she is probably the heroine of the Gospel of Mary, both dating from the late second or third centuries. Such texts portrayed Mary Magdalene as Christ's most significant follower, his leading apostle, and the one most likely to understand his secret teachings. After one of her insights in the *Pistis Sophia*, Jesus praises her, saying,

> Excellent, Mariam, thou blessed one, thou . . . all-blessed Pleroma [Fullness], who will be blessed among all generations . . . she whose heart is more directed to the Kingdom of Heaven than all thy brothers.[6]

Some controversial passages go beyond this, suggesting that Mary was closest to his heart in a romantic or even sexual sense. In the Gospel of Mary, Peter acknowledges "that the Savior loved you more than all other women." When Peter himself doubts that she was in fact so close to Jesus, another disciple rebukes him and reaffirms Peter's original statement. The disciples complain similarly in the third-century Gospel of Philip, in which we hear that Jesus used to kiss her on the mouth. She is his *koinonos*, a word that can mean consort or girlfriend (but which almost certainly does not in this context). In the *Pistis Sophia*, Peter complains that Mary does not allow the men to get a word in.[7]

Mary Magdalene's prominent role has some grounding in historical reality. All the canonical gospels agree that she was among the first witnesses of the Resurrection. Some contemporary scholars argue that she genuinely was a primary figure in Jesus's circle, but that she was excluded from a leadership role in the ensuing power struggles within the apostolic community.

We can easily find other explanations for the emphasis accorded to the Magdalene. Early sects imagined a mythological universe in which spiritual figures were paired, so that male and female figures balanced and complemented each other, making it essential for Christ to have a female counterpart, a *syzygos*. This idea was fundamental to the thought of the Egyptian Gnostic Valentinus. Searching the canonical gospels would have produced strikingly few rival candidates for such a historical role, and Mary Magdalene was duly selected. That is almost certainly the context in which we should understand the word "consort," rather than implying a sexual connection. The Gospel of Philip speaks of three Marys—Mary Magdalene, Jesus's mother, and his sister—a *syzygos* in triple form. Only in a theological sense is the Magdalene Jesus's "other half" (or third).[8]

Whatever the reason, though, the Magdalene's central role at this early stage is never in doubt, although it declined precipitously over the centuries. By the sixth century, Pope Gregory the Great identified her as the penitent prostitute who humbled herself before Jesus, and this stigma has lingered until modern times. Modern writers see the transformation not as an innocent error of interpretation, but as a cynical attempt by a patriarchal church to smear an embarrassingly powerful woman. Reporting on the work of scholar Karen King, an article in *Smithsonian* magazine remarked that Gregory's reading "simultaneously diminished Magdalene and set the stage for 1,400 years of portrayals of her as a repentant whore, whose impurity stood in tidy contrast to the virginal Madonna." The suggestion is that the church deliberately cultivated devotion to the Virgin Mary to distract attention from the subversive Magdalene.[9]

Actually, that supposed denigration is grossly exaggerated. Even in her new role, Mary Magdalene continued to be one of the most popular medieval saints—she has colleges named for her at both Oxford and Cambridge universities. Late medieval painters commonly depicted her Assumption to heaven, recalling similar stories of the Virgin, except that the Magdalene is shown nude, with only her outrageously long hair preserving her modesty. The *Golden Legend* gives her extensive coverage, as befitting a woman who still, in the late Middle Ages, was a potent source of miraculous intervention. Including a vastly expanded version of all the New Testament passages that might conceivably refer to her or her family, the *Legend* describes her career in later life after her alleged move to southern France. Strikingly, in light of modern-day debates about women's place in the churches, the *Legend* reports her mighty role as a preacher, teacher, and missionary:

And when the blessed Mary Magdalene saw the people assembled at this temple for to do sacrifice to the idols, she arose up peaceably with a glad visage, a discreet tongue and well speaking, and began to preach the faith and law of Jesu Christ, and withdrew from the worshipping of the idols. Then were they amarvelled of the beauty, of the reason, and of the fair speaking of her. And it was no marvel that the mouth that had kissed the feet of our Lord so debonairly and so goodly, should be inspired with the word of God more than the other. And after that, it happed that the prince of the province and his wife made sacrifice to the idols for to have a child. And Mary Magdalene preached to them Jesu Christ and forbade them those sacrifices.[10]

Still at this late date, the *Legend* exalts Mary as she "to whom Jesus Christ appeared first after his resurrection, and was fellow to the apostles, and made [by] our Lord apostolesse of the apostles." That hardly sounds like someone being written out of history. And yes, over five hundred years ago, the English language had a feminine form of "apostle."[11]

WHATEVER THE MAGDALENE'S HISTORICAL FATE, her erasure did not purge Christianity of extremely powerful female figures. No account of early Christian development can fail to stress the very high role accorded to the Virgin Mary from very early times. Far from offering believers a wholly masculine array of heroes and role models, the church regularly faced the danger of raising this Mary to semi-divine status. In devotional practice, for well over a thousand years the Virgin became the second Christ, a co-Christ. If the church officially drew a strict distinction between the worship due to Christ and the veneration due his mother, that division collapsed in practice.[12]

Any history of Christianity that fails to accord a central place to the Virgin Mary, and to Marian devotion, is severely flawed. Whether we are looking in Italy or France, China or India, Syria or Egypt, the Virgin is the most distinctive feature of Christian art and piety. For a large share of the world's Christians who have ever lived, this supernatural Mary—with all the legends and her ritual calendar—has been an integral part of the belief system. And contrary to the dismissive phrase about a "virginal Madonna," this Mary has been portrayed not as a passive and domestic mother figure, but as a highly active spiritual leader—in fact, a figure very much like the one the Gnostic texts imagined Mary Magdalene to be.[13]

Later Protestants often complained how devotion to the Virgin escalated over time to the point that she became a mediator and savior who usurped her son's unique functions. But whatever we think of this kind of Marian theology, it actually emerged much earlier than is commonly believed, and it was by no means a novelty in the Middle Ages. In fact, the process was well under way in the church's first centuries.

Although the canonical gospels all mention the Virgin, three of the four do not give her any kind of central role. The oldest of the four, Mark—written about the year 70—barely mentions her. By the 90s, though, Luke's gospel, however, makes Mary's experience critical to framing the gospel story, and she is made to speak words of immense theological significance in the hymn of praise that we call the Magnificat. The Book of Revelation, probably from the same decade, has a cryptic passage concerning the "woman clothed with the sun, with the moon under her feet and a crown of twelve stars on her head," who goes into the wilderness to give birth to the messianic ruler. Later generations have associated these words with the Virgin Mary herself, and that is a natural enough interpretation if we assume that the child is Jesus Christ.[14]

Mary's status rose rapidly in the late first century, and her exaltation continued apace in the coming decades. No later than 160, in his *Dialogue with Trypho*, theologian Justin Martyr presented what would become the standard medieval comparison between Eve and Mary. Although Eve's behavior had brought sin into the world, the Virgin Mary offered redemption: "For Eve, who was a virgin and undefiled, having conceived the word of the serpent, brought forth disobedience and death. But the Virgin Mary received faith and joy, when the angel Gabriel announced the good tidings to her that the Spirit of the Lord would come upon her."[15]

A few years later, the fiercely orthodox theologian Irenaeus of Lyon used the same idea when he wrote, "And thus, as the human race fell into bondage to death by means of a virgin, so is it rescued by a virgin; virginal disobedience having been balanced in the opposite scale by virginal obedience." Throughout the Middle Ages, Latin writers commonly noted that evil came into the world through "Eva," but was defeated when the angel reversed the name as *Ave*—Ave Maria, Hail Mary! By the third century, believers were praying *to* her.[16]

Meanwhile, the pseudo-gospels of the Virgin presented a complete cycle that took virtually everything attributed to Christ and transferred it to this mighty and godly woman. We cannot explain away that feminization in terms of the church compromising its

beliefs in the face of older pagan beliefs or customs. The Marian
Gospels are deeply rooted in Jewish and early Christian traditions
that began long before the church made mass conversions in the
pagan worlds.[17]

Highly supernatural interpretations of Mary's death emerged
in the third and fourth centuries, and they reached full flood in
the fifth, around the time of St. Augustine. Exalted Marian ideas
segued naturally into the rich devotion of the Middle Ages. In the
eighth century, an antiphonary credited to the English scholar Alcuin praised Mary thus:

> Blessed are you among women, through whom the curse of
>   the mother Eve is dissolved
> Blessed mother of God, you are exalted above the choirs of
>   angels to the celestial domains.[18]

JUST HOW ADVANCED MARIAN IDEAS became can be seen from the
Protevangelium, or Infancy Gospel of James, which claims to tell
the story of Christ's family. Unlike many other early Christian texts
and pseudo-gospels, this particular example can be dated with confidence, because well-known church fathers discussed and cited it.
It was probably written about 170, if not even earlier, very much in
the time of the early church.[19]

Notionally written by Jesus's brother James in the late 40s, this
gospel was in fact designed to respond to an identifiable set of historical circumstances in the 160s or 170s. As Christianity expanded,
Jewish and pagan critics formulated a well-developed repertoire
of accusations, which were summarized by the Greek philosopher
Celsus. For its enemies, Christianity was discredited by its origins among the impoverished and credulous, what we might term
an underclass. Jesus, in this hostile view, was poor, ignorant, and
semi-criminal. The story of the virgin birth was a thin disguise for
his illegitimate birth—and his mother's immorality.[20]

The Protevangelium, then, set out to disprove these charges. Poor? Nonsense. Mary's father, Joachim, was very wealthy. And her sexual purity was demonstrated by a series of fantastic stories about her birth and background. Indeed, chastity and virginity emerge as such strong themes in the work that we might well think that we are reading a saint's life written in the twelfth or thirteenth century, a world of convents and celibates.[21]

The Protevangelium applies to Mary the canonical stories about the births of John the Baptist and Jesus. As with John, Mary's parents, Joachim and Anna, are aged and childless, until a miraculous intervention causes conception. An angel appears to Anna promising, "Thou shalt conceive and bear, and thy seed shall be spoken of in the whole world." Mary herself is born following an Annunciation that prefigures her own later experience.[22]

Mary's childhood is no less special. As soon as she is able to walk, her mother prepares a special sanctuary for her in her bedroom, where she is tended by "undefiled" women. At age three, she is taken to the Temple, where the priest recognizes her special role in God's coming redemption of Israel. Because of her importance for the messianic scheme, she is set apart to be raised in the Temple, an idea that suggests total ignorance of the actual working of that institution, which had ceased to exist a century before the actual time of writing. Mary was "nurtured in the Holy of Holies, and didst receive food at the hand of an angel, and didst hear the hymns, and didst dance before the Lord." She receives her own Annunciation in the Temple, while she is making a ritual veil for the building, the same Temple veil that would be rent at her son's crucifixion.[23]

As she approaches puberty, the priests gather to decide Mary's fate. She is betrothed to an older man called Joseph, rather to his embarrassment. As he says, "I have sons, and I am an old man, but she is a girl: lest I became a laughing-stock to the children of Israel." But his advanced age is important to the narrative in order to avoid the suggestion that he might have had sexual relations with Mary at any point, whether before or after marriage. So reluctant is he to accept his new bride that he gives way only under direct orders from the priest. We then follow the familiar New Testament story of the discovery of her pregnancy, complicated by an official trial for the couple's alleged immorality. As they travel to Bethlehem, Mary goes into labor. Joseph finds a cave where she can lie, setting his own adult sons to guard her.[24]

The virginity theme dominates throughout. The midwife who delivers Mary marvels at her still-virgin state. She reports this to another woman, Salome, who scoffs at the alleged miracle. (Salome, incidentally, was the name of an early disciple of Christ's who features extensively in the alternative gospels.) This exchange leads to a scene involving a Christ parallel that strikes modern readers as grotesque. Salome declares that she will not accept such a thing unless she can insert her fingers into Mary's womb. The text precisely echoes the words of Doubting Thomas about testing Christ's wounds after the Resurrection by putting his fingers into his mangled side. And as in Thomas's case, the midwife gains faith once she has performed that test (and has in the process seen her hand wither). Mary's perpetual virginity was already a sturdy doctrine.[25]

Latin Western churches tried to suppress the Protevangelium because they did not like the accounts of Joseph's previous family history. As a result, the book disappeared in the West, leaving us with no Latin manuscripts. Only as late as 1552 did it resurface, when it was published in a new printed edition. But it had not vanished from the wider Christian world. It remained a mainstay in the Byzantine/Orthodox East and further afield, and we have translations into Syriac, Ethiopic, Georgian, Sahidic (Coptic), Old Church Slavonic, Arabic, and Armenian.[26]

EVEN IN LATIN EUROPE, one reason the Protevangelium dropped out of existence was that virtually all of its content became available through other texts, works so wholly derivative that, in modern terms, they would amount to wholesale plagiarism. Together, they constitute a family of works directly derived from the Protevangelium. We will take three chief texts together—the Protevangelium itself, Pseudo-Matthew, and the Nativity of Mary—under the general label of the Marian Gospels.

The main Western substitute for the Protevangelium was Pseudo-Matthew, probably written in the seventh century. This integrated the original Greek text of the Protevangelium with the stories of Jesus's own infancy, creating, in effect, a family history of Jesus's parents and household before the start of his ministry (it is sometimes called the *Liber de Infantia*). Ingeniously, this book dispelled doubts about its authority by forging a correspondence in which the great St. Jerome allegedly gave it his imprimatur and even described having translated it. A fake endorsement consecrated a fake text. As a result, Pseudo-Matthew and its underlying sources gained immense popularity in the Western Middle Ages. Apart from Latin, its stories found their way into many vernacular languages, including Anglo-Saxon, Old French, and Provençal.[27]

Pseudo-Matthew matters enormously as one of the primary means by which medieval European Christians learned the Christian story, in however embellished a form. By the ninth century, an abridged account of Mary's origins was circulating as the Nativity of Mary, *Libellus de Nativitate Sanctae Mariae*. Pseudo-Matthew was also incorporated into the *Golden Legend*, which recites all the familiar tales, including the doubting midwife.[28]

Pseudo-Matthew broadly follows the Protevangelium in describing Mary's beginnings, with some differences. The Temple is now explicitly compared to a medieval convent, in which the young Mary joins a "community of virgins, in which the virgins remained day and night praising God." Even in such a pious company, though, Mary stands out for her exemplary piety and hard work: she is the ideal proto-nun. Joseph, meanwhile, is even older than in the earlier account—his prospective bride, Mary, is younger than his *grand*children.[29]

Although these represent the main texts, related Marian materials surface in many other early writings. One is the puzzling Questions of Bartholomew, which might be the "Gospel of Bartholomew" cited by early commentators and probably dates from the fourth century. Mary's own account of the Annunciation takes up a major share of the document as it survives today in words that sound quite as cryptic as any of the better-known Gnostic gospels. Mary begins with a prayer or invocation, possibly a kind of speaking in angelic tongues:

> Then Mary stood up before them and spread out her hands toward the heaven and began to speak thus: *Elphue Zarethra Charboum Nemioth Melitho Thraboutha Mephnounos Chemi-ath Aroura Maridon Elison Marmiadon Seption Hesaboutha Ennouna Saktinos Athoor Belelam Opheoth Abo Chrasar.*

She reports the angelic appearance in words that echo the Protevangelium, but with added details that explicitly draw comparison to Christ's crucifixion:

> And straightway the robe [veil] of the temple was rent and there was a very great earthquake, and I fell upon the earth, for I was not able to endure the sight of him. But he put his hand beneath me and raised me up, and I looked up into heaven and there came a cloud of dew and sprinkled me from the head to the feet, and he wiped me with his robe. And said unto me: Hail, thou that art highly favored, the chosen vessel, grace inexhaustible.[30]

THE THREE KEY MARIAN GOSPELS are only the most visible signs of a vast mythological structure. We find in these works the foundation of all later theologies of Mary, including the Immaculate Conception. Although that term is often confused in the popular mind with Christ's virgin birth, what it states is that the Virgin was "preserved free from all stain of original sin." In popular piety, the idea commonly extends to the suggestion that Mary herself, like her son, was not born as the result of sexual intercourse.[31]

The idea is usually traced to the seventh century, when the church introduced a feast of Anna's conception of Mary. However, the sense that the conception was special and in some sense exalted is much older, dating to the Protevangelium itself. Reading that book's account of the Annunciation to Anna, we note that her husband "betook himself into the wilderness" around the relevant time of conception. Although it is not explicit, the text implies that Anna's conception of Mary occurred without any human intervention.[32]

Those ideas developed over the centuries. The first to propose the doctrine of the Immaculate Conception in detailed theological terms was the English cleric Eadmer, writing about 1100. Eadmer's argument, later developed by philosopher Duns Scotus, was that it was inappropriate for Christ's holy body to be born of sinful flesh. If Mary had been born under original sin, she would have been an unclean vessel of divinity; she must therefore have been born immaculate. Put succinctly, *"potuit, decuit, ergo fecit"*: God could do it, it was appropriate, therefore He did it.[33]

In 1854, Pope Pius IX formally declared the dogma:

> *From the very beginning, and before time began,* [my emphasis] the eternal Father chose and prepared for his only-begotten Son a Mother in whom the Son of God would become incarnate and from whom, in the blessed fullness of time, he would be born into this world. . . . Therefore, far above all the angels and all the saints so wondrously did God endow her with the abundance of all heavenly gifts poured from the treasury of his divinity that this mother, ever absolutely free of all stain of sin, all fair and perfect, would possess that fullness of holy innocence and sanctity.

The pope used various arguments for this doctrine, but specifically stated that "illustrious documents of venerable antiquity, of both the Eastern and the Western Church, very forcibly testify that this doctrine of the Immaculate Conception of the most Blessed Virgin, . . . always existed in the Church as a doctrine that has been received from our ancestors, and that has been stamped with the character of revealed doctrine." Those "illustrious documents" were the Marian Gospels.[34]

The idea of the Immaculate Conception attracted the scorn of Protestants, and indeed of some Catholics, but almost as sensational was the portrait of Mary as especially chosen before the beginning of time, a doctrine giving her an amazingly exalted role in the Christian scheme. Like the Torah for Jews and the Qur'an for Muslims, Mary now became a fundamental part of Creation itself. Still today, that doctrine remains set in stone as an article of faith for the world's billion-plus Catholics.

JUST AS MARY'S BIRTH ACQUIRED CHRISTLIKE DIMENSIONS, SO, too, did her death. No later than the third century, Christians were speculating about Mary's ultimate fate and whether she had suffered death in the usual human way. When, in about 370, bishop Epiphanius was struggling against heretical speculations about the Virgin, even he remarked that nobody really knew whether she had died or not, and if so, whether she had been buried.[35]

But the pressure to supply a miraculous story of her death was very strong. If she was born without corruption, then pious logic demanded that she should not be subject to corruption at the end of her life, and that she should escape the normal processes that afflicted sinful humanity. By the early fifth century, theological debates over the Incarnation had promoted an ever more enthusiastic cult of the Virgin. The Council of Ephesus in 431 marked a watershed as the church proclaimed Mary as *Theotokos*, God-Bearer.[36]

In the fourth and fifth centuries, around the time of Epiphanius, a group of related scriptures described the Virgin's passing from this world. Although scholars debate the exact sequence in which these books were written, and the relationships between them, some key scriptures can be identified.[37]

Somewhere before 400, there appeared a lengthy novelistic account of the Virgin's passing. Probably written in Greek, it spread far afield and was translated into Syriac, Ethiopic, and Arabic. We know one version called the Six Books Apocryphon, which in English translation runs to a substantial 12,000 words. The book's origins are not clear, but the Apocryphon reflects the ideas and practices attributed to the Kollyridians. To put this in context, this was written not more than twenty years or so after the Nag Hammadi texts were concealed.[38]

The Six Books Apocryphon represents a complete gospel, with many echoes of the canonical texts, only now many of those familiar themes and stories are transferred from Jesus to the Virgin herself. It describes how Mary prepares for her coming end by summoning the apostles, who are gathered miraculously from the various corners of the world. Thomas is summoned from India, while several of the group are raised from the dead for the occasion. When Mary dies, Jesus commands a chariot of light to carry her to "the Paradise of Eden." Her soul is carried through the heavens, where she encounters such great biblical figures as Elijah and Moses.[39]

Clearly, the idea of the Virgin's supernatural passing was widely held, and it attracted a sizable body of legends and stories. Another important text, *De Obitu Mariae* (On Mary's Death), was attributed to St. John himself, appropriately enough, given that the New Testament reports that Christ on the cross entrusted that apostle with the care of his mother. This book—perhaps from the fifth or sixth century—tells much the same story as the Six Books Apocryphon, including her gathering of the apostles before her death, but adds one important new detail. After her death, it is not just her soul that is carried to glory, but also her body:

> The apostles carried the couch, and laid down her precious and holy body in Gethsemane in a new tomb. And, behold, a perfume of sweet savor came forth out of the holy sepulcher of our Lady the mother of God; and for three days the voices of invisible angels were heard glorifying Christ our God, who had been born of her. And when the third day was ended, the voices were no longer heard; and from that time forth

all knew that her spotless and precious body had been transferred to paradise.

Analogies to Christ's Resurrection could not be more explicit.[40]

―――――――――――

ANOTHER BOOK THAT HAD A LASTING influence was a fifth-century
work usually referred to today as *De Transitu Virginis* (The Passing
of the Virgin). In itself, it is not much different from its competitors,
introducing few new ideas or literary devices. What gave it a wide
readership was that it took the material circulating in those rival
texts and dressed them in orthodox form. The fact that it was translated into Latin allowed it to circulate in those regions that would
soon become central to the Christian world.[41]

The *De Transitu* is presented (falsely) as the work of the pres-
tigious second-century church father Melito of Sardis, who was
supposedly writing to defeat the heretical errors of one Leucius. In
response, says Pseudo-Melito, he will write the true and authorized
version of Mary's passing, beginning with Christ's crucifixion. For
two years after the first Pentecost, he reports, Mary served the nascent church, living on Mount Olivet. She then received a visitation
from an angel, who greets her in a reprise of the original Annunciation. He brings her a palm branch from Paradise to accompany her
body at her forthcoming funeral. At that point, St. John is miraculously transported to meet Mary, followed by the other apostles, all
borne on clouds. All gather to pray:

> And when they had sat down in a circle consoling her, when
> they had spent three days in the praises of God, behold, on
> the third day, about the third hour of the day, a deep sleep
> seized upon all who were in that house, and no one was at all
> able to keep awake but the apostles alone, and only the three
> virgins who were there. And, behold, suddenly the Lord Je-
> sus Christ came with a great multitude of angels; and a great
> brightness came down upon that place, and the angels were

singing a hymn, and praising God together. Then the Savior spoke, saying: Come, most precious pearl, within the receptacle of life eternal.[42]

Christ assures Mary that Satan can have no power over her, because he and his angels will guard her:

> And when the Lord had thus spoken, Mary, rising from the pavement, reclined upon her couch, and giving thanks to God, gave up the ghost. And the apostles saw that her soul was of such whiteness, that no tongue of mortals can worthily utter it; for it surpassed all the whiteness of snow, and of every metal, and of gleaming silver, by the great brightness of its light.[43]

Christ orders Mary's body to be placed in a new tomb, while he delivers her soul to the archangel Michael.

The apostles then prepare for Mary's burial. Three virgins wash her body, recalling the three women who went to Christ's tomb on Easter morning. The Jewish chief priest is scandalized by the glorious procession into Jerusalem, and he tries to overturn the bier. He is struck down immediately by a miracle, and can only be cured by accepting Christ as savior.[44]

But Mary's burial proves only temporary. Christ agrees to the apostles' petition that Mary should be taken to heaven:

> And He ordered the archangel Michael to bring the soul of St. Mary. And, behold, the archangel Michael rolled back the stone from the door of the tomb; and the Lord said: Arise, my beloved and my nearest relation; thou who hast not put on corruption by intercourse with man, suffer not destruction of the body in the sepulcher. And immediately Mary rose from the tomb, and blessed the Lord, and falling forward at the feet of the Lord, adored Him. . . . And kissing her, the Lord went back, and delivered her soul to the angels, that they should carry it into paradise.

In a short space, we find a facsimile of the Annunciation followed by a Pentecost scene, an entry into Jerusalem, and a second resurrection.[45]

As the story evolved, it acquired even more miracles and still closer analogies to Christ's experience. According to one widespread medieval legend, all the apostles gathered to witness Mary's ascension to glory, except for Thomas, who had also been inconveniently late for Christ's Resurrection appearance. Mary, however, graciously appears to him personally, and as a token of proof, leaves her Girdle, or Belt, which became a famous relic. The scene features in the *Golden Legend* and was much used in Renaissance art.[46]

THE VOGUE FOR SUCH TEXTS might disturb many modern Christian readers. Veneration or love for the Virgin is one thing, but placing her so starkly in Christ's own role seems daring to the point of blasphemy. In the seventh century, the Qur'an denounced Christians for making divine claims both for Jesus and his mother.[47]

Some earlier Christian leaders shared these concerns about thus elevating Mary. In the sixth century, the Gelasian Decree consigned to the apocrypha a number of Marian Gospels, although we don't know exactly how they corresponded to the texts we know. They included the "*Liber de infantia salvatoris* [Book on the Savior's Infancy]; *Liber de nativitate salvatoris et de Maria vel obstetrice* [Book of the Nativity of the Savior and of Mary, or the Midwife]; also the book called *Transitus sanctae Mariae* [Passing of Holy Mary]." Probably, the third work listed refers to the *De Transitu Virginis* we know. If it was, this is yet another example of the abject failure of church authorities to suppress texts they disliked.[48]

For centuries after the appearance of the decree, pious scholars writing on Mary's passing demonstrated their skepticism with qualifiers such as "Some say that . . ." In the eighth century, the historian Bede told potential visitors to Palestine that they could see there "an empty sepulcher in which the holy Mary was once said to have rested, but it is not known by whom or when it was taken." A little later, discussing Mary's passing, the Frankish abbot Ambrosius Autpertus wrote:

> But no catholic history tells us by what means she passed hence to the celestial realms. For the church of God is said not only to reject the apocrypha [*respuere apocrypha*] but even to be unaware of these same events. And indeed there are so many anonymous writings on her Assumption against which, as I have said, one is so warned, that even for the confirmation of the truth one is barely allowed to read them. Hence many people are indeed disturbed because her body was not found in the earth, nor is her corporal assumption found in catholic history, as it is read in the apocrypha.

The English scholar Aelfric was very cautious. In a homily of about 1000 celebrating the nativity of Mary, he warned his listeners, "We do not wish to recite the narrative of the heresy that heretics composed about her birth, because wise teachers have forbidden it, and about her death, which the holy scholars have forbidden us to relate."[49]

But the core ideas went from strength to strength. At least by the sixth century, Mary's passing or Assumption was being kept as a feast in both East (Palestine and Egypt) and West (Gaul). No later than the sixth century, the idea of Mary's triumph over death was being preached by some of the church's greatest leaders. In Gaul about 600, Gregory of Tours wrote that

> the course of this life having been completed by blessed Mary, when now she would be called from the world, all the apostles came together from their various regions to her house. And when they had heard that she was about to be taken from the world, they kept watch together with her. And behold, the Lord Jesus came with his angels, and, taking her soul, he gave it over to the angel Michael and withdrew. At daybreak, however, the apostles took up her body on a bier and placed it in a tomb, and they guarded it, expecting the Lord to come.

And behold, again the Lord stood by them; the holy body having been received, he commanded that it be taken in a cloud into paradise, where now, rejoined to the soul, [Mary's body] rejoices with the Lord's chosen ones and is in the enjoyment of the good of an eternity that will never end.

In the early eighth century, St. John of Damascus reported what was by then the standard Eastern tradition, that "Mary died in the presence of all the Apostles, but that her tomb, when opened, upon the request of St. Thomas, was found empty; wherefrom the Apostles concluded that the body was taken up to heaven."[50]

ALL THAT REMAINED TO BE SETTLED was the exact nature of her passing, and whether she was carried to heaven before or after bodily death. The West developed a doctrine of Assumption, namely, that she was taken up while still alive, and did not suffer death. In the East, Orthodox churches admitted that she had died, or rather, fallen asleep, albeit in the gentlest and most soothing way. Hence the word Dormition, or Falling Asleep (*Koimesis*). However, the differences were not absolute, and plenty of Western artists depicted the Dormition. The East developed a powerful belief in her subsequent resurrection, which was symbolized by her tomb being found empty on the third day.[51]

Some of the greatest painters in Western art have treated the Assumption, including Mantegna, Titian, and Rubens. Less familiar, but more extraordinary, is the Eastern treatment that forms the subject of so many icons. The Virgin lies on her deathbed, surrounded by the mourning apostles. Nearby stands her son, receiving her pure soul. But those artists usually include a breathtaking detail without parallel in the West. The Jesus who stands at his mother's bed holds a baby girl, who represents the soul of the newly deceased Mary in a state of perfect innocence. It is attractive and moving to see Jesus as the loving guardian of the child that was his mother, who is now a New Creation.

At least in official doctrines, those mystical ideas of Mary's ending are still today firmly held by the Roman Catholic and Orthodox churches, who together compose perhaps two-thirds of the world's Christians. As recently as 1950, Pope Pius XII pronounced the "divinely revealed dogma" on Mary, stating that "the Immaculate Mother of God, the ever Virgin Mary, having completed the course of her earthly life, was assumed body and soul into heavenly glory. . . . She was not subject to the law of remaining in the corruption of the grave, and she did not have to wait for the end of time for the redemption of her body." Catholic and Orthodox alike mark the date of the Assumption, August 15, as a primary feast of the church. Because Pius's declaration gave such weight to God's feminine aspect, psychologist Carl Jung described the papal proclamation as the most significant moment in Christian history since the Reformation itself.[52]

Stories like the Assumption tell us a great deal about the formation of Christian doctrine and belief. They are not grounded in the Bible—or if so, very tenuously—but rather depend on the church's developing body of tradition and belief as argued and negotiated over the centuries. In theory, Protestants demand a scriptural basis for major doctrines, but in fact they realize that it is exceedingly difficult to rely on scripture alone even for such key doctrines as the Trinity or the Incarnation. These doctrines rely on the collective wisdom and tradition of the early church as expressed in the works of the church fathers and the great councils—especially the first four, held between 325 and 451. The churches of the fourth and fifth centuries already accepted beliefs and practices that today we might consider quite medieval, including attitudes toward the Virgin Mary. In practice, all churches depend on accumulated traditions more than they might like to admit. Where they differ is how selective they are, and at what chronological point they draw a line.

———

THE ASSUMPTION DEMONSTRATES the profound impact of the Marian Gospels on church life. Not only were the scriptures read, but they justified a structuring of time and the ritual year that for many centuries was a familiar part of the everyday lives of a majority of Christian believers. Feasts and celebrations devoted to the Virgin Mary made up a major and cherished portion of the Christian year, and at least in theory, they still occupy that status in Catholic and Orthodox nations.

The notion of a Marian ritual year begins remarkably early, stunningly so in light of what we know about the origins of the Christian calendar. At a very early stage, the church commemorated special days associated with saints and major leaders, usually marking their deaths. Special days linked to Christ's life and career were also celebrated. But the Marian calendar stands out for its complexity and its comprehensive nature.

An early draft of this ritual cycle was first described in the Six Books Apocryphon about 400. The work urges the celebration of three special days devoted to the Virgin, the first being two days after the Feast of the Nativity, and the others on May 15 and August 13. This calendar, allegedly ordained by the apostles themselves, is explicitly associated with the agricultural year. On the first day, near the Nativity, "with her pure offerings shall be blessed the seeds of the husbandmen, which they have borrowed and sown." The May event would be "on account of the seeds that were sown" and to prevent the curse of locusts. A third celebration was "on account of the vines bearing bunches [of grapes] and on account of the trees bearing fruit," with the aim of preventing trees from being crushed by hail. In advocating a specific calendar devoted to a particular individual, this odd passage really has no parallels in the vast corpus of apocryphal writings and early hagiography. It links the emerging cult of the Virgin with older nature religions, and perhaps even with the commemoration of an older Near Eastern goddess figure.[53]

Yet that seemingly bizarre format of celebrations came close to what the church actually institutionalized. By the seventh century, the Byzantine Empire had established a series of feasts to recall the Virgin's birth and other events in her life: initially, these were the Purification, the Annunciation, the Assumption, and Christ's Nativity. Others were added over time, with the Mary-besotted

English especially creative in inventing new devotions. Increasingly, too, existing feasts shifted their emphasis to become more explicitly Marian, so that Jesus's Presentation in the Temple came to be celebrated as Mary's Purification.[54]

Although in the Eastern and Western churches the details differed, the Marian year came to look like this:

February 2	Purification of Mary / Jesus's Presentation in the Temple
March 25	Annunciation
August 15	Assumption/Dormition
September 8	Nativity of Mary
November 21	Mary's Presentation in the Temple
December 8	Immaculate Conception of Mary

In addition, May was Mary's distinctive month, to a degree that would have delighted the author of the Six Books Apocryphon.

To varying degrees, each of these celebrations bears the mark of the apocryphal gospels. Although the Purification is described in the canonical Gospel of Luke (Luke 2.22), artistic depictions of it reflect apocryphal influence when they depict Joseph as an elderly widower. In four of the cases, though, the stories are based entirely on later, noncanonical gospels. The Immaculate Conception and Nativity are entirely drawn from the Protevangelium and its offshoots, as is Mary's Presentation in the Temple. The Assumption is from the Six Books, the *De Transitu Virginis*, and related noncanonical literature.

ELEMENTS OF THE MARIAN GOSPELS permeated Christian high art and popular culture. So copious are these materials that we can only touch on them here. Any full coverage, in fact, would amount to a survey of much of the art and literature of medieval Europe.

Even more than the Harrowing of Hell, Mary's passing and glorification became central to Christian devotion. The *Golden Legend* reported Mary's passing in pure resurrection imagery mimicking Christ's own:

> And then when the apostles came to the Vale of Jehosaphat, they found a sepulcher like unto the sepulcher of our Lord, and laid therein the body with great reverence, but they durst not touch it, which was the right holy vessel of God, but the sudary [cloth] in which she was wrapped, and laid it in the sepulcher. And as the apostles were about the sepulcher after the commandment of our Lord, at the third day, a cloud much bright environed the sepulcher, and the voice of angels was heard sound sweetly and a marvelous odor was felt sweet smelling.

Christ himself appears, "and He bare the body with Him of the Blessed Virgin with much great glory." One doubting apostle insists on the tomb being opened to confirm the miracle: "And at the last they opened the sepulcher and found not the body, but they found only but the vestments, and the sudary."[55]

Such stories provided a climax to the mystery plays. The English York play of the Assumption features a powerful ritual invocation of the Virgin to rise from the dead. A band of angels appears, singing lines adapted from the biblical Song of Solomon, which here becomes a liturgy devoted to the Virgin. They sing together:

> *Surge proxima mea Columba*
> *Mea tabernaculum glorie vasculum vite, templum celeste . . .*
> *[Rise up my dearest one, my dove,*
> *Tabernacle of glory, container of life, heavenly temple . . .]*

A band of angels each sing a line, each recalling the Song of Solomon:

> *Rise, Marie, thou maiden and mother so mild . . .*
> *Rise chieftain of chastity, in chering [suckling] thy child . . .*
> *Rise turtle, tabernacle and temple full true. . . .*
> *Rise up this stounde [instant]*

Come chosen child
Come Marie mild
Come flower unfiled [undefiled]
Come up to the king to be crowned
[Together]
Veni de libano sponsa, veni coronaberis
[Come forth Lebanon my spouse, come forth, thou shalt be
        crowned][56]

To the amazement of the watching apostle Thomas, her soul
rises, to become

A babbe born in bliss to be bidand [abiding]
With angels' company, comely and clean.

In an ironic reversal of the canonical gospels, it is Thomas who goes
to reveal Mary's rising to the sorrowing disciples, who doubt his
words. Ultimately, they realize the truth, as Peter declares:

Behold, now hither your heads in haste
This glorious and goodly is gone from this grave.[57]

Other stories survived in popular culture, shaping the songs that
ordinary people sang in their fields and streets. One passage in
Pseudo-Matthew has the holy family wearying on the flight into
Egypt. Mary asks Joseph to give her dates from a palm. Joseph protests that the palm is too high, but the young Jesus causes it to bow
down to give its fruit. That story, like other portions of the flight,
was often depicted in medieval art. In a somewhat different form,
this story gave rise to one of the oldest recorded English songs, the
"Cherry Tree Carol," which may date from the fifteenth century.
The carol begins with a remark on age that certainly reflects the
apocryphal tradition:

Joseph was an old man,
and an old man was he,

When he wedded Mary,
in the land of Galilee.

While en route to Bethlehem, they pass through a cherry orchard, where Mary asks for the fruit. From within her womb, Jesus performs the same miracle, causing the tree to bend. When the baby Jesus is born, he prophesies his death and Resurrection:

"Upon Easter-day, mother,
my uprising shall be;
O the sun and the moon, mother,
shall both rise with me."[58]

The Marian Gospel tradition shaped much later Christian visual art, including medieval wall-paintings, stained glass, and mosaics as well as manuscript painting and Books of Hours, no less than poetry and storytelling. Few, indeed, are the medieval images of Mary that do not draw heavily on the apocryphal gospel traditions.[59]

It is in the Marian Gospels that countless artists found the common image of a very aged Joseph marrying a sprightly young Mary. They also found here the depictions of Joachim and Anna that were so common in the Middle Ages, and the image of Mary giving birth to Jesus in a cave. Mary, of course, was accompanied by an ox and an ass, and her midwife—Salome—displays a hand withered by her blasphemous skepticism. As in the case of Mary's birth and childhood, her passing and glorification likewise became a whole cycle beloved by artists and their patrons.

The Annunciation demonstrates the systematic triumph of apocryphal imagery. Christians through the centuries have portrayed the moment when the angel tells Mary that she will bear a child, as reported in the canonical New Testament. But modern scholars have done a masterful job of analyzing medieval depictions of the various Annunciation scenes to show how heavily they deploy themes and variations from the apocryphal texts.[60]

What, in particular, is Mary actually doing at this critical moment? Many portray her in settings taken directly from the

Protevangelium or its sister texts. Sometimes, she is at a well drawing water, but commonly in the Eastern church she is seated at her
work in the Temple, making the veil. This context is easily missed if
the viewer assumes that Mary, like any diligent young woman of her
time, is simply working with textiles. But she is doing much more
than that, making something for God's Temple, already working in
a context that is both priestly and messianic. Western depictions of
the event usually show her reading or studying, again likely recalling Pseudo-Matthew, which stresses that "she was always engaged
in prayer and in searching the Law."[61]

At least by the later Middle Ages, Christian visual artists had
developed the various traditions into a whole cycle of the Life of the
Virgin. The exact themes and motifs varied in Eastern and Western
Europe, but the common core drew on both canonical and apocryphal texts. Canonical events included the Annunciation, the Visitation, the Birth of Jesus and the events of the Christmas story,
the flight into Egypt, and Jesus's crucifixion and ascension. However, these stories were flanked by others drawn from alternative
scriptures. The cycle concluded with the death of the Virgin, her
Assumption, and her heavenly coronation. One particular subcycle
drew entirely on the Protevangelium/Pseudo-Matthew tradition,
incorporating twelve episodes:

> *The marriage of Joachim and Anna*
> *Joachim's offering refused*
> *The Annunciation to Anna*
> *The Annunciation to Joachim*
> *Joachim and Anna meet at the Golden Gate*
> *Birth of the Virgin*
> *Infancy of the Virgin*
> *The Virgin's Presentation to the Temple*
> *The Virgin's life in the Temple*
> *Marriage (handing over) of Mary to Joseph*
> *The family's setting up housekeeping*
> *Distribution of alms.*[62]

These images appear at least from the early Middle Ages and reached impressive heights between 1250 and 1520. Judging by the number of artistic treatments, these themes were enormously attractive to believers, and especially to rich patrons, who sponsored magnificent artistic treatments. In Padua in about 1300, Giotto himself painted a complete cycle in the gorgeous Scrovegni Chapel. Other artists covering the subjects included Albrecht Dürer, who about 1500 produced a popular series of nineteen Marian images in woodcut. (Dürer created many other works reflecting apocryphal themes as well, including, as noted earlier, a Harrowing of Hell.)[63]

SUCCESSIVE RELIGIOUS and aesthetic revolutions have destroyed so much of Europe's pre-Reformation heritage that in only a few places can we see enough to grasp the older worldview. Even so, destruction has not been total. St. Mary's parish church in Fairford, Gloucestershire, is home to the only complete set of medieval stained glass to survive in England. Constructed in about 1490 by an unknown Flemish craftsman, the windows are remarkable not just for the artistic qualities of any one item, but for their comprehensive nature. In all, the twenty-eight windows include almost one hundred separate images and stories. Taken together, the glass offers a holistic portrait of the Christian universe as it was imagined on the eve of the Reformation.[64]

Naturally, the sequence begins with the Fall and ends with a titanic image of the Last Judgment. Throughout, though, we see the pervasive influence of alternative scriptures and traditions derived from outside the canonical Bible. In the depiction of the Fall, the Tempter appears with a woman's head and bust—an image also found in *Piers Plowman*—and the Harrowing of Hell is dramatically represented. A quarter of the windows show the heroes and villains of Christian history, both the apostles and martyrs and the church's persecutors. All of these images draw heavily on the *Golden*

Legend, and the apostolic stories are chiefly taken from the apocryphal Acts of the apostles.

Marian imagery appears very frequently at Fairford, often in contexts that seem forced to modern viewers. The second image depicts Moses, but not in the famous pose of bearing the tablets of the Law. Instead, he is confronting God in the Burning Bush, which in the Middle Ages was generally taken as a symbol of Mary. Like the bush, she "burned" with God's presence, although her virginity was not consumed. Other Marian themes are quite overt. The whole second window is drawn from the Marian Gospels, showing the embrace of Joachim and Anna; the birth of Mary; Mary's Presentation at the Temple; and the betrothal of Mary and Joseph. Another window shows the flight into Egypt, together with the apocryphal miracle of the palm tree. An image of the Assumption shows Mary standing on the crescent moon; she is accompanied by an angel and shining in glory. Those images are, of course, over and above the many Marian references taken from the canonical gospels—the stories of the Nativity and Christmas, Mary's presence at the Resurrection and Ascension. For Christians of that age, how could Mary not feature centrally in the mighty scheme of the universe's creation, fall, and redemption?[65]

AT THE BEGINNING OF THIS CHAPTER, we heard a horrified description of the Mary-worshiping Kollyridians. None of their actual liturgies survive, but if they had, perhaps they would not have looked significantly different from what was taking place in perfectly respectable Catholic churches in medieval Europe. Nor would their hypothetical holy scriptures of Mary have looked much different from the Marian Gospels of actual history.

Just imagine an alternative world in which the Christian church not only triumphed, but accepted a number of alternative gospels from the second and third centuries alongside its canonical scriptures. Imagine, further, that churches made imagery from those gospels central to their art and culture, even using their motifs in wall-painting and stained glass. And that in this world, the church presented exalted female figures for veneration and near-worship by the faithful. Actually, no great effort is needed to envision such a world, for it really existed, and we call it "Catholic Christianity."

6

The New Old Testament

Tales of Patriarchs and Prophets
That Became Christian Gospels

*Our father Adam when dying, commanded in his Testament his son
Seth and said to him, "My son Seth, lo, offerings are laid by me in
the Cave of Treasures, gold and myrrh and frankincense; because
God is about to come into the world, and to be seized by evil and
wicked men, and to die, and make by his death a resurrection for all
children of Adam." And lo, the Magi, the sons of kings, came carrying these offerings, and went and conveyed them to the Son of God,
who was born of the Virgin Mary in Bethlehem.*

The Six Books Apocryphon, c. AD 400

FOR CENTURIES, CATHOLIC AND ORTHODOX CHRISTIANS FOUND
the truths of their religion proclaimed in many texts outside the
canonical New Testament. Some of the clearest interpretations
of Christ and his work apparently came from sages and prophets
who had lived long before his birth, yet who wrote sweeping pre-
gospels. One, for instance, came from Levi, one of the twelve sons
of the patriarch Jacob. By the early Christian period, a document
purported to record the Testaments of the Twelve Patriarchs, and
Levi's seemingly spoke to the emerging religious order. In his dying
Testament, presumably composed about 1500 BC, he prophesied a

time when Israel's priesthood would become corrupted. In those last days, though, God would raise up a mighty new priest:

> And His star shall arise in heaven, as a king shedding forth the light of knowledge in the sunshine of day, and He shall be magnified in the world until His ascension. . . . The heavens shall be opened, and from the temple of glory shall the sanctification come upon Him with the Father's voice, as from Abraham the father of Isaac. And the glory of the Most High shall be uttered over Him, and the spirit of understanding and of sanctification shall rest upon Him in the water. . . . And He shall open the gates of paradise, and shall remove the threatening sword against Adam; and He shall give to His saints to eat from the tree of life, and the spirit of holiness shall be on them. And Beliar shall be bound by Him, and He shall give power to His children to tread upon the evil spirits.

It was a cause for high excitement in Latin Europe when the thirteenth-century English bishop Robert Grosseteste discovered a copy of these sensational Testaments.[1]

Obviously, the Testaments of the Twelve Patriarchs are not what they claim to be. In their present form, they were written or edited by Christians during the second century and were probably adapted from older Jewish compositions. But although Levi's Testament and the rest are spurious, they still exercised a powerful influence on medieval Christians, much like the equally ahistorical Gospel of Nicodemus, or the Marian Gospels. All that distinguished such Pseudo–Old Testament texts from the explicitly Christian gospels was that the former were couched in the future tense.

Medieval Christians knew many writings credited to such Old Testament figures as Moses, Abraham, Enoch, Ezra, Isaiah, and many others. As we have noted, these were pseudepigrapha, "falsely titled writings" (rather than false writings), and they were a common product of Second Temple Judaism between about 200 BC and AD 100. Scholars commonly speak of these works as the Old Testament pseudepigrapha, but that term is misleading because

Christians so often read them as a commentary on the New Testament and on the life and role of Christ. Although they notionally dealt with pre-Christian Hebrew times, we should properly classify many of these works alongside the Marian Gospels as Christian apocryphal literature.[2]

Through much of Christian history, the relationship between the Old and New Testaments was very different from how most imagine it today. Modern believers certainly see foretastes or prophecies of Christ in the Old, but on a tiny scale compared to anything understood by earlier generations. Early and medieval Christians found countless symbolic representations of Christ throughout the Old Testament, to the point that those stories merged seamlessly into the New, creating a single expanded gospel. For those earlier generations, Christ was how God appeared to the world, and artists usually depicted Old Testament manifestations of God with Christ's face. Naturally, then, his followers saw no paradox in writing Christ into the Old Testament narrative wherever possible. Christians would have been appalled by any suggestion that the Old Testament was in any sense a Jewish text rather than their own exclusive possession. If Jews used these texts also, then surely they had stolen and perverted them.[3]

In some cases, Christian editing of older works was relatively light. Often, though, works notionally framed in an Old Testament setting existed solely to present the work of Christ in history and to promote belief in him. Rather than merely appropriating older books, some Christian authors wrote wholly fresh works that were impressive in their own right, and in a good number, Christ himself appears overtly as a character in the narrative. One, in particular, the *Cave of Treasures*, was a heroic attempt to integrate the story of Christ into the whole human story recounted in the Bible, a sequence of stories running from Adam through the patriarchs and prophets. In terms of their position within the broader Christian canon, these texts must be counted alongside the other alternative gospels we have been considering.[4]

Like those other gospels, too, some were "lost," but usually in the limited sense of fading from use at particular times and places. If some pseudepigrapha did indeed disappear, others survived, influencing some churches rather than others. Those that ultimately did vanish often lasted far longer than we commonly think, and they survived partially in other forms, in extracts or revisions in other books. Many works from this "New Old Testament" remained in lively use long after the early Christian centuries, exercising a potent influence through the Middle Ages and beyond. Reports of their loss have been greatly exaggerated.[5]

MEDIEVAL CHRISTIANS HAD NO DIFFICULTY finding scriptural warrant for the Descent into Hell. They turned to the book of Jeremiah, where that prophet said, clearly enough, that the Lord remembered Israel's dead "and descended to them in order to make known to them his salvation, that they might be saved." As early as the second century, the church father Irenaeus had cited this straightforward text. If the scripture was so transparent, how could it be gainsaid? The problem, though, was that the text cited did not come from the Old Testament Book of Jeremiah, or at least from any version of the canonical Jeremiah known to scholars over the past 2,000 years. Like a great many other Old Testament passages that Christians long used to establish doctrine, it was apocryphal. As so often happened, an apocryphal scripture validated an apocryphal doctrine.[6]

Pseudo-Jeremiah was by no means the only work of its kind circulating long centuries after the death of the historical prophet. Christians often favored such alternative Old Testament texts on doctrinal grounds, but that does not necessarily mean that they themselves had created (or forged) those works. Often, they were unwittingly transmitting a whole tradition of Christian midrash on the original biblical texts. Given their background, Jewish Christians, in particular, were likely to create such midrashic expansions of the original texts.[7]

One example occurs in Psalm 96, which features the line, "Say among the heathen that the LORD reigneth." In the context of the

Psalms, that is not a surprising statement—but Christians borrowed and adapted it at a very early stage of the church. Already
in the second century, the Christian apologist Justin Martyr knew
the verse in expanded form as "the Lord reigns from the Tree,"
foreshadowing the crucifixion. Conceivably, that revised version
of the psalm text had Jewish origins, but it had an obvious appeal
for Christians. Justin's reading also occurs in the Old Latin version
of the Bible (pre-fourth century) and in a variety of early patristic
writings. In his debates with the heretic Marcion, the church father
Tertullian asked how his rival could possibly deny such a straightforward prophecy. Latin fathers like Augustine and Gregory the
Great continued to use the "reigns from the tree" verse through
the fifth and sixth centuries, and it survived in the Latin Psalter
until modern times.[8]

Distinguishing between faithful and false texts was not easy.
St. Jerome in the fourth century reported discovering a whole
apocryphal version of Jeremiah, *Hieremiae apocryphum*, which a
Jewish-Christian believer had given him. Jerome recognized it as
apocryphal because he was immensely learned and widely read,
with a dazzling grasp of various versions of the scriptures and of
pseudo-scriptural texts. But how were less skilled readers to respond
if a work of that kind fell into their hands? The temptation to accept
the attribution to Jeremiah, or another patriarch or prophet, was
overwhelming: people wanted to believe. In the second century, Justin Martyr fully credited such a pseudo-Jeremiah text as authentic
even though he was an excellent scholar. So convinced was he, in
fact, that he used this example to denounce Jews for concealing biblical texts that lent themselves to Christian interpretations (Grosseteste would say the same thing about the Testaments of the Twelve
Patriarchs). Justin also believed that the Jews had censored "reigns
from the Tree" for their own sinister purposes.[9]

BESIDES INDIVIDUAL VERSES, whole alternative books proliferated.
The range and variety of pseudepigrapha, Jewish and Christian,

were overwhelming. In the first century AD book 2 Esdras, which we will discuss shortly, God commands Ezra to copy the books of the Bible, including the "twenty-four" texts that make up the Hebrew Tanakh, or what we know as the modern Protestant Old Testament. But other scriptures existed over and above this, and arguably, these were the ones that really mattered:

> Make public the twenty-four books that you wrote first, and let the worthy and the unworthy read them; but keep the seventy that were written last, in order to give them to the wise among your people. For in them is the spring of understanding, the fountain of wisdom, and the river of knowledge.

This passage suggests not only the scale of the alternative texts—three times the number of the canon—but also their privileged position. Any sense of the full and true Bible, suggests Ezra/Esdras, demands a knowledge of all ninety-four scriptures.[10]

The term "pseudepigrapha" needs some unpacking. We should be careful with our vocabulary here, as modern attitudes to authorship are very different from those of bygone societies. Today, an author who presents a work under the name of some other individual is guilty of serious misconduct, and we might speak of forgery or impersonation, dismissing the work in question as bogus or false. Such judgmental language would have puzzled an early or medieval reader, who had a strong prejudice in favor of established authority over novelty. Writers commonly presented new writings under the guise of some famous or venerated figure, especially if the new work could be fitted within an existing and well-known tradition that could be traced back to that figure.

Also, to call one work "pseudo-" implies that other texts can reliably be attributed to a named person, so that, for example, the canonical Gospel of Mark really was the work of someone of that name. That idea might have been acceptable when scholars believed that the four evangelists really were the authors of the gospels with which they are credited, but modern authorities are more skeptical. You would look long and hard for a reputable biblical critic who believes that anyone named Mark or John actually wrote the gospels attributed to them. Mainly out of habit, though, neither work is usually described as pseudepigrapha.[11]

In modern times, the Old Testament pseudepigrapha have become the focus of lively scholarship for historians of both Judaism and Christianity. A standard edition of these writings, edited by James H. Charlesworth in the 1980s, is an essential feature of the scholarly library. This collection includes fifty-two texts as well as fragments of many others, mainly written between about 200 BC and AD 200. (The collection runs to some 2,000 pages, including commentary.) More recently, another group of scholars is in the process of publishing a still more extensive collection, including many works not previously available. The books thus span the period that gave rise to Christianity, and they contributed mightily to the creation of some of our canonical texts.[12]

The history of these alternative texts is curiously reminiscent of the lost gospels we have been examining in a Christian context, in that these, too, wandered far from their places of origin. Most of these pseudepigrapha originated in a Jewish world. From the third century AD onward, though, rabbinic scholars became very concerned about Jews falling into heterodoxy, and they laid down strict prohibitions against using marginal works. One rule from the collection of religious traditions known as the *Mishnah*, a codification of oral law, lists the people who have no place in God's kingdom. They include "he who maintains that resurrection cannot be proved from the Torah, [one who maintains that] the Torah was not divinely revealed, and an Epicurean [a materialist or atheist]. R. Akiba says: Also, one who reads in the outside books." Such outside reading was treated as on a par with outright rejection of the basic tenets of faith. Jews appear to have been very successful not just in prohibiting those outside books but in utterly destroying all copies, at least within their own community. Commonly, though, Christians preserved them long after they had been excluded from synagogues. These works persisted on the margins, which in that instance meant the Christian realms. Forgotten in their homelands for over a millennium, they were preserved and read in Ethiopia or in the Byzantine and Slavonic worlds. Only in modern times were they fully restored to their Jewish homes.[13]

Although the pseudepigrapha cover a huge variety of topics and approaches, some common themes emerge. Above all, they try to answer the questions that naturally occurred to readers of the mainstream scriptures but were not answered there in sufficient detail to satisfy the curious. Particularly cherished were the various accounts of supernatural visions, revelations, and ascensions, which fulfilled popular demand for ever more information about the spiritual geographies of heaven and hell. Many texts describe the realities of the unseen world, either present (visionary journeys through the heavens and the angelic universes above us) or future (apocalypses). Apocalypses, visionary accounts of the imminent end-times, enjoyed a special vogue in the Second Temple era. Although the standard Christian Bible includes just two apocalyptic texts, Daniel and the Revelation of John, the original collection edited by Charlesworth has nineteen apocalypses.

SUCH BOOKS LEFT A POWERFUL INHERITANCE in the religious fringes of early Christianity, especially in Gnosticism, which teaches that properly initiated believers can rise from the present world of illusion to the authentic realms of Light and Wisdom. Historians debate how much Gnosticism grew out of the earliest Christian movement and how much it drew on earlier Jewish currents of the kind we see in the pseudepigrapha. Certainly the Gnostic writings share many ideas with the pseudepigrapha, including the fascination with ascent through the heavens and the angelic worlds. Without the larger body of pseudo–Old Testament literature, Gnosticism is incomprehensible.[14]

At least in the form in which we have them, some of the pseudepigrapha themselves can be classified as Gnostic. Now long lost, a Gospel of Eve was a source of particular horror to orthodox churchmen, who believed it taught sexual libertinism. Several of the scriptures buried at Nag Hammadi are credited to Old Testament figures, including Shem and Melchizedek, and to Norea, who is claimed as Noah's wife. We find an Apocalypse of Adam, as delivered to his son Seth, and a treatise attributed to Seth himself. Both Jews and Christians found Seth intriguing. According to some readings of Genesis, Seth must be the ancestor of all human beings who survived the flood. Other believers saw him as the founder of a special royal race and a precursor of Christ. (In very modern times, the film *Noah* popularized this theme of a special saving role for the descendants of Seth.) Especially in Egypt, Sethians constituted an important faction within the early Gnostic movement, and the Gospel of Judas refers to "Seth, who is called Christ." When we trace the continuing power of the pseudepigrapha literature through the Middle Ages and beyond, we are following a direct line from the Gnostic story that so intrigues modern audiences.[15]

The academic jury remains out as to whether some works should properly be classified as Gnostic or as closer to the mainstream position of the Great Church. Still vigorously debated are the Odes of Solomon, a hauntingly beautiful collection of religious poetry that probably reflects the liturgical life of the Syriac church in the second or third centuries. Some of the imagery startles:

> *A cup of milk was offered to me,*
> *And I drank it in the sweetness of the Lord's kindness.*
> *The Son is the cup,*
> *And the Father is He who was milked;*
> *And the Holy Spirit is She who milked Him.*

Some scholars believe that the Odes are Jewish in origin, or at least adapted from a Jewish original. Even the Jewish sect of the Essenes—the likely authors of the Dead Sea Scrolls—have been credited as authors.[16]

———————

THROUGHOUT CHRISTIAN HISTORY, churches have varied in their attitudes to the pseudepigrapha, which remain unknown to most modern-day Catholics and Protestants. Matters were different in bygone eras, when churches approved the reading of such texts. Some works are included in Bibles as fully credentialed scripture.

In Latin Western Europe at least, many such texts played little role after the end of antiquity. The fact that these alternative texts are scarcely mentioned in the lists of approved and forbidden scriptures that churches issued so frequently from the sixth century onward suggests that they were not seen as a threat in anything like the same way as the old Gnostic works. Not until the Renaissance did thinkers in Latin Europe begin to rediscover these long-lost works on any scale.[17]

But any description of the Christian world needs to go beyond Western Europe. The "falsely titled" works were much better known in regions speaking Greek, Coptic, Syriac, and Armenian than they were in the Latin West. We have already made the acquaintance of the list of approved and condemned scriptures known as the Stichometry of Nicephorus, probably a seventh-century document. Besides the Deuterocanonical books, the list of Old Testament works that were respectable but disputed (*antilegontai*) also included "the Psalms and Odes of Solomon." In the inferior category of apocrypha, the stichometry listed a solid library of pseudepigrapha that included the Testaments of the Twelve Patriarchs (a lengthy 5,100 lines) and Enoch (4,800) as well as the Testament and Assumption of Moses and pseudepigrapha of Baruch, Habakkuk, Ezekiel, Daniel, and others. If these works were not canonized, they were at least preserved. Like the alternative gospels, their "loss" was a relative and limited phenomenon.[18]

By far the most remarkable example of survival was in the Orthodox churches of Eastern Europe, where a great many obscure pseudepigraphical works were translated into Slavonic languages in the early Middle Ages. There they remained in regular use, as a well-known genre of pious reading, until scholars rediscovered them in the nineteenth century. That find sparked a minor revolution in our knowledge of Second Temple Judaism and Christian origins, one that continues to produce new insights even today. (I will discuss those texts and their history in the next chapter.)[19]

We can trace the fate of these ancient works from three figures who were all credited with deeply impressive publication records: Ezra, Baruch, and Enoch. Their "falsely titled writings" ended up in mainstream Bibles over large parts of the Christian world—although in very different and widely separated regions. Their story tells us much about the quite different Bibles available to varying groups of Christian believers. All three prophets, moreover, were appropriated to become Christian evangelists.

IN MODERN PROTESTANT BIBLES, Ezra (Esdras in Greek and Latin) is the main character of an important but short book that describes the restoration of Jerusalem in the fifth century BC following the Babylonian exile. Traditional Jewish Bibles merged the texts of Ezra with Nehemiah to become a single canonical book. But that coverage gives a very poor idea of Ezra's profound importance in Jewish and Christian history. His legendary wisdom made him an attractive candidate for false attributions, as did his special association with the Temple and an epochal act of religious restoration. Perhaps in some future apocalyptic age he would be the initiator of a renewed Temple. In later centuries, he was credited with numerous writings that have survived in multiple languages—apocalypses, visions, and books of "questions." (See Table 6.1, "Books Attributed to Ezra/Esdras in Various Bible Translations.")[20]

Especially important for Christians was 2 Esdras, sometimes called the Fourth Book of Ezra, quoted earlier. Much of the text is taken up by a series of visions known as the Apocalypse of Ezra. The work was probably written around the year 100, close to the composition of the biblical Book of Revelation. It was likely written in Palestine, and possibly in Hebrew. At an early stage, it was adopted by Christians, and copies survive in multiple languages—Latin, Syriac, Arabic, Armenian, and Ethiopian.[21]

Through the mid-sixteenth century, 2 Esdras was included in most Christian Bibles, and it did much to shape medieval concepts of the Last Things, the world's end and the Judgment. It also

---

**TABLE 6.1   BOOKS ATTRIBUTED TO EZRA/ESDRAS IN VARIOUS
BIBLE TRANSLATIONS**

	Septuagint Greek	*Vulgate Latin*	*English*
"The Greek Ezra"	I Ezra	III Esdras	I Esdras
Canonical Ezra	II Ezra	I Esdras	Ezra
Canonical Nehemiah	III Ezra	II Esdras	Nehemiah
Apocalypse	—	IV Esdras	II Esdras

Chapters 1–2 of this work are also known as 5 Ezra

Chapters 3–14 are the Jewish Apocalypse of Ezra

Chapters 15–16 are known as 6 Ezra

Source: Based on James King West, *Introduction to the Old Testament* (London: Macmillan, 1981), 469.

---

influenced the Roman Catholic liturgy. One of the book's greatest legacies survives in a Catholic context, where the traditional response to death involves the liturgical phrase "Eternal rest grant unto them, O Lord, and let perpetual light shine upon them." This is adapted from 2 Esdras 2.34–35. Christopher Columbus used a passage from the book (6.42) to support his geographical views and to convince the Spanish monarchs to sponsor his transatlantic voyage. From the sixteenth century, 2 Esdras was generally demoted to apocryphal status, but that did not mean that it disappeared from Christian usage, or from some Bibles, and it is still canonical in Ethiopia.[22]

Ezra's "additional" writings remained quite mainstream throughout the Christian world, including the Latin West. But much more obscure pseudepigrapha survived in the Syriac world, among some of the world's oldest churches. Throughout the Middle Ages, these Syriac-speaking churches spread far beyond the Middle East and across much of Asia. Even allowing for the massive destruction of Christian texts in this region over the centuries, we still find evidence of Christian scholars reading and citing an impressive range of Old Testament pseudepigrapha throughout the Middle Ages. These were the books that Syriac-speaking churches carried with them as they expanded across Asia into India and China. They retained their following at least into the thirteenth century.[23]

The Odes of Solomon are another case in point. Although they were popular in the third and fourth centuries, evidence for them becomes very thin in later years. Yet scribes took the trouble to make complete copies of them long afterward. One Egyptian manuscript probably dates from about 1000, while the main Syriac version is from the fifteenth century. We have no idea why such copies were made, whether they were intended for the personal devotion of one small group or for a wider group of churches, or if in fact they were still used in liturgies. But over a thousand years after their supposed disappearance, someone cared enough to preserve them.[24]

One enduring work was the apocalypse known as 2 Baruch, which dated from not long after the fall of Jerusalem in 70. It presents a searing vision of the end-times, with appalling destruction that culminates in the coming of the Messiah and the eternal restoration of the Temple. The book thus represents the concerns of a Jewish author of the late first century AD, but meshes perfectly with Christian apocalyptic expectations. Whatever the original author intended, Christians had no doubt of the identity of the Messiah described in those passages.[25]

Apart from a couple of quotations in the church's Latin fathers, 2 Baruch was not known in the West. Even so, right through the Middle Ages, at least up to the fifteenth century, we find readings from "Baruch the prophet" in Syriac lectionaries. In about the year 600, the Syriac Bible known as the Codex Ambrosianus included 2 Baruch, 2 Esdras / 4 Ezra, and part of Josephus's *Jewish War*, a section that circulated as scriptural under the name 5 Maccabees. These additional books were included as integral portions of the manuscript, not as appendices, as we would expect if they were being treated as marginal or apocryphal.[26]

Syriac churches also knew and copied the Book of Jubilees, which we have already encountered as a sacred book in Ethiopia. Despite its sometimes bizarre perspectives, and its hostility to Gentiles, a major portion of the book is included in a Syriac Christian chronicle as late as the thirteenth century.[27]

Also much read in various parts of the world was the literature associated with the ancient figure of Enoch, who reputedly lived before the Flood. He is described very briefly in Genesis, where his main achievement is disappearing to be with God, seemingly without dying. That description, though, gave him an impressive role as an intermediary between human and divine worlds. Even more promising for astronomical and astrological speculations, his age was given as 365 years.[28]

From the third century BC onward, Enoch became the subject of several writings using his name, probably written in Aramaic. Indeed, scholars now speak of Enochic Judaism as a significant form of religious dissidence and connect it with the movement represented at Qumran, where several of these works survived among the Dead Sea Scrolls. Probably by the first century AD, various segments were brought together to form a work called 1 Enoch. Modern scholars have rediscovered 2 Enoch, probably also dating from the first century AD. The author of 2 Enoch claims that 360 books were written in the prophet's name; medieval Muslim historian al-Tabari knew an impressive "thirty scrolls" credited to Enoch.[29]

As we saw earlier, 1 Enoch in particular was enormously influential in its time, especially for its account of the "Watchers" during the time of Noah and their semi-human offspring. This book also gave scriptural foundation for the obsession with angels and archangels, such as Michael and Gabriel. The whole work sounds like a manual for an ancient magician who needed a script to conjure up angels and spirits, which may have been one of the book's early functions.[30]

The book has a complex history in the mainstream church. It certainly had devotees in the earliest Christian community. Our canonical Epistle of Jude quotes it as inspired prophecy—which poses massive problems for modern-day fundamentalists who want to draw a sharp distinction between canonical and noncanonical texts. Some modern commentators go to improbable lengths to show that Jude cannot have meant to cite the work in this way, but he assuredly did. A series of church fathers from the second and third centuries also treated Enoch as canonical. So, also, on occasion, did the brilliant critic and controversialist Origen, although he later became skeptical. Enoch, for these thinkers, was a fully accredited part of the Old Testament, and in about 200, the African theologian Tertullian called Enoch "the oldest prophet."[31]

Their successors became more suspicious. In the fourth century, the Alexandrian church leader Athanasius scorned the additional writings credited to Enoch, Moses, and Isaiah. While giving some credit to Enoch's writings, Augustine rejected most of his alleged works, placing them in the same category as those "many writings . . . produced by heretics under the names both of other prophets, and, more recently, under the names of the apostles, all of which, after careful examination, have been set apart from canonical authority under the title of apocrypha." By the fifth century, 1 Enoch duly faded from use, becoming another lost scripture.[32]

Or at least that was true in much of Europe. But 1 Enoch retained followers elsewhere. The Ethiopian church, in particular, was highly conservative in its reluctance to abandon ancient texts. It thus preserves in a fossilized form what would have been the canonical tastes and preferences of the Egyptian and Syriac churches of Late Antiquity. Even today, the Ethiopian church's Old Testament canon includes 1 Enoch, which only survives in full in the ancient Ethiopian language of Ge'ez. Western Europe rediscovered the work when a British traveler brought back an Ethiopic copy in the eighteenth century. Also in the Ethiopian canon we find Jubilees, which Ethiopians call the Book of Division, as well as 2 Esdras.[33]

Nor were the old pseudepigraphical works wholly purged from Europe itself. As late as the eighth or ninth centuries—three or four hundred years after its supposed "loss"—1 Enoch was still known to the author of *Beowulf* in the orthodox and Roman-leaning Catholic culture of Anglo-Saxon England. Genesis reports, cryptically, that Enoch "walked with God: and he was not; for God took him." But his books endured.[34]

FROM LATE ANTIQUITY ONWARD, Christians never ceased to write ancient/new documents producing texts notionally credited to earlier prophets or patriarchs but actually presenting a thoroughly Christian message. The history of Jesus Christ expanded almost indefinitely, as his Second Coming was constantly reimagined to fit into the context of contemporary events.[35]

The long-familiar genre of apocalyptic allowed anonymous and deniable commentary on current events. The turbulent events of the seventh-century Islamic conquest naturally spawned several such works. One of the most enduring and widely read, the Apocalypse of Pseudo-Methodius, was firmly grounded in the Old Testament apocryphal scriptures, especially the alternative literature on Adam and Seth that we will discuss shortly. It offered a complete history of the world from the time of Adam, but focused chiefly on conditions in the Muslim-dominated world around 690. "Methodius" foresaw the rise of a Greek King who would slaughter the Muslim Ishmaelites, reconquer Jerusalem, and liberate Christians, before the final Judgment.[36]

Through the seventh and eighth centuries, various apocalypses were credited to Ezra and Enoch, who now appeared as acute commentators on contemporary Islam. So did Daniel, the alleged author of a seventh-century Syriac Apocalypse. About 800, another Greek work of the same name described the catastrophes that Christians would encounter at the hands of the "sons of Hagar," the name the author gives to the Arab Muslims, together with their Jewish allies. Worldly disasters grow worse until the final Judgment and coming of Christ. So long did such apocalyptic efforts persist that they raise in acute form the question of just when, if ever, we can place an end to the process of producing scriptures.[37]

SOME OF THE NEWER WRITINGS offered frank statements of Christian doctrine placed in the mouths of pre-Christian figures. In at least one instance, they drew rich doctrinal support from a source that was ostensibly pagan and non-Christian.

For a millennium, one of the most beloved Christian "gospels" was the prophecy of the Sibyl, which claimed to date from pagan antiquity. The ancient world knew a number of prophetesses, or Sibyls, and oracles circulated widely under their name. The most significant were composed between about 150 BC and AD 300 and were eventually collected in the sixth century. As we examine them today, we can trace their very diverse origins, and some at least were composed by Jews or Jewish Christians.[38]

The Sibyllines exercised such power because they apparently represented a firm prediction of Christian truth stemming from sources that were pagan, and so, presumably, objective. If even the pagans acknowledged this fact, who could gainsay it? Adding to the appeal of these works in the Jewish and Christian worlds, a powerful tradition claimed that "the Sibyl"—or at least, one of that title—was the sister of Enoch, from the ancient pre-Flood world.[39]

The Sibyllines attracted much interest from Christian scholars, but one particular oracle exercised a lasting allure. This is the eighth oracle, a second- or third-century AD text attributed to the Erythraean Sibyl. It offers an epic poetic rendering of the apocalypse and the Day of Judgment:

> Sounding the archangel's trumpet shall peal down from
>   heaven,
> Over the wicked who groan in their guilt and their
>   manifold sorrows.
> Trembling, the earth shall be opened, revealing chaos and
>   hell.
> Every king before God shall stand in that day to be judged.
> Rivers of fire and brimstone shall fall from the heavens.

But beyond these poetic qualities, it also has a feature that impressed later generations. In Greek, the poem is an acrostic, and the first letter of each line spells out the words Ἰησοῦς Χριστος Θεοῦ υἱὸς σωτηρ, σταυρός—Jesus Christ, Son of God, Savior, Cross. The modern English rendering quoted here tries to reproduce this effect by spelling out the word SOTER, Savior. If we further reduce *that* phrase to its initials, and omit the "cross," then we are left with the word *ichthyos*, or fish, which is why early Christians used the fish symbol for Christ. A huge amount of symbolism and doctrine is thus crammed into a short space.[40]

Other Sibylline texts were cited as prophecies of Christ, but this one in particular—the *Versus Sibyllae de die iudicii*, Sibylline Verse on the Day of Judgment—enthralled readers and artists for well over a millennium. Augustine gave a Latin rendering of this, the *Iudicii Signum*, in the *City of God*, and the acrostic was a source of wonder to prominent medieval scholars across Latin Europe.[41]

Even such hints of the larger texts were enough to make the Sibyl's words a cultural icon, beloved by artists and composers. The poem is referenced famously in the thirteenth-century hymn of the Last Judgment, the *Dies Irae*, in which the world's fiery destruction is prophesied by David and the Sibyl: *Teste David cum Sibylla*. In that form, the Sibyl has reached worldwide fame through Requiem settings by Mozart, Verdi, and many other composers. The *Iudicii Signum* also circulated in popular culture. Medieval translations appeared in French as well as Provençal and Catalan, which in the Middle Ages were among Europe's great literary languages. The Sibyls found a lively following in Slavic Orthodox countries, above all Russia. Although interest developed more slowly in Russia than in Western Europe, the Sibyllines permeated seventeenth-century tsarist culture.[42]

The enormous power of these Sibylline prophecies is suggested by the ceiling of the Sistine Chapel, painted about 1510, and commonly acknowledged as one of the greatest works of visual art ever created. In this vast composition, Michelangelo included portraits of twelve prophetic figures who foretold Christ. Twelve is a routine symbolic number, and it would be easy enough to compile such a list from the canonical prophets of the Old Testament. Michelangelo, though, uses only seven of the Hebrew prophets, who are accompanied by five of the Sibyls, including the Erythraean. That choice speaks to the scriptural authority of the Sibyllines, particularly the *Iudicii Signum*. They were an integral component of the Christian scriptural universe.[43]

BY FAR THE MOST SIGNIFICANT Old Testament figure appropriated to Christian use in pseudo-scriptures was Adam. Together with his immediate family, particularly Eve and Seth, the patriarch attracted an enormous body of later literature that expanded greatly on the slim Genesis account. In fact, the surviving pseudepigrapha demonstrate a powerful taste for the characters in the opening pre-Flood chapters of Genesis, from Adam through Enoch and Noah.

Adam himself features in the New Testament in a critical passage in Paul's Letter to the Romans, where he becomes a forerunner and counterpart of Christ. As Adam fell and brought sin and death into the world, so Christ reversed those curses when he redeemed the world. That parallelism was an irresistible call to Christian storytellers, who framed a complex theology in terms of identifiable human characters with their own faces and voices.[44]

This literary Garden of Eden is complex territory, with many unresolved questions about dating and original languages, but we can map its general development with some confidence. Adam was already attracting a substantial Jewish literature during the Second Temple era, between about 200 BC and AD 100. This included a Life of Adam and Eve, which Christians adopted enthusiastically. The corpus expanded the biblical account of the expulsion from Eden, supplying substantially more information about the first human generations. This primary literature then grew into a series of secondary texts with titles such as the Apocalypse of Adam, the Penitence of Adam, the Testament of Adam, the Cave of Treasures, and the Conflict of Adam and Eve with Satan. And that does not include the sizable literature devoted to other family members, including Seth, Eve, Cain, and Abel. (For a listing and chronology of the apocryphal Adam literature, see Box 6.1.)[45]

Box 6.1   The Apocryphal Adam Literature

Life of Adam and Eve (first century AD?)
Known in multiple languages, including Greek, Latin, Armenian, Coptic, and Georgian. Includes the lives, deaths, and funerals of Adam and Eve, including detailed accounts of the Fall and prophecies of future events.

Book of Adam (Ginza Rba) (second or third centuries AD)
Sacred text of the Mandaean religion. Includes Sethian material.

Apocalypse of Adam (pre-third century AD)
Found at Nag Hammadi. Adam reveals to Seth the origins and nature of the Gnostic universe.

The Books of the Daughters of Adam (Date very uncertain)
Does not survive. Condemned in the Gelasian Decree of the sixth century AD.

Testament of Adam (fourth century)
Preserved in Syriac and Arabic. Adam reveals the future to Seth, including the coming of the Messiah.

Conflict of Adam and Eve with Satan (fifth or sixth century AD)
Preserved in Ge'ez (Ethiopic). A history of the world from the Garden of Eden to the Fall of Jerusalem in AD 70.

The Cave of Treasures (sixth century AD?)
Survives in Syriac. Recounts the history of the world from the Fall to the death of Christ.

No later than the third century, Christians began adapting existing Adam texts for their own ends, making them ever more explicit in their Christian theology. One exemplar is appropriated from an original Jewish Testament of Adam. Originally written in the Syriac language, this work in its Christian form survives in several languages. In this short "Testament," or neo-gospel, Adam tells his son Seth that

God is going to come into the world after a long time. [He will be] conceived of a virgin and put on a body, be born like a human being and grow up as a child. He will perform signs and wonders on the earth, will walk on the waves of the sea.[46]

In a later variant, Adam's prophecy is very specific, and entirely Christian:

And God said that He should go about with people on the earth, and grow in days and years, and should perform signs and wonders openly, and should walk upon the sea as upon dry land, and should rebuke the sea and the winds openly, and they should be subject unto Him, and that He should cry out to the waves of the sea and they should make answer to Him speedily. And that He should make the blind to see, and the lepers to be cleansed, and the deaf to hear, and the dumb to talk, and should raise up the paralytics, and make the lame to walk, and should turn many from error to the knowledge of God, and should drive out the devils from men.

God foretells the future to Adam, with the stunning promise of future deification:

Do not fear. You wanted to be a god; I will make you a god, not right now, but after a space of many years. . . . For your sake I will be born of the Virgin Mary. For your sake I will taste death and enter the house of the dead . . . and after three days, while I am in the tomb, I will raise up the body I received from you. And I will set you at the right hand of my divinity, and I will make you a god just like you wanted.[47]

In the Eastern churches, the years between 350 and 600 were an exuberantly productive era for serious theology and scholarship, and also for popular religious writing of all kinds. Probably in Egypt, a substantial Christian expansion of the Adam legend developed into a full literary cycle. Adam was also central to an emerging

mythology crafted by Syriac writers, which included the Conflict of Adam and Eve. This work presently survives only in the
Ethiopian language of Ge'ez, and it was not rediscovered until the
nineteenth century. Although the Conflict is classified as an "Old
Testament"–related text, its Christian credentials are beyond doubt.
When Adam and Eve are in Eden, for instance, they complain that
they lack the Water of Life. The Word of God replies:

> It cannot be this day, but on the day that I descend into hell
> and break the gates of brass and bruise in pieces the king-
> doms of iron. Then will I in mercy save thy soul and the souls
> of the righteous [to give them] rest in my Garden. And that
> shall be when the End of the World is come. And again, as
> regards the Water of Life thou seekest, it will not be granted
> thee this day; but on the day that I shall shed my blood upon
> thy head in the land of Golgotha. For my blood shall be the
> Water of Life unto thee, at that time, and not to thee alone
> but unto all those of thy seed who shall believe in me; that it
> be unto them for rest forever.[48]

IN ITS CHRISTIAN FORM, the Adam mythology reached its full-
est and most systematic form in the *Book of the Cave of Treasures*,
also known as *The Book of the Order of the Succession of Generations*.
This was a Syriac work credited to the fourth-century church father
Ephrem Syrus, but it was more likely written somewhat later—
estimates range from the late fourth century through the end of
the sixth (although some of its sections might have been written
considerably earlier). This new quasi-gospel had a vast influence
on Syriac literature over the next thousand years; it was translated
into Greek, Armenian, Georgian, Ethiopic, Coptic, and Arabic.
Through its incorporation into the seventh-century Apocalypse of
Pseudo-Methodius described earlier, it penetrated the Greek- and
Latin-speaking worlds.[49]

Although so much of its material concerns Old Testament characters and settings, the *Cave of Treasures* is utterly focused on the core Christian narrative. It frames the Christian story in a cosmic context, depicting the life and death of Jesus as the summary and essence of meaning of all that has gone before. It offers a narrative of human history from the Creation through the time of the apostles and the Day of Pentecost. The author believed this history covered a time span of 5,500 years, and so the narrative is divided into five millennia, with Christ's life fitting into the final half-millennium.

As a faithful Christian, the author knows that Christ's sacrifice on the cross redeemed humanity, but he presents this concept very literally through the story of Adam, the epitome of the whole race. In his life, Adam was "the prototype of Christ in every respect," at once priest, prophet, and king. Adam and Christ are one, and all realities meet at Calvary:

> Eden is the Holy Church, and the Paradise that was in it is the land of rest, and the inheritance of life, which God hath prepared for all the holy children of men. And because Adam was priest, and king, and prophet, God brought him into Paradise that he might minister in Eden, the Holy Church. . . . That Tree of Life that was in the midst of Paradise prefigured the Redeeming Cross, which is the veritable Tree of Life, and this it was that was fixed in the middle of the earth.[50]

But Adam's role is no less significant after death. The work describes his burial in the Cave of Treasures on the holy mountain, into which he is eventually followed by his descendants—Seth, Enosh, Jared, Methuselah, and the rest. Finally, though, Noah exhumes the bodies, and his son Shem relocates them where Adam had specified, at the world's center. This center is Golgotha, later to become the site of the crucifixion, where a cross-shaped grave awaits them:

> And when they arrived at Gâghûltâ [Golgotha], which is the center of the earth, the Angel of the Lord showed Shem

the place [for the body of Adam]. And when Shem had deposited the body of our father Adam upon that place, the four quarters [of the earth] separated themselves from each other, and the earth opened itself in the form of a cross, and Shem and Melchizedek deposited the body of Adam there. . . . And that place was called "Karkaphtâ" [Skull], because the head of all the children of men was deposited there.

Three of the canonical gospels explain that Golgotha (Calvary) means "place of the skull." The *Cave* adds the vital information about just whose skull is referred to, namely, Adam's.[51]

Shem further appoints his colleague Melchizedek as priest to minister at the place. Melchizedek is crucial to the Christianized Old Testament mythology and appears frequently in apocryphal texts. In the canonical Bible, he is a king and priest who meets Abraham following a battle and blesses him with bread and wine. Melchizedek also appears cryptically in the New Testament, where the Epistle to the Hebrews makes him a forerunner of Christ.[52]

In the narrative of the *Cave of Treasures*, the universe was thus preparing for the day of crucifixion, when human history would come full circle:

Know also that Christ was like unto Adam in everything, even as it is written. In that very place where Melchizedek ministered as a priest, and where Abraham offered up his son Isaac as an offering, the wood of the Cross was set up, and that self-same place is the center of the earth, and there the Four Quarters of the earth meet each other. . . .

When Shem took up the body of Adam, that same place, which is the door of the earth, opened itself. And when Shem and Melchizedek had deposited the body of Adam in the center of the earth, the Four Quarters of the earth closed in about it, and embraced Adam, and straightway that opening was closed firmly, and all the children of Adam were not able to open it. And when the Cross of Christ, the Redeemer of Adam and his sons, was set up upon it, the door of that place was opened in the face of Adam. And when the Wood [the Cross] was fixed upon it, and Christ was smitten with the spear, and blood and water flowed down from His side, they ran down into the mouth of Adam, and they became a baptism to him, and he was baptized.[53]

The *Cave* goes to fantastic lengths to draw parallels between the crucifixion and the biblical narrative that has preceded it, back to the Creation, and indeed especially to that event:

> For three hours Adam remained under the Tree naked, and for three hours was Christ naked on the wood of the Cross. And from the right side of Adam went forth Eve, the mother of mortal offspring, and from the right side of Christ went forth baptism, the mother of immortal offspring.
>
> On Friday Adam and Eve sinned, and on Friday their sin was remitted.
>
> On Friday Adam and Eve died, and on Friday they came alive.
>
> On Friday Death reigned over them, and on Friday they were freed from his dominion.
>
> On Friday Adam and Eve went forth from Paradise, and on Friday our Lord went into the grave.
>
> On Friday Adam and Eve became naked, and on Friday Christ stripped Himself naked and clothed them.
>
> On Friday Satan stripped Adam and Eve naked, and on Friday Christ stripped naked Satan and all his hosts, and put them to shame openly.
>
> On Friday the door of Paradise was shut and Adam went forth, and on Friday it was opened and a robber went in.
>
> On Friday the two-edged sword was given to the Cherub, and on Friday Christ smote with the spear, and broke the two-edged sword.
>
> On Friday kingdom, and priesthood, and prophecy were given unto Adam, and on Friday priesthood, and kingdom, and prophecy were taken from the Jews.

> At the ninth hour Adam went down into the lowest depth
> of the earth from the height of Paradise, and at the ninth hour
> Christ went down to the lowest depths of the earth, to those
> who lay in the dust, from the height of the Cross.

This catalog of parallels cries out to be set to musical form, either a hymn or a responsorial chant. Not coincidentally, the early Syrian church was famous for its innovations in Christian music and hymnody.[54]

FOR SYRIAC CHRISTIANS, the stories of the *Cave of Treasures* became part of the inevitable apparatus of mythology. Although not mentioned in canonical scripture, these tales became an integral part of faith. We recall, for instance, the gifts that the Magi from the East brought to the newborn Jesus according to Matthew's gospel. Famously, these were the gold, frankincense, and myrrh that they bore in their treasure chests. In the West, the Magi are usually numbered as three, hence the "Three Kings" of countless Christmas pageants. But this number has no scriptural warrant. The Western number is based on the assumption that each magus must have brought his own distinctive present, of which three are listed. Eastern churches think of twelve Magi, and the Irish envisage seven. Nor does Matthew call them kings.[55]

Matthew's account left much to the imagination, permitting authors and pseudo-historians to speculate freely about the gifts and their origins. Yes, they were fascinated by the Magi, and debated furiously over their names and origins. But what about the gifts themselves? Ideally, they should be located firmly in the broader biblical story, and preferably given some world-historical significance.

How better to do this than to link them to Adam, and to the original Paradise that had been lost through his sinful disobedience? In the Testament of Adam, Seth describes the death and burial of the first man. After Adam's death, Seth places his last testament in the legendary Cave of Treasures, "with the offerings Adam had taken out of Paradise, gold and myrrh and frankincense." The Conflict of Adam and Eve with Satan ends with a description of the coming of Christ, and here, the Magi deliver the three gifts "that had been with Adam in the Cave of Treasures."[56]

SUCH TEXTS FOUND CHRISTIAN PARALLELS and precedents on almost every page of the Old Testament. This went far beyond the well-known concept of typology, in which themes in the Old Testament prefigure the New. For example, Moses raising his arms to support the Israelites in victory prefigures Christ spreading his arms on the cross; but patristic writers used every possible Old Testament image of water and wood as a foretaste and prophecy of blood and the cross in the New. What we have here is a much more direct and material way of reading the biblical tradition, a method we might call material typology.

Not only did Old Testament concepts prefigure the New, but there was a material, physical continuity of objects and places. An event in Christ's time happened at a particular place because this was the exact site of another Old Testament phenomenon, for instance, the grave of a particular (and highly relevant) biblical figure. Christ's cross stood over Adam's grave. In Armenian tradition, Adam's submission to Satan was formalized in a contract that was signed on a stone and buried under the river Jordan. That contract was negated when Christ was baptized in the river, standing on the very same stone. That kind of scriptural expansion is of course a very Jewish approach, recalling patterns of midrashic interpretation. Without seeing those long-term continuities, claimed Christian writers, we can scarcely understand the deeper meanings of the New Testament text.[57]

Such linkages are constantly stressed in the thirteenth-century work called *The Book of the Bee*, a collection of Bible legends compiled by Solomon, bishop of Basra (in modern Iraq). The collection provides lengthy summaries of older materials utterly forgotten in Latin Europe, including narratives and tales associated with Adam and Moses and the Cave of Treasures. Solomon's work shows us just how thoroughly the Adam mythology had permeated Syriac Christian culture.[58]

Solomon loved deep connections and continuities. We know, for instance, that Moses owned a rod, which appears several times in the canonical text. In one miracle, it becomes a serpent. But where did this rod come from? Solomon had an answer:

> When Adam and Eve went forth from Paradise, Adam, as if knowing that he was never to return to his place, cut off a branch from the tree of good and evil—which is the fig-tree—and took it with him and went forth; and it served him as a staff all the days of his life. After the death of Adam, his son Seth took it, for there were no weapons as yet at that time. This rod was passed on from hand to hand unto Noah, and from Noah to Shem; and it was handed down from Shem to Abraham as a blessed thing from the Paradise of God. With this rod Abraham broke the images and graven idols which his father made, and therefore God said to him, "Get thee out of thy father's house." It was in his hand in every country as far as Egypt, and from Egypt to Palestine.[59]

The story then proceeds through Isaac, Jacob, and their descendants, and thence to Moses, and the rod ultimately reaches the hands of Christ himself.

Describing the crucifixion, Solomon explains the detailed Old Testament connections back to Moses and beyond:

> Some men have a tradition that the stone that was laid upon the grave of our Lord was the stone that poured out water for the children of Israel in the wilderness. The grave in which our Redeemer was laid was prepared for Joshua the son of Nun, and was carefully guarded by the Divine will for the burial of our Lord. The purple that they put on our Lord mockingly, was given in a present to the Maccabees by the

emperors of the Greeks; and they handed it over to the priests for dressing the temple. . . .

As to the tree upon which our Redeemer was crucified, some have said that He was crucified upon those bars with which they carried the ark of the covenant; and others that it was upon the wood of the tree on which Abraham offered up the ram as an offering instead of Isaac. His hands were nailed upon the wood of the fig-tree of which Adam ate, and behold, we have mentioned its history with that of Moses' rod.[60]

If this seems phantasmagoric, it has a deadly serious point. Solomon is showing that in every sense, Christ was the culmination of the Old Testament narrative. In this story, Christ is the point and the rationale—truly the Alpha and Omega.

THESE IDEAS HAD AN ENDURING influence into the Middle Ages and beyond, and not just in the Syriac world. Once established in the literature, these *Cave*-derived themes influenced other texts, including the mythologies surrounding the Virgin Mary. The Armenian version of the Infancy Gospel presents the standard account of the Virgin Mary in the cave with the midwife. In this instance, though, she has a visitor, Eve herself, the foremother of all humanity. "And the foremother entered the cave and took the infant into her lap, hugged him tenderly and kissed him and blessed God . . . and she wrapped him in swaddling clothes and laid him in the manger of the oxen." It is Eve, not the midwife, who warns Salome about her dangerous skepticism concerning Mary's perpetual virginity.[61]

In his guise as Christian prophet and evangelist, Adam appears in the Gospel of Nicodemus. Bound in hell, Adam recalls how he was once sick, and sent Seth to seek "the oil of the Tree of Mercy" to anoint his body. Seth, though, is prevented by the Archangel Michael, who warns him that this oil would not be available to humanity for over 5,000 years, not until after the coming of Jesus:

Then shall the most beloved Son of God come upon the earth to raise up the body of Adam and the bodies of the dead, and he shall come and be baptized in Jordan. And when he is come forth of the water of Jordan, then shall he anoint with the oil of mercy all that believe in him, and that oil of mercy shall be unto all generations of them that shall be born of water and of the Holy Ghost, unto life eternal. Then shall the most beloved Son of God, even Christ Jesus, come down upon the earth and shall bring our father Adam into paradise unto the tree of mercy.

Partly through Nicodemus, Christian Europe knew Adam as a vital precursor of Christ. In later stories, Michael gives Seth seeds that he is to plant in Adam's mouth, from which will spring the Tree of Good and Evil—the ultimate source of Christ's cross.[62]

At least from the eleventh century, England especially had a lively mythology of the origins of the cross, "the Rood," which originated in Eden. The English traced the object's history through the eras of Moses, David, and Solomon and made the cross itself a speaking character in some great medieval poems. A poetic debate between the cross and the Virgin Mary includes a shocking image as Adam's bite of the apple morphs into the bloody wound in Christ's side. Quoted in the *Golden Legend*, the Adam/cross narratives became available to any reader, in both Latin and the vernaculars.[63]

The cross's later story was a centerpiece of European visual art in the early Renaissance. The most celebrated moment was the cross's discovery by Helena, mother of the Emperor Constantine, but depictions of that event customarily included a prehistory dating back to the *Golden Legend* account of Seth. Seth features in such commemorations of the True Cross as the frescoes in Florence's chapel of the Santa Croce, from the 1380s, and their several imitators. In the 1460s, Piero della Francesca painted his masterpiece, the spectacular frescoes of the True Cross in St. Francis's church in Arezzo. The first image in the series is the death of Adam and the meeting between Seth and Michael.[64]

If whole works were not read, then extracts certainly were. The Life of Adam and Eve had a special impact because it was available in Latin at least by the sixth century. It was then translated into many vernacular languages, including French, German, English, and Italian. In Ireland, a number of Adam-related works influenced the tenth-century *Saltair na Rann*, a staggeringly ambitious account of the whole history of the world and its people. Because of the link to Seth and the cross, the Life of Adam and Eve was much reproduced in scholarly and popular works and was included in miracle plays.[65]

BEYOND ITS CORRECT SENSE of "hidden," the word "apocryphal" sometimes implies something marginal, or even trivial. When we are considering texts that influenced long-gone societies, the term can also imply superstitious accretions to faith. In the case of the "lost" Old Testament writings, though, these texts did much to form Christian religious consciousness right up to modern times. The strength of that influence is all the more striking when we recall the horrific divisions between Christians and Jews throughout the Middle Ages. Despite the enduring bitterness, right through to Reformation times, Christians continued to draw far more heavily on Jewish sources and traditions than they might ever have dreamed.

Beyond their undeniable influence in the churches, the Old Testament–related writings contributed to the popular Christian movements that so troubled orthodox institutions. At least some of these heretical medieval sects carefully studied these pseudo-scriptures.

7

Out of the Past

The Heretical Sects That Preserved Ancient Alternative Scriptures for a Thousand Years

Then did the contriver of Evil devise in his mind to make paradise, and he brought the man and woman into it.

The Secret Supper (Book of John the Evangelist), c. 1100

IT WAS A BOOK EIGHT HUNDRED YEARS OUT OF ITS TIME, AND ONE with a remarkable history.

In the thirteenth century, the Catholic Church across Western Europe was struggling against what it believed to be a widespread religious insurgency, the alternative Dualist church called the Albigensians (or, less commonly, Cathars). Reputedly, these Western heretics were an offshoot of a still older Dualist church, the Bulgarian Bogomils, making them part of a vast transnational conspiracy. To suppress these feared enemies, the church set up a new institution called the Inquisition, equipped with draconian powers that made it far more intrusive—and more lethal—than its later Spanish counterpart. The Inquisition had a base of operations at Carcassonne in southern France, deep in what had been heretical territory.[1]

At the archives of Carcassonne, from about 1270, we find a manuscript introduced thus: "This is the secret book of the heretics of Concoreze, brought from Bulgaria by their bishop Nazarius; full of errors." This entry describes a gospel written in Bulgaria and stemming from the Bogomil church. The note suggests a Dualist bishop carrying that text to Concorezzo near Milan, Italy, from whence it was taken to southern France. As we will see, we actually know a great deal about Nazarius and his incredible career.[2]

Nazarius's faith was shaped by a pseudo-gospel called the Secret Supper, or the Book of John the Evangelist. Like the Gnostic gospels of old, it presents distinctive views by putting them into Jesus's own mouth, in the form of a dialogue with one of his apostles. Also resembling those early texts, it borrows an actual setting from the canonical gospels and uses it as the setting for an extended account. In this instance, the "secret book" reports the scene at the Last Supper, when the apostle John lies upon Jesus's breast. The book was probably written in the eleventh or twelfth century, and a Dualist congregation could have used it for decades or centuries before it was finally seized. Mere possession of the book would likely have meant death.[3]

The Secret Supper challenges our expectations about old and new scriptures. It was a newly written text, created almost a millennium after the closure of the canonical New Testament. Yet it followed a truly ancient model. In its format and the broad outline of its teachings, this is the sort of text we might expect from the third or fourth century, and it carries exactly the same spirit of Gnostic assemblies in Syria or Egypt during Roman times. If we came across such a book in the Egyptian desert, it would not be surprising in the slightest. But here we find it in Western Europe, a full millennium afterward, in the era of Thomas Aquinas and Francis of Assisi.[4]

This upstart neo-gospel illustrates the thriving market for new and alternative scriptures many centuries after the fading of the early church. As we have seen, quite orthodox churches sometimes preserved older scriptures because they simply were not aware that they had become controversial elsewhere, or had even been declared heretical. In other cases, though, we can trace the survival of much more controversial texts that the orthodox churches really did loathe and want to suppress. They failed because these texts were preserved by the alternative Christian movements that persisted so stubbornly. In some surprising instances, medieval heresies were inspired by scriptures that dated back even before the Gnostics—Old Testament pseudepigrapha from the era of the Jewish Second Temple.

Nor are we dealing solely with clandestine subterranean movements living in perpetual fear of orthodox Inquisitors. Radical and wildly unorthodox Christian sects dominated whole territories, even in the heart of Europe itself. In cities and villages, alternative institutional networks often amounted to parallel churches with national and international ties. These underground churches existed over several centuries and used their own secret codes and languages. Heretical ideas remained in constant dialogue with what we think of as mainstream Christianity, cropping up among bishops and clergy of the established churches, to say nothing of the ordinary faithful. The abundance and diversity of the continuing heresies means that there was a continuing market for the consumption of alternative texts, and thus an incentive to produce them.

My approach here contradicts what a number of modern historians have come to believe. Many are rightly skeptical of evidence derived from the records of courts and Inquisitors, who twisted the evidence they received to fit their particular interests and prejudices. Some historians, though, take this doubt still further, arguing that the heresies scarcely existed as real movements, except as constructs in the minds of obsessed Inquisitors. According to these modern scholars, official persecutors used the poor suspects who fell into their hands to establish a written record of bogus and bizarre doctrines. To the contrary, though, the European heretical movements of the twelfth and thirteenth centuries not only existed much as depicted, but their ideas and beliefs can be traced to the church's very earliest ages. That continuity is reflected in the sacred books they preserved and cherished.[5]

WE HAVE ALREADY ENCOUNTERED the Manichaeans, who inherited the Dualist and Gnostic beliefs of early Christian times. So strong and so widespread were broadly similar movements, though, over such a lengthy time span, that they must have been responding to powerful impulses within the Christian faith itself, and especially within the New Testament. It was (and is) possible to read the gospels in ways very different from what the church approved, and to find there an irreconcilable opposition between Christ and the World, between Light and Darkness, Spirit and Matter. Over the centuries, a great many thoughtful Christian readers—especially the monks and clergy, who were the literate class—found themselves rediscovering that troubling alternative Christ. Quite apart from such devout individual thinkers, Dualist ideas were upheld and transmitted by potent sects and movements.[6]

These movements did not draw on the elaborate mythological world of the Manichaean faith; nor did they use its distinctive scriptures. As far as we can tell, few Western sectaries had even heard of Mani himself, still less did they view him as a prophet. But we can see continuity in terms of an intermingled group of very early traditions dating back to apostolic times—Marcionism, Docetism, Adoptionism, Encratism, Gnosticism. However we label those views—whatever "-ism" we give them—they commonly existed together as an identifiable and highly consistent package, a Dualist synthesis that can be summarized thus:

> *The visible material world was created by Satan, who also created Adam and Eve, and who inspires the continuation of the human race. Conception and birth are tools of the Devil. Mary was an angel, rather than a human woman, and Jesus was not born from her in any conventional human sense. The Crucifixion and Resurrection both occurred only as illusions rather than material realities. As Satan is the God of the Old Covenant, true Christians must reject the Old Testament and its prophets. Christians should reject material symbols, including the water of baptism, the sacrament of the Eucharist, icons, and the cross. The institutional church and its liturgy must be condemned as diabolical, and*

contrary to the wishes of the true God, who sent Jesus to enlighten
and free the world.

I stress that this is my own reconstruction, synthesized from multiple sources.

These ideas closely resemble the ancient Gnostic worldview that was reflected in the early lost gospels. The true Christ was purely spiritual, and his church was an inward reality. Christian truth was found in the spiritual and psychological realms, and only the vulgar took the gospel stories in a material sense. If this set of ideas was not Manichaean, it was definitely Dualist. And the "package" was very widespread. Common on the eastern fringes of the Roman Empire in Late Antiquity, it subsequently appeared all over Europe, both east and west. This was the belief system that united sects like the Paulicians, Bogomils, and Albigensians over a span of eight hundred years.

In 1163, a group of Dualists was tried in Cologne, and ultimately they were executed. Denying that their belief was any kind of lately arising heresy, they traced it to apostolic times. As they argued, their doctrines "had been hidden [*occultatam*] from the time of the martyrs to the present day, and had survived in Greece and certain other countries."[7]

They were right to stress those Eastern connections. One early Dualist-inclined movement was the Paulicians, who originated in Armenia in the seventh century, and who troubled the eastern borders of the Byzantine Empire. Although the exact nature of their ideas is disputed, they seem to have been Marcionites, rejecting the Old Testament. From the eighth century onward, the empire transported thousands of these tough border peoples to the Balkans, where they could help guard against barbarian assaults. However, relocating the Paulicians into Europe also meant importing their heretical beliefs. By the tenth century, Bulgaria was the center of a full-fledged Dualist heresy that took its name from an obscure priest called "Bogomil." That word, meaning "Beloved of God," might have been an actual name, but it could have been a title or nickname. (The movement's founder lived under a Bulgarian king who reigned from 927 to 969.) Although the exact process is not clear, somewhere around 950 Paulicianism was transformed into Bogomilism.[8]

A little after 970, the Orthodox presbyter Cosmas preached furiously against the heretics, who were gaining ground rapidly across the Balkans and in the Byzantine realm itself. These Bogomils condemned the material world as the Devil's. "And what word of the scriptures have they not perverted?" asked Cosmas. "What have they not defamed in this God-created world? They direct their blasphemies not only toward the earth, but toward the heavens, saying that everything is according to the will of the Devil: the sky, the sun, stars, air, earth, man, churches, crosses, and every divine thing they attribute to the Devil, and simply everything that moves on the earth—with and without a soul—they call the Devil's."[9]

According to later reports, Bogomils taught that God the Father had two sons, and the elder, Satanael, was cast out of heaven for his pride, together with the angels who followed him. Falling into the lower regions, he created the heaven and earth we know, and this Satanael thus became the God of the Old Testament. Satanael's name, incidentally, has a lengthy pedigree in Jewish and early Christian apocrypha. As "Satanail," it appears in the Slavonic version of 2 Enoch.[10]

About 1080, another Cosmas, the patriarch of Constantinople, issued official condemnations (anathemas) against the Bogomils, and these offer a useful epitome of their doctrines. The anathemas were restated in later decades, including in the Bulgarian Synodikon (church council) of 1211. Among other things, the Bogomils were reported to believe the following:

> That Christ our God was born of the Holy Mother of God and Ever-Virgin Mary as an illusion, and as an illusion he was crucified, but that he took this assumed flesh up with him, leaving it in the air. . . .

[They] call Satan the creator of the visible world, and name him the master of rain, hail and of everything that crawls out of the ground. . . .

[T]hat Satan created Adam and Eve. . . .

[They] reject Moses the God-seer and Elijah the Tishbite, as well as the holy prophets and patriarchs and their sacred writings, which are from God, saying that they come from Satan and that these men were moved by him to write what they wrote and said about Christ, and that they were speaking involuntarily and under compulsion, and for this reason the Bogomils reject what is written in the Old Testament, as well as the holy prophets who are illumined in it. . . .

[They] revile John the Baptist and say that he is from Satan, as is baptism with water, and who baptize without water, saying only the "Our Father."[11]

Bogomils rejected crosses, icons, churches, and all sacraments, including the Eucharist and baptism. As the presbyter Cosmas asked, "And how can they call themselves Christians, when they don't have priests to baptize them, when they don't make the sign of the cross, when they don't sing priestly hymns and don't respect priests?" They scorned the veneration of the Virgin Mary. About 1100, a Byzantine writer recorded a Bogomil leader who "called our sacred churches the temples of devils, and our consecration of the body and blood of our one and greatest High Priest and Victim he considered and condemned as worthless." By the standards of the time, that was a deadly assault against the most fundamental beliefs of a Christian society; even expressing such views threatened to invoke divine fury against the whole nation.[12]

SIMILAR DUALIST VIEWS SURFACED in France and Italy, where followers eventually became known as Albigensians. Western writers usually dated the movement's dramatic expansion to the early and mid-twelfth century. The spread of the movement reflected growing

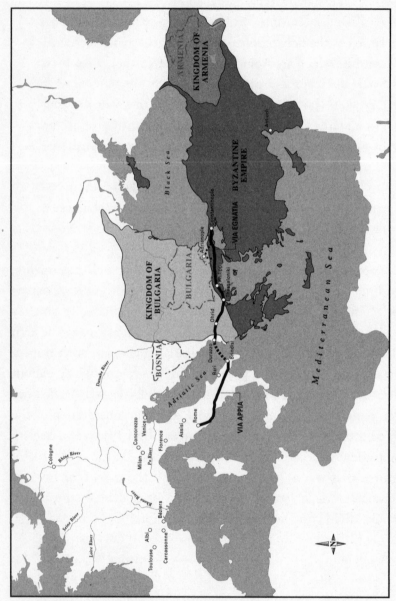

Mediterranean World from Byzantium to Southern France, with Via Egnatia

Western contacts with Byzantium following the Crusades and the establishment of Western colonies in Constantinople itself.[13]

Once westerners acquired an interest in these powerful spiritual ideas, it was not difficult for them to remain in contact with the Byzantine world. In the third century BC, the Romans had built a road across their newly won possessions in the Balkans, and this Via Egnatia remained a crucial avenue of communication long afterward. It ran from Constantinople through Adrianople, Philippi, and Thessalonika to Ohrid, and then to Durazzo [Durrës] on the Adriatic. A short sea journey then supplied the connection to Brindisi in Italy, and thus to the Appian Way leading to Rome itself. The road was enormously significant, in religious affairs no less than in trade and politics. The New Testament preserves St. Paul's correspondence to churches he had visited at Philippi and Thessalonika. In later years, the Via Egnatia offered a high road for Eastern evangelists carrying their Dualist beliefs and texts to Italy and the West.[14]

By 1150, these views were so strong in southern France that they represented a full-fledged alternative church with its own hierarchy and institutional structures. Medieval Europe, in other words, contained two—at least—radically different churches, each denying the Christian credentials of the other. According to Catholic observers, the Western heretics, the Albigensians, preached a package of doctrines that would have made wonderful sense to second-century heretics like Marcion. In the words of the chronicler Raynaldus:

> The heretics held that there are two Creators; viz. one of invisible things, whom they called the benevolent God, and another of visible things, whom they named the malevolent God. The New Testament they attributed to the benevolent God; but the Old Testament to the malevolent God, and rejected it altogether, except certain authorities which are inserted in the New Testament from the Old; which, out of reverence to the New Testament, they esteemed worthy of reception. They charged the author of the Old Testament with falsehood. . . . They also call him a homicide, as well

because he burned up Sodom and Gomorrah, and destroyed
the world by the waters of the deluge, as because he overwhelmed Pharaoh, and the Egyptians, in the sea.[15]

The Catholic Church responded with a brutal crusade in southern France. Not until the early fourteenth century did Catholics
succeed in eliminating the rival creed in Western Europe by means
of the ruthless Inquisition. But as late as the fifteenth century, Dualist beliefs still survived in Bosnia and the Balkans.[16]

I HAVE ARGUED THAT MEDIEVAL Dualism bears many resemblances
to much earlier Christian heresies, but this view of long continuities
is deeply unfashionable in modern scholarly circles. Let me summa-
rize the two competing schools of thought:

a. Dualist Reality?

For much of the twentieth century, scholars confidently drew
links between the various Dualist movements, including the
Albigensians. The roots of such groups can be traced back to
the early centuries, and their views were heavily influenced by
Manichaeanism. A classic 1947 book on these currents was
entitled *The Medieval Manichee*, and Bogomil ideas have been
labeled "Balkan neo-Manichaeism."[17]

b. Dualist Myth?

More recent scholars disagree totally, and their views currently
dominate the field. Some leading medieval historians urge us to
see heresy charges in the context of the Inquisitors investigating
dissident groups and of the social and political conflicts that
gave rise to heresy trials. Such writers agree that ordinary French
and Italian people protested against the church hierarchy of
their day, and turned to the New Testament to do so, but in no
sense should we see these people as Dualists or Manichaeans.
Rather, their views were anticlerical and anti-sacramental, or
even proto-Protestant.

Other historians of the Albigensian struggles minimize the presence of real organized heresy and reject the notion of an alternative religious system with deep Near Eastern roots. Perhaps elite members of the sect, the so-called *perfecti*, might have been Dualist, but they concealed their views from ordinary believers, who favored more mainstream church reform. When people confessed to bizarre heresies, they did so under coercion or torture, and they were simply responding to leading questions made to them by Inquisitors who knew about Dualism or Manichaeanism from literary sources. From this perspective, the "medieval Manichee" is a modern myth.[18]

Resolving that debate is essential for understanding attitudes toward alternative scriptures.

Revisionist historians deserve praise for their critical skills and their ability to interrogate documentary sources: they are careful and cautious. Yet they pay too little regard to the theological content of the views they are discussing. Nor do they appreciate the radicalism of the views that accused heretics expressed quite spontaneously, without the slightest coercion. Such modern writers also do not acknowledge the clear evidence of contact between distant regions, and particularly between Western Europe and the indisputably powerful heretical movements of the Balkans. Western Albigensians were nicknamed Bulgarians far more than they were ever labeled Cathars.

The revisionists deploy a scholarly method called "constructionism." In order to understand a social problem, say constructionists, we should spend less time on the issue at hand than on the responses of official agencies and, to use an anachronism, the media. Why did states and churches feel the need to identify and combat the supposed problem at the time? To give an analogy, early modern Europe devoted massive effort to fighting witch-cults that never really existed. You can have a great deal of smoke with no fire at all.[19]

Even on the basis of the evidence the revisionists present, though, we repeatedly encounter Albigensians spontaneously and undeniably expressing views that fit perfectly with the Dualist hypothesis.

Throughout the eleventh and twelfth centuries, such believers advocated a consistent body of teachings that held, for instance, that marriage and sexuality are evil, that Christians are not permitted to eat meat, and that the sacraments are diabolic inventions. In some of the best-documented encounters between Catholics and heretics, and not under coercion or torture, Albigensian leaders openly rejected the Old Testament. Those heretics worshiped instead the good "God of Light" revealed in the New Testament.[20]

The Albigensians were indeed firmly part of the Christian tradition, and their recorded rituals draw entirely on the New Testament as they understood it. Some believers were reluctant to accept any scripture as authoritative beyond the four gospels, although others read at least some of the epistles. Beyond those texts, they dismissed any alleged scriptures as *affitilhas* (a modern translation might be "bells and whistles"). They rejected the Old Testament as well as the Incarnation. Albigensians recounted the Creation in terms of fallen angels who forgot their origins and became trapped in human form—classic Gnostic formulations. Their elite believers, the *perfecti*, followed the ancient Encratites in rejecting any sexual contact and the eating of any food apart from vegetables and fish. Believers entered the state of perfection by accepting spiritual baptism, the *consolamentum*, which involved a laying on of hands in the presence of the Gospel of John.[21]

If historians of the early church found accounts of such a group in 250 or 350, they would not hesitate to locate them on the well-known Gnostic/Dualist spectrum. The group's use of familiar heretical scriptures would leave that identification beyond doubt.[22]

The Albigensian persecutions should not then be compared to the witch trials but rather to the Spanish Inquisition's later assaults on Protestants and Jews. Although those later Inquisitors undoubtedly invented and circulated many horror stories about both groups, we never doubt that Jews and Protestants really existed to be libeled and persecuted. Similarly with the Albigensians or Cathars. Whatever miscarriages of justice the medieval Inquisition perpetrated at particular times and places, a sizable volume of solid evidence really does suggest that the Albigensians existed as a distinct movement with a broadly Dualist theology and a characteristic structure and organization. They were in touch with like-minded believers elsewhere, especially in southeastern Europe. And they did in fact constitute a rival church. Bogomils were Dualists, and so were Albigensians.[23]

THE DUALIST THEOLOGICAL PACKAGE was deeply rooted in scriptures; indeed, in quite a complex mixture of writings old and new.

At least in part, Dualists relied on familiar canonical scriptures, especially the gospels. Orthodox believers had long protested against heretical misuse of scripture, although reasonable people might disagree as to whether the standard, approved readings of such passages were automatically correct and self-evident. As far back as the second century, Irenaeus complained that "in like manner do these persons patch together old wives' fables, and then endeavor, by violently drawing away from their proper connection, words, expressions, and parables whenever found, to adapt the oracles of God to their baseless fictions." Medieval Dualists likewise creatively rooted their doctrines in scripture. One reason that heresy spread so rapidly among the Bulgarians and other Slavic peoples was that they already had vernacular translations of the scriptures at an early date—from the ninth century, long before their Christian counterparts in Western Europe. This removed a potent obstacle to quite ordinary believers both gaining access to biblical texts and interpreting them in their own way. In turn, these interpretations passed easily to congregations in Western Europe.[24]

Dualists could cite a surprising number of texts to support the idea that the Devil is the Lord of the present world. Bogomils cited the Temptations in the Wilderness to prove that the Devil held power over the world, or else he could not have offered it to Jesus. Jesus himself speaks of the Devil as Lord of the World, and the canonical Book of Revelation likewise offers several passages that can be read to justify Dualist theology.

Many of the texts commonly used since the Reformation to support predestination also lend themselves to Dualist purposes, especially the frightening parable of the wheat and the tares. Although rarely a popular sermon text today, this parable has inspired and puzzled readers through the centuries. Following on directly after the much more famous parable of the sower, this story tells of a man sowing good seed in a field. In the night, an enemy sows tares (weeds) among the wheat, and the two kinds of plants grow up together. The farmer tells his servants not to purge the tares immediately, or they will certainly damage the wheat in the process:

> Let both grow together until the harvest: and in the time of harvest I will say to the reapers, Gather ye together first the tares, and bind them in bundles to burn them: but gather the wheat into my barn.

In a Dualist reading, the world and its people include the materials of both Light and Darkness, between whom there can be no compromise. They will exist together until the God of Light, or perhaps Christ himself, intervenes directly in the world, to separate out the forces of Light and to bring salvation. For the children of Darkness, which includes the institutional church, there is no hope, only the prospect of fire.[25]

The presbyter Cosmas reports another distinctive reading, presumably of the story of the Prodigal Son:

> Having heard the parable in the gospels about the two sons, they consider Christ the older son, and the younger one who deceived his father they consider the Devil, and they call him Mammon, and they call him the creator and builder of the things of the earth. And he commanded men to marry, to eat meat, and to drink wine. And while simply defaming everything of ours, they consider themselves heavenly dwellers, and people who marry and live in this world they call the servants of Mammon.[26]

Bogomils liked the puzzling parable of the unjust steward in Luke 16, which they saw as an account of the revolt of the fallen angels. In this reading, Satan/Satanael himself was the "steward," and he used material promises to lure other angels into rebellion, forgiving their "debts." Albigensians cited the story of the Good Samaritan, which moderns might find hard to relate to any kind of cosmological scheme. As Dualist readers noted, though, the man going down from Jerusalem to Jericho actually symbolized Adam descending from the heavenly Jerusalem. The robbers who took his clothes and belongings were the evil spirits who stripped him of the divine light that belonged to his true nature.[27]

In familiar scriptural texts, heretical thinkers found meanings utterly at odds with what mainstream Christians have come to regard as normal. Arguably, though, such "alternative" readings of the parables make as much sense as the conventional ones. They also follow on precisely from the interpretations that prevailed among the Gnostics and other heretics of the earliest centuries. In that sense, medieval heretics found in canonical gospels such as Luke and John precisely the same warranties for belief as their predecessors a thousand years earlier. They read the same New Testament.

Bogomils drew on their own body of scriptures, and the case of the Secret Supper shows that texts were certainly imported into Western Europe. Although most books in their libraries are now lost to us, we see many intriguing survivors.[28]

When we say that texts survive, the danger is to imagine the literary works themselves somehow moving under their own steam from country to country, as of course they did not. They were carried by people, as individuals and groups, as spiritual entrepreneurs or as organized churches, and in some cases we actually can trace the trajectories of individual texts across the civilized world. Over the centuries, manuscripts were carried (often as contraband) from ancient Syria or Palestine to the borderlands of the Roman Empire, to the kingdoms of the Caucasus, to Bulgaria and the Balkans, and on into France, Italy, and Germany.

We have already seen that the Bogomils used ancient Gnostic works, including the Apocalypse of Peter and (probably) the Gospel of Thomas. Other very early texts survived among the rituals and liturgies used by the Western Albigensians. They claimed scriptural authority for beliefs that hark back to the primitive age, including Jesus's intimacy with Mary Magdalene, a view reflected in the Gospel of Philip. About 1215, a Catholic critic described the Albigensian view that "the Christ who was born in terrestrial and visible Bethlehem and crucified in Jerusalem was evil, and that Mary Magdalene was his concubine and the very woman taken in adultery of whom we read in the gospel." That does not mean that any early Gnostic gospel still circulated in its entirety, but extracts or summaries might have.[29]

Dualist churches used truly ancient liturgies that reflected the practice of the church of the earliest centuries. Although they are preserved only in late medieval copies, they maintain archaic forms. From fifteenth-century Bosnia, a Slavic document preserves what is termed the Ritual of Radoslav the Christian, probably a remnant of the once-standard Bogomil liturgy. It impresses by its simplicity, so radically unlike a typical medieval church liturgy, which had over time acquired so many additional prayers and rituals. In scriptural terms, Radoslav's text is based chiefly on the Lord's Prayer and the Prologue to John's Gospel, both beloved by Dualist churches.[30]

That Slavic ritual was the basis for liturgies used by Western European believers. We note the amazing Lyon Ritual, which surfaces among the Albigensians in thirteenth-century France. This includes a procedure for confession and the *consolamentum*, a ceremony also known as the Immersion in the Perfect Community. Neither draws on any text except the New Testament, chiefly the gospels and epistles, and the closest parallel to the Immersion comes in Jesus's commissioning of the apostles in Luke 9.[31]

So close, in fact, is the Albigensian ritual to the Baptism of the Catechumens practiced in the very early church that modern scholars have suggested a direct inheritance, possibly by means of ancient texts that were still available to these alternative believers. This seemingly medieval artifact may be a direct translation of a Greek document from the second century. If it were not for the Encratite oath, an unsuspecting reader would assume that these texts were expressions of rigorous Christian piety, carrying the authentic mark of the earliest apostolic church. Would they have been wrong to do so? As late as 1200, in southern France, there were still believers using the ancient liturgies of the apostolic church.[32]

DUALISTS USED ALTERNATIVE scriptures that dated back even before the Gnostic gospels to reach into pre-Christian times. We have already seen the importance of the Old Testament pseudepigrapha, the sizable body of scriptures attributed to one or other of the great figures of the Hebrew Bible. In modern times, one very large collection of this material was rediscovered in Eastern Europe, in exactly the regions where the great Dualist heresies were then rampant.

The Slavonic lands were converted under the influence of the Byzantine Empire from the ninth century onward, and they followed the Orthodox version of the faith. Remaining in close touch with Constantinople and other great intellectual centers, their churches preserved and translated older Greek texts, including some that had long since vanished from other areas. Even as other churches became nervous about these works, they remained widely available in monasteries and churches spread over Eastern Europe and the Balkans.

From the end of the nineteenth century, scholars were astonished to discover the wealth and range of the Old Testament pseudepigrapha that existed in the old Slavonic languages. Many of these works, moreover, do not survive in other languages, including in their (usually) Greek originals. Among the works that today exist only or chiefly in Slavonic forms, we find, for instance, the Apocalypse of Abraham, the Ladder of Jacob, 3 and 4 Baruch, and the Martyrdom and Ascension of Isaiah. Others bear such suggestive titles as the Testament of Job, Joseph and Aseneth, the Apocryphon of Zorobabel, and the Sea of Tiberias. Some exist in multiple versions, and they have in the process acquired a good deal of extraneous material and folklore.[33]

One example will show how the material was recovered. In the nineteenth century, Russian scholars were researching a medieval judicial codex called the *Just Balance* (*Merilo Pravednoe*), which was mainly a collection of historical laws and commentaries. It was not surprising that a legal work compiled in the fourteenth century should include abundant religious and biblical-sounding material, but much of it sounded bizarre. The manuscript proved to contain an important pseudo-biblical book, 2 (Slavonic) Enoch, or the Book of the Secrets of Enoch, with its vertiginous accounts of heavenly visions and angelic encounters. Different versions of the work survive in twenty Slavonic manuscripts.[34]

Although its dating is controversial, 2 Enoch was probably written in Greek in the first century AD. It was then translated into other languages, including Coptic, but the vast majority of what we know comes from Slavonic texts. The book offers a fine illustration of how manuscripts evolve over time. In Slavonic, it survives in both longer and shorter versions, and the longer has clearly been adapted for Christian purposes. The shorter version is much older and closer to the Jewish original, lacking references to a Messiah or the resurrection of the dead. This form may take us back to a work written by an Alexandrian Jew somewhere around the first century AD.

Taken together, these materials give a staggering picture of the kaleidoscopic thought-world of Second Temple Judaism with all of its diverse voices, some of which would develop into full-blown Dualist thought. These "lost" texts survive in such profusion because they were accepted and cherished by the mainstream Orthodox Church of the Slavonic lands, where they were read for almost a millennium.

We still do not fully understand the means by which those arcane texts found their way into Slavonic languages, but some likely centers of transmission stand out. Where might someone have had access to the treasures of Byzantine libraries but in a Slavonic setting with rich access to Jewish resources and scholarship? We naturally look to the Bulgarian kingdom, which accepted Christianity in the ninth century, and which in 919 became the seat of an autonomous patriarchate. That kingdom had two major cultural and literary centers, namely Ohrid and Preslav, both of which had schools dating from the 880s. Preslav was critical to the development and spread of Cyrillic script, but Ohrid outpaced it in learning and influence. By the turn of the millennium, Ohrid was both the capital of the Bulgarian empire and the seat of the patriarchate. The Byzantines recaptured the city in 1018, reducing the patriarchate to an archbishopric, but Ohrid remained a powerful ecclesiastical seat through the next two centuries. It also stood on the Via Egnatia, the heretical high road to the West.

Ohrid was a center for biblical scholarship, both Jewish and Christian. One famous archbishop was Theophylact (1055–1107), who made his church a center of biblical exegesis. We have already met Theophylact denouncing heretics who regarded the Gospel of Thomas as a fifth gospel; the fact that he felt the need to make these comments suggests how widely deviant works circulated in this region. After he died in 1107, his successor as archbishop was Leon Mung, a Jewish philosopher who converted to Christianity. In the same era, one of Leon's old schoolfellows was the city's senior rabbi, himself a noted biblical scholar. That is not to suggest that either Theophylact or Leon Mung was personally responsible for the process of translating the pseudepigrapha, much of which was already accomplished well before that point. Even so, Ohrid would certainly have provided the right cultural milieu for such an endeavor.[35]

Incidentally, investigating the Slavonic pseudepigrapha offers sobering lessons for what we can and can't know about the existence of texts in earlier ages. Based on the substantial volume of contemporary writings from the Slavonic churches of the Middle Ages, we would never have dared suspect the existence of libraries that contained such a wealth of ancient Jewish writings, whether at Ohrid or anywhere else. Scholars were only alerted to these survivals by applying the modern critical skills that allowed them to rediscover the documents themselves. This story must caution us against any temptation to argue from silence about the disappearance or nonexistence of supposedly "lost" scriptures.

As scholars explored these ancient Slavonic texts, they were struck by resemblances to the doctrines and imagery of the Bogomils. Some Old Testament apocrypha suggested that the material world was created by an inferior God, a Demiurge or Craftsman-Creator. The Bogomils thus originated and flourished in exactly those regions in which these enticing texts circulated in Slavic languages. Those Dualists had a special taste for several ancient works, including the Apocalypse of Abraham, 2 Enoch, and especially the Vision of Isaiah, to which we will return shortly. These works offered ample materials about angels both good and evil, with a roster of names that would reappear throughout the Middle Ages—Michael and Gabriel in God's legions; Satanael/Satanail, Sammael, and Azazel in the cause of evil. Readers could easily conclude that one or more of those dark angels was the sovereign of this fallen world, the one who had sowed tares in the farmer's field.[36]

The similarity between the pseudepigrapha and much later Dualist ideas could be a coincidence, but other possibilities suggest themselves. One is that the texts as we have them in their present forms have over time been adapted or edited by writers with a Bogomil axe to grind. In other words, claim some scholars, ancient Jewish texts have been subjected to medieval Dualist editing. That theory has become less fashionable over time, and the alternative is quite evocative. Instead, perhaps the apocrypha themselves helped Eastern European clerics move in Dualist directions during the tenth century. Whether or not those Slavonic texts actually inspired Bogomil dissidence, those scriptures contributed to the movement's growth and expansion. That would mean a direct influence from the long-extinct fringes of Second Temple Judaism through the heresies of medieval Europe. Perhaps thirteenth-century Inquisitors were struggling against ideas that originated in Alexandria and Jerusalem at a time when the Second Temple still stood.

LIKE THEIR ANCIENT PREDECESSORS, medieval Dualists had a special taste for works notionally associated with the great prophet Isaiah. The canonical Book of Isaiah was enormously influential in shaping Christianity, but other later works purported to give extra information about the prophet's martyrdom and his ascension through the heavens. The Ascension of Isaiah, a puzzling work that probably dates from the first or second centuries AD, follows the standard patterns of apocryphal works popular in Jesus's own time. Although it draws on older Jewish materials, in its present form it is obviously Christian, and it includes typical prophecies of Christ's life and career:

> [Gabriel] the angel of the Holy Spirit, and Michael, the chief of the holy angels, on the third day will open the sepulchre: And the Beloved sitting on their shoulders will come forth and send out His twelve disciples; And they will teach all the nations and every tongue of the resurrection of the Beloved, and those who believe in His cross will be saved, and in His ascension into the seventh heaven whence He came: And that many who believe in Him will speak through the Holy Spirit: And many signs and wonders will be wrought in those days.

Both Jerome and Epiphanius quoted the Ascension in the fourth century. Suggesting its wide influence, copies survive in multiple languages, including Greek, Latin, Coptic, Ethiopic, and Old Slavonic.[37]

Chapters 6 through 11 of the Ascension circulated independently as the Vision of Isaiah, and as such it played a special role in inspiring dissident Christian movements. The Bogomils used their Slavonic version, while Western Albigensians referred to the Latin translation. In 1240, Inquisitor Moneta of Cremona reported that heretics used "a certain book in which it is recounted that the spirit of Isaiah, being drawn out of his body, was taken up to the seventh heaven."[38]

The Vision's appeal for Dualists is not hard to grasp. As Isaiah describes his successive visions in the heavens, it is obvious both that Satan is the Prince of the World and that the world is the scene of constant warfare between the supernatural forces of good and evil. "Isaiah" reports:

> And we ascended, [the angel] and I, upon the firmament, and there I saw the great battle of Satan and his might opposing God's faithful followers, and one surpassed the other in envy. For just as it is on earth, so also is it in the firmament, because replicas of what are in the firmament are on earth.

He says further:

> And I saw there a great battle of Satan and his force, who were opposing piety. And one was vying with the other, because on the firmament it is just the same as on earth, for the images of the firmament are here on earth. And I said to the angel: "What is this warfare and vying and battling?" And answering me, he said: "This warfare is the Devil's, and it won't cease until there comes the One whom you will see, and He kills him with the spirit of His power."

The struggle will end only with Christ's triumph:

> When He descends and will be in your form, the Prince of the World will lay his hands on Him, because He is [God's] Son, and they will hang Him on a tree and kill Him, not knowing who He is. And He will descend to hell and will render naked and useless all those phantoms, and He will take prisoner the Prince of Death and will wipe out all his power.

The Isaiah literature offers a link between the fringes of Judaism and Christianity in the earliest era and the heretical dissidence of the High Middle Ages, a direct conduit from AD 200 to 1200.[39]

OVER AND ABOVE SUCH SCRIPTURES, the Bogomils also composed their own texts. Given the movement's clandestine nature, the Secret Supper might have been one of many, but others have been lost, at least to date.

Besides using the same canonical texts as earlier heretics, the Dualists also noted the same holes in the narratives, which it was natural for later writers to exploit. The Gospels often report instances when Jesus expounded special teachings to his closest associates, suggesting that he might also have done so on other unrecorded occasions. The Secret Supper is one of many efforts to imagine what he might have said at such times.

This gospel is a classic summary of Dualist teaching. John begins his report with the words, "Lord, before Satan fell, in what glory abode he with thy Father?" Jesus then describes Satan's former condition. After his Fall, Satan created the material universe, he reports, in words that clearly echo those of Genesis, but with Satan firmly identified as the God of the Old Testament. Satan, not God, created humankind:

> The Devil entered into a wicked serpent and seduced the angel that was in the form of the woman, and he wrought his lust with Eve in the Song of the serpent. And therefore are they called sons of the Devil and sons of the serpent that do the lust of the Devil their father, even unto the end of this world. And again the Devil poured out upon the angel that was in Adam the poison of his lust, and it begetteth the sons of the serpent and the sons of the Devil even unto the end of this world.[40]

John then asks, "How say men that Adam and Eve were created by God and set in paradise to keep the commandments of the Father, and were delivered unto death?" Jesus replies,

> Foolish men say thus in their deceitfulness that my Father made bodies of clay: but by the Holy Ghost made he all the powers of the heavens, and holy ones were found having

bodies of clay because of their transgression, and therefore were delivered unto death.

Matter is death; the body is death.

From this Dualist standpoint, the whole history of the world is a story of Satanic deceit. Significantly, this mythological system refers to Enoch, although this time the prophet appears in a diabolical role. According to this account, it was the evil Enoch who inspired the practice of sacrifice and ritual law:

> Then did the Devil proclaim unto [Moses] his godhead, and unto his people, and commanded a law to be given unto the children of Israel, and brought them out through the midst of the sea which was dried up.[41]

Liberation and salvation come only from the other God, the good God of Light, who intervenes to send Jesus, but assuredly not by putting him in the form of polluted matter: "When my Father thought to send me into the world, he sent his angel before me, by name Mary, to receive me. And I when I came down entered in by the ear and came forth by the ear." Jesus's followers must reject such Satanic snares as baptism and the Eucharist.[42]

USUALLY, WE KNOW NEXT TO NOTHING about the readers or owners of particular alternative scriptures, or their attitudes to the text they possessed. We have no idea whether the owners of the Nag Hammadi scriptures regarded those documents as prized revelations or as loathsome heresy, or indeed as financial investments that could be sold to dealers. Did they constitute a scriptural library, or were they inventory? Might they even have been grave goods, reverently deposited to accompany a pious believer into the afterlife? Much later, the Carcassonne Inquisition owned the Secret Supper not as improving spiritual reading, but as potentially useful evidence against likely suspects.[43]

That said, we do in fact know a great deal about the man who owned the Secret Supper before it was seized and why he valued it so highly. The resulting picture is profoundly revealing about the underground spiritual culture of the Middle Ages and the pseudo-scriptures on which it was based.

The Inquisitor's note on the manuscript refers to the northern Italian heretical leader Nazarius, who stands out among nonelite medieval people in that we can know so much about what he thought and believed. (Although he is called a bishop, his title did not of itself suggest any particular wealth, and most definitely it did not imply official status in mainstream society.) In the late thirteenth century, two Inquisitors described him and his career. One was Rainier Sacconi, himself a converted Cathar, who met Nazarius toward the end of the bishop's life around 1250. According to Sacconi, Nazarius "said in my presence, and that of many others, that the Virgin Mary was an angel, and that Christ did not take on human nature, but an angelic nature and a celestial body. And he said that he learned his error from the Bishop and the Elder Son of the Church of Bulgaria, now almost sixty years ago." (The "Elder Son" was a senior rank in the Bogomil hierarchy.) That would place Nazarius's conversion to Bogomil views somewhere in the 1190s. We hear nothing more of his conversion or where it occurred. Nazarius probably encountered these views in Bulgaria itself, but on occasion Bogomil emissaries made the trek to Italy. Just conceivably, Nazarius had traveled east during the Third Crusade of the early 1190s.[44]

About 1270, Inquisitor Anselm of Alessandria sketched the Cathar church structure in Lombardy, specifically mentioning the church based in Concorezzo. Anselm describes Nazarius as fourth bishop in the succession in this region and says he held that rank for forty years. As a rough estimate, we might date his life from about 1175 to 1250, with his elevation to bishop's rank around 1210. (To put that in context, he was a rough contemporary of Francis of Assisi, 1181–1226.) Nazarius's whole career was not only clandestine but thoroughly illegal, but only after his death did the church take action against him, in the form of burning his remains. Probably, it was also Anselm who took possession of the Secret Supper, which ultimately found its home in France.[45]

Inquisitorial accounts allow us to reconstruct the Concorezzo church in some detail. Rainier credited the group with a membership of about 1,500 of both sexes spread over a wide area. He described the church's views as solidly Dualist, saying it taught that the Devil formed the body of the first man, "and into it infused an angel who had already sinned slightly." The group rejected the Old Testament, especially the works of Moses.[46]

Anselm tells us a great deal more about Nazarius himself. In his day, about 1270, the Concorezzo church was starkly divided between so-called ancients and moderns, with one party following the old-fashioned opinions held by Nazarius, a thoroughgoing Dualist, while others adhered to a more moderate younger rival, Desiderius. Nazarius himself did not believe that Christ truly ate material food, that he actually died or truly rose again, or that he performed actual miracles. He preached "that Christ brought His body down from heaven, entered into the Virgin through her ear and emerged from her ear and in His ascension bore the same body." Christ was not God, and not one with the Father. (Desiderius was closer to orthodoxy on all these points.) On scriptural matters, the Concorezzans agreed that the biblical prophets were good men, but they believed that their writings were sometimes guided by the Devil. Like other Dualists, Nazarius was deeply suspicious of the popular saint John the Baptist, who was, after all, responsible for the material sacrament of baptism. Nazarius held that the same spirit was in John as was in the prophet Elijah, but that it was a diabolical being.[47]

NAZARIUS's VIEW OF THE COSMOS gives us remarkable insight into a medieval mind. Obviously, we have to be careful in using such a hostile source as Anselm, who wanted to make his subject appear variously ignorant, superstitious, or deranged. Perhaps Nazarius really did believe that the sun and moon were not just living beings, but sexually active, and that dew and honey resulted from their intercourse; or, just as likely, Anselm was conflating and distorting some of the heretical bishop's actual views. One of Nazarius's alleged views, though, deserves quotation: "Nazarius believes that from Adam's crown, the Devil made the sun, that is, from one part of it, and from another he made the moon; from the crown of Eve, he made the moon and the stars and the five stars which are not in the firmament [the planets]. From another part [of Eve's crown], he believes that the Devil made the throne where Satan sits in the starry heaven and from which he rules over all the world below, with the exception of good souls." If Anselm's account is even partly correct, we glimpse Nazarius's vision of a cosmos that was wholly alive, where all of heaven and earth filled some symbolic purpose deeply rooted in faith, and where even the skies constantly taught scriptural truths.[48]

Although Nazarius's universe might be the product of an idiosyncratic poetic imagination, some of its features recall truly ancient layers of Christian tradition, not to mention Jewish and Manichaean precedents. Where, for instance, did he find the story of the crowns of Adam and Eve? Crown imagery has a long history in Christian churches, chiefly those of Eastern derivation. In the *Cave of Treasures*, God sets a crown of glory on the head of the newly created Adam as a symbol of his sovereignty over the world. This infuriates Satan: "When Satan saw Adam seated on a great throne, with a crown of glory on his head and a scepter in his hand, and all the angels worshipping him, he was filled with anger." Adam's crown of glory recurs as a characteristic item of his regalia prefiguring Christ's crown of thorns.[49]

Some related associations occur in the Old Testament pseudepigrapha, although they are quite remote from Nazarius's ideas. The Greek Apocalypse of Moses describes two dark figures who appear at Adam's funeral. In response to Eve's question to her son Seth, he tells her "that they are the sun and moon and themselves fall down and pray on behalf of my father Adam." The sun and moon darken at Adam's death in the Latin Life of Adam and Eve. Ethiopian churches still hymn "the Glory of Adam and the Crown of Eve."[50]

Jewish mysticism offers much closer parallels, with a telling juxtaposition of the ideas of Adam, crown, and creation. In the potent tradition of the Qabala, thinkers imagined the universe to be structured on the pattern of a human body, which together constitutes Adam Kadmon, Primordial or Original Man. Superimposed on that body is the chart of the divine radiances, or attributes, known as the Sefirotic Tree. At the summit of this figure is the divine Crown (Keter or Kether) through which the lower spheres of reality are generated. This Primordial Man, Adam Kadmon, creates the first human being reported in Genesis, Adam ha-Rishon ("First Man"). The different spheres are usually identified with cosmic bodies, with Keter as the stellar sphere. In other words, God created the world through Adam's Crown. As a good Dualist, Nazarius believed that creation was the work of the Devil rather than of God, but the model is similar. We also note that Eve's Crown gives rise to the stars and planets, all of which have their place in the Tree.[51]

The image of Adam Kadmon is described in the Zohar, an awe-inspiring Qabalistic text that originated in Spain in the thirteenth century. Although these ideas were not fully codified until shortly after Nazarius's death, they were percolating in Jewish mystical circles in Spain, Italy, and elsewhere across the Mediterranean world. We know that conversions occurred between faiths, and not just out of Judaism: some prominent Italians converted to Judaism, including one archbishop of the great city of Bari. Italy at this time also had Judaizing heretical movements very much like the Jewish-Christian sects of old that insisted on full obedience to the Jewish Law. Might we then imagine Nazarius stemming from a Jewish background? Militating against such an idea is the lack of reference to such a heritage in any of the Inquisitors' accounts. Surely, if they were dealing with a converted Jew, they would have highlighted this fact in the harshest and most offensive terms.[52]

More plausible, given the Bogomil connection, is the parallel with Manichaean ideas, which drew on much earlier versions of this Jewish system. From early times, Gnostic sects had drawn a crucial distinction to separate Primordial Adam (*Anthropos*) from the first human being recorded in Genesis. For Mani, likewise, Primordial

Man was a creature of the kingdom of light, while material Adam was a product of darkness. Following that principle, it would make sense for Adam to be a vehicle for the creation. The tenth-century Islamic text known as the *Kitab al-Fihrist*, "Catalogue of Books," records an ancient Manichaean creation epic in which the forces of Light create the sun and moon as refuges for the Light that has been liberated from its captivity in matter. It would not be a distant reach to imagine someone speaking of the sun and moon as part of that primordial creation. Although it is not directly linked to the creation episode, the ensuing passage reports a heavenly being investing Adam with a crown of splendor to help protect his son Seth.[53]

Whether Nazarius's sources were Manichaean or Qabalistic, the "Adam" he was crediting with the heavenly creation was almost certainly not the familiar first man of the Bible. It is most unlikely that this subtle distinction between Adams would have been apparent to the Inquisitors of the day.

We can argue, then, about exactly where Nazarius found his ideas, and he may well have invented parts of his system. But his thought often suggests a wider intellectual world, including some of the age's most intriguing undercurrents. We can easily understand why he would be so attracted to the pure Bogomil doctrine summarized in the gospel that he brought back with him from Bulgaria.

HOWEVER DANGEROUS TO ORTHODOXY they may have been, the Dualists were only one strand of medieval heresy. There were also, for instance, proto-Protestants, groups like the Waldensians and Lollards, who insisted on translating the scriptures into the vernacular and drawing their own daring conclusions from the text. With these other movements, however, we are on shakier historical grounds about their actual beliefs and their access to alternative gospel traditions.

Historians who debate the existence of medieval Dualism agree that dissidents existed in some number, however they interpret their beliefs. In the case of another heresy, the so-called movement of the

Free Spirit, there is intense disagreement as to whether the deviant faith ever existed at all, or whether it was, like the witch-cults, wholly invented. We can nevertheless find some authentic core, some fire amid the billowing smoke.

The Free Spirit movement allegedly existed from the early Middle Ages into the seventeenth century and beyond. At least according to official accounts, the group taught an exhilarating blend of pantheism and antinomianism. As pantheists, they held that God is Nature and Nature God. Once believers realized that God really was all things, and all things were God, then they, too, became God ("autotheism"). As God, they were not subject to the Law or to mere human laws; at least in theory, they claimed the right to do anything they chose. This view was antinomian, literally, "against the Law." Knowing that the present world was all that existed, they spurned fables of Judgment or an afterlife: heaven and hell were here and now, and, like God himself, those states existed only within us. Free Spirit adepts scorned the church and all its teachings and sacraments. According to investigators' accounts, the Free Spirit was an organized movement, if not an alternative church. While rejecting all hierarchies, adepts maintained impressively innovative structures, clandestine networks connecting cells of believers across nations and continents.[54]

If official accounts are even partly accurate, then the Free Spirit was not only a thoroughly radical outgrowth of mainstream Christianity, but a close facsimile of the libertine Gnostic movements in the early church. Free Spirit believers reputedly held that everything reported in the Bible applied to inner, spiritual realities rather than to events in historical Palestine. The Resurrection of Christ took place within the ordinary believer, who could return to the Garden of Eden, and who was incapable of sin. This was exactly the psychologizing approach that Elaine Pagels highlighted as characteristic of the ancient Gnostics, and it was proclaimed in ancient Gnostic scriptures, such as the Gospel of Eve. In the words of some eleventh-century French dissidents, Christian orthodoxy was no more than "the fictions of carnal men, scribbled on animal skins," and it was worthless in comparison with the law that the Holy Spirit wrote on the believer's heart.[55]

However intriguing the movement, though, many historians doubt whether it ever existed outside the minds of Inquisitors. Much of our evidence for heretical views comes from criminal trials, in which accused individuals were interrogated under extreme pressure or outright torture, and often they agreed to statements put to them by Inquisitors. Beyond question, many accusations of Free Spirit activism were false or exaggerated, and we know that Inquisitors had lists of standard questions to which suspects were induced to agree. Naturally, then, confessions from all over Europe tended to sound much the same, seemingly confirming the existence of a vast, unified conspiracy.

Moreover, Inquisitors reported heretical views in extreme and fantastic ways, making dissidents sound as dangerous and lunatic as they could. Contemporary exposés naturally made much of the grotesque sexual excesses charged against the group, inventing a kind of puritan pornography. No reasonable historian would accept such evidence without very careful qualifications. If early Protestantism had been snuffed out in the sixteenth century, we can only imagine how church historians might have presented its teachings based on forced confessions.

But if many myths surrounded the Free Spirit, some individuals genuinely and spontaneously uttered or wrote such opinions, and in many different historical and cultural settings over several centuries. The Ranter movement carried Free Spirit ideas forward into seventeenth-century England, and John Wesley, founder of Methodism, still had to contend with Ranters in the age of the Industrial Revolution. Some Free Spirit reality did exist, and some kind of underground continuity.[56]

In a few cases, we hear the movement speaking in its own unmediated voice, and a startling voice it is. Apart from a few quite substantial writings, investigations reveal accused individuals discussing their views freely, with little or no official prompting, and this despite the suspects' knowledge that they were facing imminent death. Not only do such cases confirm that Free Spirit theories existed much as claimed, but they offer tantalizing glimpses of ongoing religious debates based on wholly unexpected access to scriptural traditions.[57]

One well-known example involves John Hartmann, who was interrogated in Erfurt in 1367 and who shared his views quite frankly. In providing us with a glimpse of alternative religious consciousness, he parallels Nazarius in the previous century. Hartmann's advocacy of a spiritually based communism has made him something of a hero in historical accounts of the Middle Ages, and Marxists long claimed him as a predecessor. But the greatest surprises come from Hartmann's religious thoughts. If they were just his eccentric musings, they are surprising enough, but if he was drawing on a wider tradition, his remarks suggest that some truly weird beliefs circulated in medieval Europe.[58]

As in most such instances, the interrogator established that the heretic rejected standard moral laws. He then pushed that admission to secure detailed statements about scandalous conduct that the suspect refused to condemn, usually sexual acts. Could any reasonable person *really* believe that consensual sex was not a deadly sin? But in Hartmann's case, the exchange then moved into stranger territory. Seemingly out of nowhere, the interrogator asked whether Christ had himself been a Free Spirit. Hartmann's reply was nuanced. Not at first, he said. Jesus was clearly a regular human when he prayed to his Father in Gethsemane asking that the cup might pass away from him. But at his crucifixion on Good Friday, he became truly free.

The interrogator then asked whether, after the Resurrection, Jesus had sex with Mary Magdalene. Despite his previously outspoken answers, Hartmann now became evasive, and oddly so, as he must have known that he had said more than enough to consign himself to the flames. Even so, "he replied that this was the subject of serious and profound research, and though he well knew the answer, he preferred not to give his opinion."[59]

We might read Hartmann's words as those of a madman, or even of a creative religious entrepreneur. But his views also had a very long and distinguished historical pedigree, and his comment about

Jesus's human stature reflects countless debates through the centuries on the nature of the Incarnation. Nor was he the first to claim that Jesus's divinity had not belonged to him throughout his earthly life, but was rather bestowed later—usually at the Resurrection. Many Gnostics had likewise believed that the gospel stories were purely symbolic representations of inner psychological realities.

But it is the Magdalene passage that baffles. Ancient scriptures commonly presented a Jesus who gave lengthy speeches and teachings in post-Resurrection appearances to a body of disciples, usually faithful women, including Mary Magdalene. But here we find an Inquisitor asking a question about Jesus's sexual relationship with the Magdalene in 1367, a thousand years after we assume the matter was long since settled and forgotten. The exchange is mysterious— unless we assume that the interrogator was addressing an issue that was under discussion in the Free Spirit subculture.

Perhaps these views were surfacing independently, based on critical readings of the church's approved gospels. But such beliefs might indicate the existence of subterranean traditions, possibly mediated through later pseudo-gospels like those used by the Bogomils and Albigensians. Of their nature, such texts were unlikely to survive church investigations, and were likely to have been burned, and it is remarkable enough that we still possess treasures like the Secret Supper. But the Hartmann exchange again makes us wonder what other texts might once have existed, either as a whole or in fragments, or even in oral transmission.

LOOKING AT SUCH EXAMPLES, we are led to wonder just how many churches existed in medieval Europe, and whether we might even think of them in the modern sense as competing denominations. Despite all the vigilance of bishops and Inquisitors, a significant number of alternative gospels circulated in European Christendom. Still others existed beyond the limits of the Christian world.

Beyond the Horizon

Muslim and Jewish Versions of the Earliest Christian Traditions

Then said the priest: "How shall the Messiah be called, and what sign shall reveal his coming?" Jesus answered: "The name of the Messiah is admirable, for God himself gave him the name when he had created his soul, and placed it in a celestial splendor. . . . Muhammad is his blessed name."

Gospel of Barnabas, c. 1300?

JESUS AND A SELECT GROUP OF FOLLOWERS WENT UP TO A HIGH mountain. There, "his garments became white like snow and his face glistened as the sun, and lo! there came Moses and Elijah." After this stunning moment of Transfiguration, Jesus sat with the whole band of disciples to expound the truths of what would soon come to pass:

> Then Jesus said: "And the Messenger of God when he shall come, of what lineage will he be?" The disciples answered: "Of David." Whereupon Jesus said: "You deceive yourselves. . . . Believe me, for truly I say to you, that the promise was made in Ishmael, not in Isaac."

He foretells the coming of God's great Messenger:

> O blessed time, when he shall come to the world! Believe me
> that I have seen him and have done him reverence, even as
> every prophet has seen him: seeing that of his spirit God gives
> to them prophecy. And when I saw him my soul was filled
> with consolation, saying: "O Muhammad, God be with you,
> and may he make me worthy to untie your shoe-latchet; for
> obtaining this I shall be a great prophet and holy one of God."
> And having said this, Jesus rendered his thanks to God.[1]

That declaration of faith makes it obvious that this account is not
drawn from the canonical New Testament. But the larger framework sounds oddly familiar to Christian readers. When he is not
prophesying the coming of Muhammad, this Jesus sounds unnerv-
ingly like someone we know well.

The account is taken from the Gospel of Barnabas, a lengthy
version of the story of Jesus that in most ways recalls the canonical
gospels, but at critical points has clearly been subjected to Muslim editing. The exact date of this compilation is uncertain, but it
probably took this Islamicized form sometime in the fourteenth
century. The underlying Christian materials being edited are much
older, possibly harking back to the old Jewish-Christian sects.
Barnabas still continues to find many readers around the Muslim
world, and the text has gained a new lease on life in modern-day,
inter-religious polemic.[2]

Barnabas reminds us that rival accounts of Jesus were not confined to heretical Christian sects, but also existed in the other religions that were the neighbors and rivals of that faith. We have
already noted the Manichaeans, but the most significant rivals to
Christianity were of course Islam and Judaism. Each faith in its different way was concerned about Jesus and produced writings about
him. Islam, especially, produced or preserved a substantial body of
writings. Each faith also had a deep vested interest in combatting
or undermining Christianity, encouraging the creation of ferocious
polemic in the form of what were in effect anti-gospels.

EVER SINCE THE BIRTH OF ISLAM in the seventh century, that faith has existed in dialogue with Christianity. For much of Muslim history, Christians composed a large proportion of the population of what we now think of as "Muslim countries," such as Egypt, Syria, and Mesopotamia/Iraq. In turn, Muslim populations existed across Europe. In the early Middle Ages, Spain and Sicily were both ruled and settled by Islamic populations. From the fourteenth century through the twentieth, Ottoman Turkish power stretched deep into Europe, leaving the continent's southeastern quadrant under Islamic rule for most of that time. Wherever the crescent flag waved, Christian subjects were free to read old texts that would have been suppressed in Catholic or Orthodox lands. Who was to stop them?[3]

Muslims, meanwhile, read their own scriptures and holy texts, works influenced by diverse Christian traditions. The faith of Islam emerged in a largely Christian milieu obsessed by apocryphal writings, some of which have left a profound mark on the Qur'an itself. So substantial, in fact, is the Qur'an's account of Jesus that these passages represent a whole alternative gospel very different from the canonical Christian stories, one that drew heavily from early apocryphal scriptures. At different times, that apocryphal/Islamic Jesus was proclaimed in Qur'anic recitations across much of Europe, in the mosques of Toledo and Palermo, Seville and Sofia, Athens and Budapest, Belgrade and Bucharest.

Some political background is necessary in order to understand that Christian inheritance. We have already noted the role of the minor kingdoms that served as buffer states between the great empires of Rome and Persia. Long before the rise of Islam, Arab tribes and ethnic groups formed influential states in the lands that we today think of as Jordan, Iraq, and Syria. To the west, in the sixth and seventh centuries, stood the Ghassanid kingdom, which was allied with Rome, while the pro-Persian Lakhmids dominated the East. Both states had a strong Christian presence, and the Lakhmid capital of al-Hira was an important bishopric of the

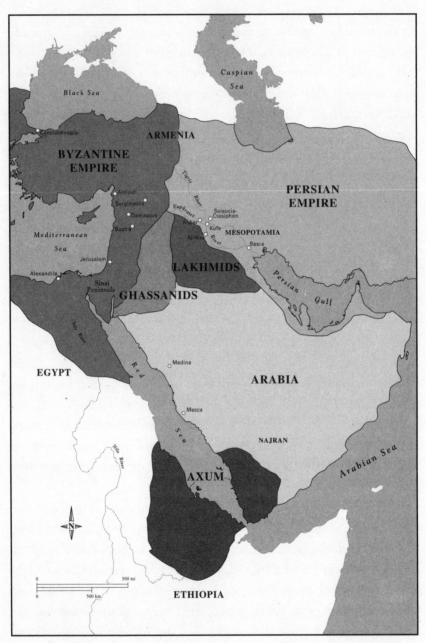

Middle East c. 550, Showing Ghassanid and Lakhmid Realms

Church of the East. The two kingdoms included several cultural and religious centers that would be critical for both Christianity and early Islam, including Bostra and Sergiopolis. (The same areas also had sizable Jewish communities.)[4]

These early kingdoms provided a template for the rise of Islam. In later legend, Bostra featured as the place where the prophet Muhammad met the Christian monk Bahira, who foretold his prophetic role. In the East, al-Hira was supposedly the place where the Arabic alphabet was invented. It is close to the city of Kufa—hence the name "Kufic" script. Others attribute that script to the Christian Arabs of Anbar.[5]

Apart from those immediate neighbors, the Arab world also existed in close proximity to Christian Ethiopia, with its copious libraries of texts both approved and suspect. Ethiopian kings repeatedly intervened in Arabia, and when Muhammad's early followers were persecuted in Mecca, they found refuge in Ethiopia.[6]

The Christian context of early Islam is indisputable. This does not mean, though, that the region's Christians adhered to later ideas of church orthodoxy, and Near Eastern Christianity in the centuries before the rise of Islam was very diverse. As early as the fifth century, one church leader denounced Arabia as a breeding ground of heresies, *Arabia haeresium ferax*.[7]

That teeming diversity was reflected in the presence of multiple gospels and apocryphal texts. A hundred years ago, scholars were already noting that the pre-Islamic Christian East was "literally inundated" with apocryphal works of both the Old and New Testaments. In the Qur'an itself, scholars have claimed to find traces of the Apocalypse of Adam, 1 Enoch, the *Cave of Treasures*, the Protevangelium, the Infancy Gospel of Thomas, the Arabic Infancy Gospel, and the Gospel of Barnabas (the early apocryphal text of this name, rather than the Islamicized version quoted above). When reading Qur'anic citations to such seemingly familiar works as the Torah, the gospels, and the Psalms, we should be cautious. We are not always dealing with the canonical versions of these texts, but rather, with apocryphal versions or adaptations.[8]

We also find mysterious references to gospels circulating in the region, texts that we cannot fully identify. Muslims venerate the Hadith, collections of stories and sayings attributed to Muhammad. One tale reports how, after the prophet received his initial revelations, he was deeply puzzled, indeed frightened, about what had happened. His wife, Khadija, took him to her cousin Waraqa, a Christian who "used to write the writing with Hebrew letters. He would write from the gospel in Hebrew as much as Allah wished him to write." Although the story is difficult to date, it suggests that a Jewish-Christian text, perhaps the Gospel of the Hebrews, was being used in Arabia in the seventh century.[9]

Some scholars go further in proposing Christian influence over the emerging faith of Islam. For German scholar Christoph Luxenberg, the Qur'an demonstrates a Christian Syriac literary background that certainly could not have arisen in Mecca or nearby parts of Arabia, which had no adequate schools or libraries at that time. Instead, he suggests, the Qur'an originated in a Christian environment in al-Hira or Anbar, and so, by implication, did much of the faith of Islam. Any such suggestion about Islamic origins is of course deeply sensitive, so much so that the name "Luxenberg" is a pseudonym for an author whose real identity is a closely guarded secret.[10]

WE SEE THE INFLUENCE of alternative Jewish and Christian scriptures throughout the Qur'an, especially in the accounts of Old Testament patriarchs and prophets. This is understandable when we look at what Christian authors in Syria and Mesopotamia were studying and writing in the years that Islam was emerging: the Cave of Treasures may well date from the 590s, when Muhammad himself was a young adult. The Qur'an's account of the fall of Satan stems from the Life of Adam and Eve. The Qur'an's Allah tells how

> We said unto the angels: Fall prostrate before Adam, and they
> fell prostrate, all save Iblis [Satan]. He was of the Jinn, so he
> rebelled against his Lord's command.

Almost certainly, a strange mystical figure who appears in the Qur'an's Sura 18 is Melchizedek, who so often starred in the Jewish and Christian pseudepigrapha. (Under the title el-Khidr, he is still a focus of popular devotion across the Middle East.)[11]

Such noncanonical sources dominate the extensive Qur'anic portrayals of Jesus and Mary. Some of their differences from the canonical gospels can easily be understood in terms of the establishment of a new faith—or, as Muslims would say, the purification of an age-old faith. It is not surprising, then, to find the Qur'an's Jesus explicitly rejecting the claims of contemporary Christians. He affirms clearly that he is not God and shares nothing of divinity.[12]

In other cases, though, we see the influence of alternative traditions that originated within Christianity itself and that were imported through apocryphal gospels. Such a source supplies the Qur'anic account of Mary, whose virginity is a tenet of faith for Muslims as well as Christians. Mary's life is described in the Qur'an's third Sura, *Imran*. Her mother prays for a child, and then delivers a girl, who is promised to God. Mary is raised in the sanctuary of the Temple under the guardianship of Zechariah. There she receives her food miraculously, by divine gift. Zechariah prays to God for the gift of offspring, and the story then follows the canonical account of the conception of John the Baptist. We then return to Mary, to the angelic promise that she will bear a child, Jesus: "He will speak unto mankind in his cradle and in his manhood, and he is of the righteous."[13]

Medieval Christian believers would immediately have recognized the backstory supplied here for Mary. Every one of the Qur'an's statements is rooted in the Protevangelium—from the initial prayer for a child uttered by Mary's mother to her decision to pledge Mary to a life of service to God and Mary's childhood in the Temple, where she receives food from the hand of an angel.[14]

The Qur'an recalls other apocryphal scriptures, too. In Sura 5, *al-Ma'idah*, God calls on Jesus to recount the wonders he has wrought with divine power. Some of these deeds are familiar enough to Christians, including healing lepers and the blind, but the verse goes on:

> Remember My favor to you and to your mother: how I
> strengthened you with the Holy Spirit, so that you spoke to
> mankind in the cradle as in maturity; . . . and how, by My
> permission, you shaped the likeness of a bird out of clay, and
> blew upon it, so that it became a bird.

Again, there is no mystery in finding the originals of these stories. The Arabic Infancy Gospel describes Jesus in his cradle telling his mother of his divine identity and mission. The tale of the birds features in the Infancy Gospel of Thomas.[15]

Other Christian contributions abound. The Qur'an tells the story of the Seven Sleepers, youths miraculously preserved after being walled up alive in a cave. In its origins, this is certainly a Christian story, reported by the fifth-century Syrian Father Jacob of Serugh, and well known throughout the European Middle Ages.[16]

The Qur'an drew on ideas of Christian apocrypha that were distantly removed from orthodoxy. On the crucifixion, the Qur'an declares,

> They slew him not nor crucified, but it appeared so unto
> them; and lo! those who disagree concerning it are in doubt
> thereof; they have no knowledge thereof save pursuit of a
> conjecture; they slew him not for certain but Allah took him
> up unto Himself.

Such a denial of Christ's human reality is pure Docetism of a kind that had existed for centuries in Christianity's Eastern regions. It is an open question which of a number of alternative gospels circulating in the region might underlie this text.[17]

Although parallels do not of themselves indicate direct influences, the evidence for Jewish-Christian survivals into Islam is quite strong. About 690, the caliph Abd al-Malik built the magnificent Dome of the Rock in Jerusalem, which today is one of the holiest places of Islam. The Dome's inscriptions contain some of the earliest written evidence of the Qur'anic text, most visibly the passage from 4.171–172, in which Jesus denies his divinity. Depending on the translation, God declares:

> Christ Jesus the son of Mary was [no more than] an apostle
> [messenger, *rasul*] of Allah, and His Word, which He be-
> stowed on Mary, and a spirit proceeding from Him.

Or, alternatively,

> The Messiah, Jesus son of Mary, was only a messenger of Al-
> lah, and His word which He conveyed unto Mary, and a spirit
> from Him.

Plenty of Eastern sects would have agreed wholeheartedly with that
non-divine understanding of Jesus's role and nature, but it would
have been particularly congenial to Jewish Christians, such as the
Ebionites.[18]

THE INFLUENCE OF NONCANONICAL Christian sources on the Qur'an
is obvious enough, but the Muslim-Christian dialogue did not end
with the Islamic conquest of the Middle East: rather, it intensified.
When Muslims occupied the Eastern Christian territories, they
were still more intensely exposed to the writings they found in such
ancient centers of Christian heterodoxy as Syria, Egypt, and Mesopotamia. In consequence, the Islamic world became a treasury of
writings otherwise lost or suppressed in Latin Europe. Almost certainly, Islamic scholars preserved some significant documents from
the earliest church, texts that were lost to Christendom.[19]

Jesus was and remains one of the greatest prophets of Islam, with
a status only exceeded by Muhammad himself. Other well-known
figures from the New Testament, including Mary and John the
Baptist (Yahya), are also esteemed, and early biographies suggest
that Muhammad himself had a remarkable sympathy for Mary.
When his forces destroyed hundreds of idols in Mecca, he reverently
preserved an image of the Virgin and Child. So abundant were the
ancient memories of Jesus recorded within Islamic writings outside
the Qur'an that scholars like Tarif Khalidi speak of a whole Muslim Gospel, offering a Jesus quite different from that of Christian

Europe. Khalidi's 2001 collection, *The Muslim Jesus*, catalogs more than three hundred relevant stories and sayings.[20]

The Jesus of Muslim tradition is a fierce ascetic, far more severe than the figure of the canonical gospels. As one of those tales records, "Jesus used to eat the leaves of the trees, dress in hairshirts, and sleep wherever night found him." He slept with only a stone for his pillow, until he saw another man who used no support whatever for his head. Angry at being bested, he then threw away his own stone. Ninth-century commentator Ahmad ibn Hanbal reported a saying typical of this world-rejecting Jesus: "I toppled the world upon its face and sat upon its back. I have no child that might die, no house that might fall into ruin." When Jesus was questioned about whether he would take a wife, he answered, "What do I do with a wife that might die?" No sane person would have invited this Jesus to a wedding at Cana, or indeed anywhere.[21]

Some of these Jesus stories can certainly be traced to controversies within Islam itself, and specifically, to the rise of the mystical Sufi movement from the late seventh century onward. More than just a model for Sufis, indeed an ideal Sufi himself, Jesus became a weapon in debates between rival Islamic schools. In that sense, we should see the Jesus traditions as late and distinctively Muslim innovations. But the fact that this Jesus looks so alien, and so alarming, does not mean that he is not rooted in ancient Christian tradition and alternative gospel traditions.

Often, the Muslim Jesus closely recalls the language and thought world of early Christian scripture, with only the slightest modifications from the familiar gospels. This is particularly true in the oldest layer of Jesus sayings and stories recounted by Muslim scholars from the ninth century. Jesus points to the birds of the sky and speaks of how God cares for them; he urges his followers to lay up treasures for themselves in heaven; he tells them to fast and pray in secret, and not like the hypocrites do; that they should repay cruelty with kindness; and that they should not cast pearls before swine. He declares that "he who has not been born twice shall not enter the kingdom of Heaven." In perhaps thirty cases, we see overwhelming resemblances to the Synoptic gospels, the title that scholars give to the three intimately related canonical books of Matthew, Mark, and Luke. Though we cannot reconstruct the Greek originals precisely from the Muslim accounts, we come close in terms of their spirit.[22]

These texts seem to take us back to an authentically primitive stage in the formation of the New Testament. Scholars agree that the earliest records of Jesus took the form of sayings, or sequences of sayings, lacking the narrative that we know from the canonical gospels. Christians remembered Jesus's words, and only later did authors sew those isolated fragments into more complete units, which were then written down. One such (hypothetical) sayings collection was Q, which was a critical source for both Matthew and Luke. Based on its similar format, some believe that the Gospel of Thomas might preserve such an early document. Sayings that did not find their way into the canonical text continued to float free as *agrapha*, "unwritten" or unrecorded words. We know them because they appear quite frequently in quotations by early church leaders or in alternate manuscript readings of the New Testament.[23]

That point takes us back to the Jesus sayings recorded by early Muslim commentators, which in their style and format bear a surprising resemblance not to the canonical gospels, but to a sayings source like Q. It looks as if those scholars had access to sayings, around which they constructed a plausible narrative, which was not necessarily the same framework provided by the Christian evangelists. Might they have used something like Q, perhaps even a Jewish-Christian sayings source? (As we will see, the theory that Islam might have preserved elements of primitive Christianity dates back at least to the Enlightenment.) The limited nature of the evidence does not allow us to say for sure, but what Khalidi calls the Muslim Gospel is an intriguing phenomenon.

Other Muslim Jesus sayings do not appear in our canonical New Testament. Might they have been based on noncanonical Christian scriptures, or isolated agrapha? Some seem to belong to those traditions, and sound very much like sayings in early alternative gospels. Jesus proclaims, for example, that "the world is Satan's farm, and its people are its plowmen." He warns his disciples not to build a house upon the waves of the sea, to beware the world and not make it their abode. Jesus meets a man and asks him, "What are you doing?" "I am devoting myself to God," the man replies. Jesus asks, "Who is caring for you?" "My brother," says the man. Jesus answers him, "Your brother is more devoted to God than you are." Very few of these early-attested sayings make the slightest bow to Islamic doctrines, or mention Muhammad or the Qur'an.[24]

To illustrate the "early Christian" feel of the sayings from the Muslim Gospel, let us look at a random mix of them, with half taken from the early Christian agrapha, and the rest from Jesus's words in the Muslim Gospel.

> Be in the middle, but walk to the side. (M)
> Become passers by. (C)
> Those who are with me have not understood me. (C)
> Blessed is he who sees with his heart, but whose heart is not in
> what he sees. (M)
> Do not own any wealth. (M)
> I am near you, like the garment of your body. (C)
> Satan accompanies the world. (M)
> Why do you marvel at my signs? I am giving a great inheritance to
> you, which the entire world does not have. (C)
> Be skillful moneychangers. (C)
> If people appoint you as their heads, be like tails. (M)

I have identified the source of each saying—whether it stemmed from Christian (C) or Muslim (M) tradition—but without such indicators, it would be difficult to tell the two categories apart. Other than New Testament textual specialists, even most scholars of early or medieval Christianity would not get a perfect score in deciding which was which. This degree of similarity is remarkable given the chronology. All the Christian examples date from the second or third centuries. None of the Muslim examples is recorded before the ninth century.[25]

It would not be hard to explain how old gospels or even pre-gospels might have entered the current of Islamic spirituality. Significantly, in terms of what we noted earlier about Christian influences on emerging Islam, the Muslim Gospel tradition almost certainly originated in southern Mesopotamia, and especially in Kufa itself. That was near al-Hira, an episcopal seat of the Church of the East, and presumably the home of a solid Christian library.[26]

Christian monasticism might well have provided the vehicle by which Jesus traditions were transmitted into an Islamic context. Many of these Muslim Gospel sayings preach asceticism and rejection of the world. In one striking passage quoted by Ibn Hanbal, Jesus says that God most loves the strangers. When he is asked whom he meant by this, he replies, "Those who flee [the world] with their faith [intact]. They shall be gathered together with Jesus on the Day of Judgment." That vision of the Christian fleeing the world is a commonplace of early Syriac literature, dating back to early texts like the Gospel of Thomas and the Dialogue of the Savior, in which Jesus blessed "the elect and solitary." The Muslim Jesus likewise teaches his disciples to "be ascetics in this world, and you will pass through it without anxiety." That is presumably the message of other Muslim Jesus sayings, including, "The world is a bridge; cross this bridge but do not build upon it." Such sayings would have had a special appeal for monks and hermits in Syria and Mesopotamia in the centuries before Muhammad.[27]

We know that some Christian ascetics became Muslims. The Qur'an praises Christian monks and clergy who accepted Islam, reporting that their eyes filled with tears as they prayed, saying, "We do believe; make us one, then, with all who bear witness to the truth!" We also know that monks in those same regions had collected substantial libraries of alternative scriptures, including apocalypses and gospels, although they might have had to remove some in times of repression. (That is one likely interpretation of the concealment of the Nag Hammadi texts.) Those convert monks presumably brought some of their old scriptures with them into their new faith. Although this is speculative, such former monks might have been among the early founders of Sufi movements. Basra, in Iraq, was an important base for the Church of the East, but subsequently it became the earliest center of Islamic Sufism. Not surprisingly, then, the Muslim Jesus bears a strong resemblance to the monastic ideal of Christian Late Antiquity.[28]

TEXTS LIKE THOSE SUMMARIZED by Khalidi stood in the Islamic mainstream, but the Muslim world also preserved other, more controversial ideas derived from the Christian fringes. Besides mainstream Christian influences, we also see continuities from the old Gnostic/Dualist worlds into sectarian Islam, and especially into some Sufi orders. Gnostic images and themes abound in the eighth-century Islamic text *Umm al-Kitab*, the Mother of Books, which recalls the Nag Hammadi writings.

Apart from the Sufis, such ideas manifest themselves among the various esoteric (*batiniya*) sects of Islam. Syria's Alawites follow several Gnostic ideas, including the transmigration of souls, to the point that many orthodox Muslims do not consider it Islamic. Equally suspect from that point of view are the Druze of Lebanon and Syria. If, in fact, we can see a Gnostic inheritance in such movements, then it is reasonable to suggest that it was transmitted through surviving scriptures and early texts, although none are presently known. Both Alawites and Druze, though, are famous for the extreme secrecy of their faith and its practices.[29]

In later centuries, too, the Islamic world received new waves of dissident ideas and texts from Christian Europe. In the fourteenth and fifteenth centuries, Catholic and Orthodox churches completed their suppression of Europe's Dualist movements. Those alternative churches found their last bastions in the Balkans, where Bosnia was often mentioned as a land of refuge for heretics fleeing persecution elsewhere. In these same years, Islamic forces were conquering large swaths of southern and eastern Europe, and by 1480 they controlled most of the Balkans. Bosnia itself was under full Ottoman control by 1451.[30]

That coincidence of chronology makes us wonder about the fate of the heretical movements. In the West, the groups probably were suppressed utterly, but they lasted longer in the East, long enough to fall under Muslim rule. We still do not know if some or all of the old sects might have merged into the new religious order, accepting conversion to Islam. In many ways, Islam offered a religious message appealing to the old Dualists, who had preached a visceral hostility to priests, institutional churches, and all their works.

From the fourteenth century, older religious ideas—possibly including Dualist themes—survived among Sufi groups such as the great Bektashi order that became so powerful throughout the Balkans and Anatolia. Although scholars have examined these connections, we do not yet have clear evidence about the preservation of clandestine gospels or other scriptures. It is wildly unlikely, though, that such venerated treasures would have been discarded lightly. We might even speculate that some such writings might still exist today in old mosques in Macedonia or Bosnia. When we consider such possible survivals, perhaps we should rather be speaking of Muslim Gospels, plural.[31]

THROUGHOUT MOST OF THEIR HISTORY, Muslims were so thoroughly confident in their culture, no less than their political power, that they saw little need to debate Christian religious claims. They cherished Jesus because he was their prophet, and it was only natural that his quoted words would reflect the Islamic worldview. In the late Middle Ages, though, some Muslim writer produced a text specifically intended to score controversial points against Christians. This is the book we have already met as the Gospel of Barnabas.

Over the past few centuries, Barnabas has been rediscovered periodically, and it has been lauded as an explosive demolition of Christian orthodoxy. In 1709, Deist skeptic John Toland found a copy in Amsterdam, and it formed the basis of his book *Nazarenus, or Jewish, Gentile and Mahometan Christianity* (1718). In Barnabas, Toland thought he had found an account of primitive Christianity as it really was before the invention of Jesus's deity, with such attendant delusions as the doctrine of the Trinity and the supersession of the Jewish Law. For Toland, Barnabas represented the original ideas of "Jewish Christianity"—a phrase he apparently invented—and of groups like the Ebionites. It was thus "THE ORIGINAL PLAN OF CHRISTIANITY" (capitalized thus), which was distorted and betrayed by the evil Paul. This interpretation is evident from the title, which rediscovers Jesus as the original Nazarene rather than the later Christ. Toland's ideas became commonplace in radical Enlightenment circles.[32]

When a scholarly English translation of Barnabas appeared in 1907, it created a sensation in Islamic lands, especially India. Soon, it was widely reproduced in pirated and abridged copies. Modern-day Muslims present the work as the only true account of the prophet Jesus, the authentic *Injil* (*evangelion*, or gospel), and it is a powerful argument in street-level Islamic proselytizing. Christians traveling in the Muslim world today are surprised to be asked their opinion of Barnabas, which is regarded as the decisive knockdown argument against Christian beliefs.[33]

The work does look very much like a canonical Christian gospel, with miracles and sermons taken wholesale from the Synoptics. Where it differs from the familiar texts, though, is partly in its length—over 80,000 words in English translation—but more glaringly, in the claims that Jesus makes for himself. In Barnabas, Jesus says firmly that he is a prophet, not the Son of God. And this gospel includes the frank declaration that "there is only one God, and Muhammad is the Messenger of God."

As it is "an orphaned text," with no obvious precursors or relatives, the Gospel of Barnabas is puzzling and controversial. In its present form, it was probably written about 1600, either in Spain or Italy; a text that sounds much like it was first described in the early seventeenth century. Some scholars argue for a significantly earlier dating, suggesting that the text appeared in its present Muslim form in the early fourteenth century. We know nothing certain about the work's authorship. It certainly was written or edited by a Muslim, but one with a thorough knowledge of Christian literature and access to some unconventional texts. Given the abundant evidence for religious conversions in the Mediterranean world, we might imagine the author or editor as a Christian convert to Islam, perhaps a former cleric.[34]

Beyond question, Muslim controversialists have at some point doctored an existing Christian text to create the overtly Islamic Gospel of Barnabas that we know today, and the references to Muhammad are clearly a late insertion. But no less certainly, those Muslim scholars and apologists did not invent the book out of whole cloth. They had at least one original text to play with, and that original might have been very old indeed. If Toland was wrong to claim it as a primitive Ebionite manifesto, it might indeed preserve the views of other early sects.[35]

In the 1980s, Muslim media sources excitedly reported the discovery of what was initially claimed to be an early Syriac manuscript of Barnabas, seeming proof that the text was authentically ancient. That story still surfaces regularly on the Internet, where it has become intertwined with other conspiracy theories. Allegedly, it was the challenge to faith caused by the finding of such early Islamic-leaning manuscripts that forced Pope Benedict XVI into early retirement in 2013. Of course, that rumored proto-Barnabas was no such thing. The text as it stands simply cannot be claimed as primitive, if only because of its frequent and significant errors about Jesus's time and about early Judaism. Directly or indirectly, though, it does incorporate ancient sources.[36]

For one thing, Barnabas draws on the Diatessaron, that lost second-century synthesis, or harmony, of the four canonical gospels discussed earlier. We find multiple readings that conflict with the Latin Vulgate Bible, but which recall the Diatessaron. Scholars disagree over whether that early stratum of text in Barnabas amounts to a few verses and motifs or a substantial portion of the work as we have it, but the parallels are there. Very likely, Barnabas drew on a vernacular Italian gospel harmony that itself was made from a medieval copy of the Diatessaron.[37]

IT IS IN BARNABAS'S LENGTHY ACCOUNT of the crucifixion that we most clearly see the influence of older alternative Christian scriptures. This narrative reads oddly to Christians because it is Judas, rather than Jesus, who suffers, after his tormentors have been deceived by a divine illusion. We see the whole story through the eyes of a baffled Judas, who struggles to convince successive hearers of his true identity. The sequence cries out to be filmed:

> The soldiers took Judas and bound him, not without derision. For he truthfully denied that he was Jesus; and the soldiers, mocking him, said: "Sir, fear not, for we are come to make you king of Israel, and we have bound you because we know that you do refuse the kingdom." Judas answered: "Now have you lost your senses! You are come to take Jesus of Nazareth; with arms and lanterns as [against] a robber; and you have bound me that have guided you, to make me king!" . . . Judas spoke many words of madness, insomuch that every one was filled with laughter, believing that he was really Jesus, and that for fear of death he was feigning madness.

Even the Virgin and the apostles shared the illusion. Jesus, though, had already made his escape from Gethsemane beforehand, as the Temple guards approached:

> Then God, seeing the danger of his servant, commanded Gabriel, Michael, Raphael, and Uriel, his ministers, to take Jesus out of the world. The holy angels came and took Jesus out by the window that looks toward the South. They bare him and placed him in the third heaven in the company of angels blessing God for evermore.[38]

Jesus then descends from heaven to appear to his faithful disciples, who listen to his teachings and eat with him. Finally, he returns to heaven. In the work's final section, the supposed author, Barnabas, writes that,

> after Jesus had departed, the disciples scattered through the different parts of Israel and of the world, and the truth, hated of Satan, was persecuted, as it always is, by falsehood. For

certain evil men, pretending to be disciples, preached that Jesus died and rose not again. Others preached that he really died, but rose again. Others preached, and yet preach, that Jesus is the Son of God, among whom is Paul deceived. But we—as much as I have written—we preach to those that fear God, that they may be saved in the last day of God's Judgment. Amen.[39]

Barnabas's crucifixion story is difficult to trace to any obvious single source, but its tone and general content recall actual alternative gospels from the early Christian centuries. This resemblance might be a matter of coincidence. Conceivably, a medieval Muslim took the familiar crucifixion story and imaginatively rewrote it to bring it into conformity with the brief Qur'anic text quoted earlier. If that is the case, he has succeeded magnificently in reproducing what a heretical Christian sect might have put together a millennium before. In Chapter 1, we encountered the ancient Gnostic Apocalypse of Peter, in which the true Jesus mocks the deluded persecutors who are actually crucifying his illusory self. (Ebionites likewise dismissed Paul as an apostate and a spinner of improbable tales.)

Other Christian sects had cultivated such ideas about Jesus's end, although they differed as to who might have substituted for Jesus on the cross. Some early readers of the Synoptic gospels noted the account of Simon of Cyrene, who is forced to carry Jesus's cross on the way to Calvary, and suggested that subsequent references to what "he" suffered referred to Simon rather than Jesus. Already in the 170s, the anti-heretical writer Irenaeus knew of such an interpretation, which he credited to the Egyptian Gnostic Basilides. Jesus, in this account, stands by the cross and laughs at the error. Among the Nag Hammadi gospels, we find a Sethite Gnostic work, called the Second Treatise of the Great Seth, in which Jesus says,

Yes, they saw me; they punished me. It was another, their father, who drank the gall and the vinegar; it was not I. They struck me with the reed; it was another, Simon, who bore the cross on his shoulder. It was another upon Whom they placed the crown of thorns. But I was rejoicing in the height over all

the wealth of the archons and the offspring of their error, of
their empty glory. And I was laughing at their ignorance.

The prophet Mani wrote of "the Son of the Widow, . . . the crucified
Messiah whom the Jews crucified." Probably, this refers to the son
of the widow of Nain, whom Jesus had miraculously raised from the
dead. Barnabas differs from these accounts in choosing Judas as the
victim, on the moral principle that he suffers the evil he intended
for another.[40]

We find more parallels in another recently published account
preserved in Coptic. Probably in the ninth century, a narrative of
Christ's Life and Passion was falsely credited to the early church father Cyril of Jerusalem. Among the fragment's surprising features,
we read that Pilate and Jesus were on excellent terms, to the extent
that the two dined together the night before Jesus's arrest. Pilate
even offered to give his only son to be crucified in Jesus's place.
Apart from reinforcing the substitution theme, that also makes us
think of Barnabas's otherwise surprising statement that Pilate "se-
cretly loved Jesus."[41]

THE MUSLIM BARNABAS is not drawing directly on any specific
Gnostic work that we know. Nor did its author find this Judas material in the Diatessaron, which faithfully followed the canonical
accounts. As an intellectual exercise, let us imagine that among
the multiple sources of Barnabas was an unknown pseudo-gospel
account of the crucifixion—we'll call it the Gospel of the Crucifixion of Judas. Let us say that it originated in early Gnostic
or Docetic circles, but was rewritten and retranslated over the
centuries. Whatever its geographical origins, it must have been
available in Italy or the western Mediterranean by the thirteenth
or fourteenth centuries, because that is where Barnabas probably
was compiled.

If we assume that such a gospel existed, then we have a natural way of explaining its existence in Italy or neighboring regions

at just that time. As we have seen, Italy was a stronghold of the Albigensian sect, which obtained texts from Bulgaria and the Byzantine world, and among these, one gospel—the Secret Supper—survives intact. It is extremely improbable that this was the only such pseudo-scripture to reach the West. What else did the heretical Bishop Nazarius have on his bookshelves? We also know that the Albigensians held Docetic views about Christ and the crucifixion. Like their Bogomil forefathers, they held that "Christ our God was born . . . as an illusion, and as an illusion he was crucified." They would have welcomed a gospel that reported the triumphant escape from death of the true spiritual Christ.[42]

To wander still further into the realms of speculation, even of historical fiction, might a converted Albigensian have carried such a gospel into the world of Islam? Might someone rather like Nazarius have so despaired of the orthodox Christian world that he abandoned the faith altogether?[43]

The gospel described here is wholly imaginary, and perhaps no such complete text ever existed. But a fragmentary gospel, even an extract included in some other work, would go far toward explaining how, around 1300, a Muslim author succeeded so immaculately in re-creating the ideas of a millennium before. If, indeed, he had no such sources, he was the most creative historical novelist who ever lived.

When modern Christians around the globe are presented with polemical claims that Barnabas is the "true gospel," they might well be confronting truly ancient heretical traditions. Sometimes, it seems as if the churches must continually refight the battles of the second century.

———————

JEWS, TOO, PRODUCED "GOSPELS" OF JESUS, and, like Barnabas, some of these probably preserve memories of older scriptures. In an earlier chapter, we encountered the Jewish-Christian gospels written in the early church, stemming from groups like the Ebionites. The Gospel of the Hebrews was the most celebrated. Little apparently survives of these gospels, but there are speculative claims that portions survived in Jewish circles.[44]

Talmudic references preserve memories of early Hebrew versions of the gospels circulating among Jews in early centuries, but it is very uncertain whether any survived through the Middle Ages and beyond. At various points through history, we find Hebrew versions of the canonical gospels, especially Matthew. Some of these versions were made by followers of Jesus who were trying to evangelize Jews, while Jews themselves produced translations for the purpose of research or, more commonly, interfaith controversy. The most famous is a translation of Matthew written in fourteenth-century Spain by the Jewish physician Shem Tob, which has some odd variations from the standard New Testament text.[45]

Repeatedly through the centuries, writers have claimed that such texts might not actually be translations, but instead represented lost Hebrew originals. In that view, the Shem Tob Matthew might preserve a supposed Hebrew original of Matthew, or even a lost work like the Gospel of the Hebrews. (The idea that Matthew might initially have been written in a language other than Greek is fiercely controversial.) Generally, attempts to trace continuity with earlier works have proved unsuccessful. Despite optimistic claims, few scholars think that these translations contain authentic versions of any lost Hebrew gospel.[46]

JEWS, THOUGH, LIKE MUSLIMS, did compose at least one wholly new gospel, or anti-gospel, for polemical ends. Hostile depictions of Jesus are found in the Talmud, but in the *Toledot Yeshu* (Life of Jesus), Jewish scholars recounted Jesus's life and career in the most negative and shameful terms, radically contradicting the Christian texts. It is an angry and bitter work. It would, of course, be legitimate to counter that this Jewish work was a paltry riposte to the flood of vicious anti-Jewish propaganda produced by Christians through the centuries.[47]

Because the Christian church was so bitterly hostile to the *Toledot Yeshu*, the work circulated underground, and much about its origins remains uncertain. It was written later than the sixth century, because it describes Christian customs and festivals that could not have originated before that time. But it cannot have been written much after the ninth century, because that is when Christian clergy began denouncing the tract in shudders.[48]

Although banned in the Christian world, it was popular in medieval Jewish communities, and perhaps a hundred manuscript copies survive. Prior to the fourteenth century, it was probably available in virtually any large or medium-sized town across Europe wherever a Jewish community existed. After the horrific massacres and ethnic purges around the time of the Black Death, the Jewish center of gravity shifted to Eastern Europe, which is where we should look for the text in later periods.

The Life takes the form of a gospel in that it covers the same general ground as one of the canonical Big Four, although inverting every significant element in the story. It begins with a virtuous woman named Miriam, who is betrothed to the noble Yohanan, a descendant of David. However, Miriam attracts the lustful attention of the vile Joseph Pandera, who seduces her by disguising himself as her husband. Their offspring is Jesus. Discovering the sordid truth, Yohanan flees in horror.[49]

Jesus launches his mission with extravagant messianic claims, supported by genuine miracles. He owes these powers to having entered the Temple and read the secret name of God on the foundation stone. In order to discredit Jesus, Jewish authorities commission another man, Iskarioto (presumably Judas Iscariot), to learn the same letters and thereby gain the same miraculous powers. In passing, we hear an echo here of the tradition found in Barnabas, that Judas was in some sense a shadow of Jesus, even a substitute. In the Jewish narrative, the two men fly toward heaven, but then plummet to earth, scattering and defiling the letters of the sacred Name. Without his occult powers, and lacking the protection offered by the Divine Name, Jesus can be arrested and crucified—on a cabbage stalk. After Jesus's death, a gardener steals and hides his body, giving rise to stories of a Resurrection. The corpse, however, is recovered and taken to the queen, Helena, tied to the tail of a horse.

Jesus's followers remain faithful and spread their message throughout the world. This begins a period of thirty years of conflict between Jews and Christians. The strife is resolved only through the machinations of a man named Simeon Kepha, who also accomplishes miracles through the power of the Divine Name. This Simeon is better known under another name, which is not, as Christians might assume, Simon Peter, but Paul. This Paul institutes the full separation of Jewish and Christian ways. Christians, the Life says,

> were now to observe the first day of the week instead of the seventh, the Resurrection instead of the Passover, the Ascension into Heaven instead of the Feast of Weeks, the finding of the Cross instead of the New Year, the Feast of the Circumcision instead of the Day of Atonement, the New Year instead of Chanukah; they were to be indifferent with regard to circumcision and the dietary laws. . . . All these new ordinances that Simeon Kepha . . . taught them were really meant to separate these Nazarenes from the people of Israel and to bring the internal strife to an end.

Ultimately based on a deceptive Jesus, historic Christianity, according to this text, was at best a parody religion, a pallid imitation of authentic Judaism.[50]

WE WOULD BE RASH TO SEEK any hints of historical truth in a work that is chiefly of interest in suggesting some of the rival views of Jesus circulating long before the modern era. It also makes us ask just what other alternative views might have existed if we were able to excavate below the layers of church censorship.

As with Barnabas, the *Toledot* has some connections with known alternative Christian texts. This is not just a case of Jewish scholars creating a blasphemous parody of the four canonical gospels. Rather, the author seems to be drawing on a range of earlier lost gospels and folktales, some Gnostic or Jewish-Christian, and some of which influenced the accounts of Mary and Jesus in the Qur'an. Portions of the *Toledot* story certainly date back to the early Christian centuries and surface in the works of Celsus, Justin Martyr, and others.[51]

The story of Joseph Pandera has an ancient pedigree. As early as the second century, Jewish critics of Christianity argued that Jesus was not the son of a virgin, *parthenos*, but rather of a man called Pantherus or Panthera, perhaps a Roman soldier. His name has here been expanded to agree with the tradition that Jesus's earthly father bore the name Joseph—hence Joseph Pandera. The *Toledot* is making a polemical point: Jesus was the son of a seducer, and he would himself seduce many of the people of Israel to an abhorrent new faith. Like the Secret Supper and the Gospel of Barnabas, the *Toledot Yeshu* was restating ideas and themes that would have been very familiar in the second or third centuries, but repackaging them for a latter-day audience.[52]

PICTURE A GREAT WESTERN EUROPEAN CITY at the height of the Middle Ages, say about 1320 in Dante's own lifetime. Groups like the ancient Gnostics have long since vanished into oblivion, as (surely) have their scriptures. In the city's Catholic churches, though, sumptuous paintings celebrate such ancient texts as the Gospel of Nicodemus and the Marian Gospels. Those and other not-so-lost gospels have now reached an unprecedented market through the newly published *Golden Legend*. In cathedrals and universities, scholars pore over newly translated texts in which Old Testament patriarchs and prophets deliver powerful testimonies to Christ.

Outside the mainstream church, other readers meet other Christs. In and around the city, clandestine circles meet to read other venerable pseudo-gospels long proscribed by the church. Some of those documents reveal a Jesus who never took material form. Others suggest a very human Jesus, with his sexual partner, Mary Magdalene. In the Jewish ghetto, equally daring readers explore their own counter-gospel, encountering ideas that outraged the mainstream church a thousand years before. From a Mediterranean city, one would not have to go far to encounter Muslims with their own memories of Jesus, and their own gospels.

A thousand years after Constantine's Council of Nicea, there were still many gospels, and many Christs.

9

After Darkness, Light

How the Reformation Era Drove the
Ancient Gospels from the Churches

*Such monstrosities did we believe in Popedom, but then we under-
stood them not. Give God thanks, ye that are freed and delivered
from them and from still more ungodly things.*

Martin Luther, c. 1540

IN 1505, THE YOUNG LAW STUDENT MARTIN LUTHER was caught
in a dreadful thunderstorm while traveling. Terrified by a light-
ning strike, he made a vow: "Help me St. Anne, I will become a
monk!" He kept his promise. On this occasion, at least, the Luther
who would insist on such rigid reliance on the canonical scriptures
turned to a saint whose existence was attested only by alternative
texts, mediated through popular religious fiction.[1]

Long after the time of Constantine, Christians around the world
continued to value alternative scriptures, but a time did come when
many of those texts really were suppressed, and more thoroughly
than the medieval church or state could ever have achieved. Today, Protestants, Catholics, and Orthodox believers agree that the
concept of scripture applies only to a strictly defined biblical canon,
although the three traditions differ somewhat on its contents.

Although literally hundreds of popular books claim to offer alternative gospels or scriptures, no modern church could incorporate them into its liturgy or services without risking its claim to be a mainstream Christian organization. No respectable church veers from a (more or less) generally agreed canon.

When did this transformation occur, this massive loss of diversity? The key moment was the Reformation of the sixteenth century, which marked a fundamental reorientation in attitudes toward the whole concept of scripture and on authority in religion more generally. While we know the movement stressed the absolute authority of scripture, it is easy to forget that it rewrote the rules of how that Bible was constituted. The Reformation was a war on the alternative gospels and their influence, and its battles involved violent attempts not just to suppress the texts, but also their countless visual representations in churches and public places. In fact, the Reformation created the Bible that we have known ever since. In terms of chronology, then, we have our story wrong by over a thousand years. The Christian church did indeed demote the ancient alternative scriptures, but in the sixteenth century, rather than the fourth.[2]

That said, obviously the old texts did not vanish overnight. How could they, when they had been so ingrained in Christian culture for so long? Even in the Protestant heritage, we are not so far removed from the old gospels as we might think.

The Reformers' triumph was less absolute than it initially appeared in other ways, too; in retrospect it even seems like a Pyrrhic victory. The Reformers sought a sweeping revolution in religious consciousness in which faith was a matter of the educated mind and will—to the absolute exclusion of external images and ritual acts. Protestantism was a faith of the text rather than of icons, shrines, or relics. But this commitment to education and intellect placed no limits on where reading and inquiry might lead, and Europe's leading Protestant nations eventually became the centers of the skeptical Enlightenment. Perhaps Reformation is the essential precondition for Enlightenment.[3]

The history of the alternative scriptures amply illustrates that paradox, that story of unintended consequences. Underlying the rejection of those texts was a radical new attitude toward the authenticity of historical documents and the criteria used to assess them. It was not long, though, before those very same standards were applied to the Bible itself, ultimately laying a foundation for secularism. In the post-Enlightenment world, both mainstream and alternative scriptures found themselves the subject of academic study as much as faithful inquiry. In retrospect, the unscalable wall that the Reformers sought to erect between true and false scriptures seems much less intimidating. In the contemporary world, in fact, a common belief holds that the authentic message of Christianity may be more fully present in noncanonical texts than it is in the New Testament itself. We have truly come full circle.

THE REFORMATION SPARKED a cultural and spiritual revolution in multiple ways. Long before the movement began, however, Western culture was already being transformed, and those changes radically affected attitudes toward scripture and canon. The emerging intellectual world had much stricter attitudes toward authenticity, insisting that texts could (and must) be assessed and evaluated according to their date, content, and authorship. Any document claiming spiritual authority was now expected to meet the highest possible standards. Medieval writers had not been incompetent or uncritical in these matters, and they had been quite prepared to reject allegedly ancient documents on shrewd historical grounds. Quite apart from their own common sense, they took inspiration from the critical faculties demonstrated by such well-known ancient fathers as Jerome. Still, even with the best intentions, they had nothing like the scholarly resources that quite suddenly became available from 1300 onward.[4]

Well before the Reformation, European scholarship was expanding in scale and sophistication, largely based in the universities that had begun appearing from the twelfth century onward. Universities proliferated, with some eighty operating across Western and Central Europe by 1500, and a flourishing university became the essential badge of status for every aspiring state or dynasty. Even so, a few of the older established places enjoyed a special elite status, notably Paris. Moreover, the intellectual level of these institutions was rising steadily as scholars built on the texts and translations acquired via the Islamic world. From the fourteenth century, critical scholarship revolutionized the study of classical texts, and at the same time, searches of old libraries rediscovered many long-lost classical manuscripts. The progressive collapse of the Byzantine political world from the fourteenth century onward dispersed Greek scholars across Europe and with them the knowledge of the Greek language.[5]

Scholars struggled to distinguish between historical and bogus documents. Although this did not involve a pseudo-scripture, one sign of the new mood was the critical investigation of the forged text known as the Donation of Constantine, which supposedly gave imperial authority for the establishment of the Papal States. According to the text, the fourth-century Pope Sylvester had healed the Emperor Constantine of leprosy, and in his gratitude, the emperor gave Sylvester sovereignty over a large portion of the Western Roman Empire. The document appeared in the eighth century, which was presumably the time at which it was forged in order to support papal territorial claims. Although the Donation repeatedly faced critical challenges, it was generally accepted as historical until the mid-fifteenth century, when several acute scholars independently proved it to be bogus.[6]

Often, a given document might not be judged to be either wholly genuine or completely false. It might contain several different strata, reflecting the work of multiple authors, who could be distinguished by painstaking critical scholarship. Establishing the unity and integrity of a text was crucial to gauging its authenticity and historicity. Western scholars honed their skills in evaluating the many new manuscripts that flowed west in this era. In the 1490s, for instance, the West discovered collections of letters attributed to the early church father Ignatius. The ensuing debate over their authenticity lasted for over three centuries.[7]

Religious attitudes were changing long before the era of the Reformation strictly defined. From the fourteenth century, the West

European church was dealing with a more educated and confident laity as literacy became more commonplace. Believers both lay and clerical were often critical of corruption and scandal within the church, and they demanded higher standards of learning and piety. They wanted direct, unmediated access to the writings on which the faith was based, and in their pristine forms.[8]

Printing had its impact in supplying the needs of this concerned readership. Modern people find it difficult to imagine just how very different the experience of reading was before that fifteenth-century innovation—or rather, before the whole media revolution. As we have seen, one early consequence of printing was the massive availability of noncanonical texts. It was in precisely the same years that scholarship and literacy were growing so impressively in the universities and elsewhere that volumes like the *Golden Legend*, and Ludolphe's Life of Christ, undertook their cultural conquest of Latin Europe. In popular devotion, stories like the Harrowing of Hell and the Cycle of the Virgin reached their apex of popularity in the century or so before the Reformation. Gradually, the rise of printing raised challenging questions about the Bible itself and exactly what it should contain. In the days of manuscript production, actually seeing or handling a complete Bible was a rare experience outside the confines of a great church or monastery. So, obviously, was any critical sense of exactly which books did or did not belong within that volume: Bibles varied according to place and time.[9]

But printing demanded standardization, and issues of canon now became central to religious debate. In the early sixteenth century, scholars applied to biblical texts the rigorous methods that had become popular in reading classical works. Tracing the development of manuscript traditions over time showed how biblical texts had evolved, and in some cases, how they had been distorted. In 1516, Erasmus of Rotterdam produced a revolutionary critical edition of the Greek New Testament, eliminating many passages that had long been included in Latin texts. The following year, French humanist Jacques Lefèvre d'Étaples sparked a bitter controversy through learned tracts that sought to disentangle the myths that had grown about the biblical figure of Mary Magdalene.[10]

The goal of restoring the original texts now became common—and, for the first time, possible. In terms familiar to American judges and politicians, Christians now began an intense search to recover the original intent underlying the scriptures.

THE YEAR 1517 IS CONVENTIONALLY taken as the start of the Reformation movement. Luther and other Protestant Reformers stressed the Bible as the sole and absolute source of authority in religion: their principle was "scripture alone," *sola scriptura*. But that meant defining what the scripture was, and precisely which books belonged in it. The result was the creation of a much shorter Bible than what had been known over the previous millennium.

Steeped in the ancient fathers, the Reformers had an excellent sense of the historical debates over the canon and specific books, and when in doubt, they followed the most rigorous and exclusive criteria. Usually, that meant following Jerome, who had little time for controversial or debated scriptures or pseudo-gospels. When it came to the Old Testament, Protestants had to choose between the stringent approach used by Jewish authorities in defining their Bible (the Masoretic text) and the more inclusive attitude of the medieval church, which had used the Greek Septuagint translation. Protestants chose the Jewish criterion, and thus excluded the so-called Deuterocanonical books, so that Judith, Tobit, Maccabees, and the rest were now designated apocryphal. Although Martin Luther and other Reformers urged people to read these texts for historical information or moral improvement, they were no longer to be considered scriptural.[11]

Historical criteria apart, Luther and his contemporaries had a natural prejudice against books that contradicted their theological approaches. Even if the historical credentials of these works had been stronger, the Reformers would scarcely have approved texts favoring the cult of Mary or the veneration of saints. Luther himself, in fact, would have been even harsher in his attitude to what we today know as the canonical scriptures, applying the same critical razor to the New Testament as the Old. He termed his message "evangelical," meaning it was absolutely rooted in the gospel, the *evangelium*, as presented in pristine form in the canonical gospels themselves and in such core Pauline texts as the Epistle to the Romans. Other scriptures had to be judged by their conformity to the central narrative of faith as Luther understood it. He would ideally have placed a number of New Testament works into a category of disputed books, the *antilegomena*. These included such books as Revelation, Hebrews, and the Epistle of James, which most modern readers assume to be integral parts of the biblical text. In practice, that segregation never gained favor. The New Testament therefore remained very much what the Western church knows today.[12]

Although Luther wasted little time condemning the self-evidently late and spurious pseudo-gospels, one medieval text did draw his special attention. He was appalled by the *Toledot Yeshu*, which seemed to prove the wider Jewish loathing for Christ and Christians. The discovery poisoned his attitude to Jews and Judaism, which in his early years had been relatively tolerant. By the 1540s, his vicious screeds urged that Jews be expropriated and subjected to forced labor, and that the practice of their faith should be utterly forbidden. In Germany, above all, his anti-Jewish fury had a long and hideous afterlife.

WRITINGS BY SCHOLARS and theologians might have a limited impact, but across northern and western Europe, the Reformers' views were enforced through decisions by national churches.

England offers one example of the spiritual revolution in progress, the war against material symbols of faith. In the century after 1540, English Christians gained much greater access to the Bible than they had had in the past, chiefly in the Protestant form of the Geneva and King James versions. These Bibles transformed social attitudes toward literacy as well as piety. In the same years, strict new official attitudes all but eliminated such once-universal manifestations as images of the Virgin Mary or the Harrowing of Hell in stained glass and statuary. Local officials were instructed to "take away, utterly extinct and destroy all shrines . . . pictures, paintings and all other monuments of feigned miracles, pilgrimages, idolatry and superstition so that there remain no memory of the same in walls, [and] glass windows." Books that reflected these stories were burned or discarded as trash. The great York Mystery Plays were suppressed in 1569, the Coventry cycle a decade later.[13]

This new biblical emphasis also reshaped the liturgy, the common means by which most ordinary people were exposed to scriptures of all kinds. In England in 1549, Archbishop Thomas Cranmer lamented what had become of the liturgy in recent years, suggesting how apocryphal and marginal texts had virtually taken it over: "These many years passed, this godly and decent order of the ancient fathers hath been so altered, broken, and neglected, by planting in uncertain stories, legends, responds, verses, vain repetitions, commemorations, and synodals, that commonly when any book of the Bible was began, before three or four chapters were read out, all the rest were unread."[14]

Even Cranmer's strenuous attempts to return to authenticity did not satisfy more zealous believers, who wanted the purge of non-biblical and apocryphal materials to go still further. The urge to cleanse England's liturgy and prayer book of Catholic and medieval elements was the issue that spawned the Puritan movement.[15]

FUNDAMENTAL TO PROTESTANT reform was the expunging of what Reformers saw as superstitious accretions to the true faith, including the cults of the Virgin and saints. Reformed and reforming churches purged the visual representations of the alternative gospels, radically transforming the worship environment for ordinary believers.[16]

From the 1520s through the mid-seventeenth century, Protestant states engaged in a systematic war on old popular devotions. Sometimes such campaigns were the work of organized state activity, but commonly they involved popular mob activism. In destroying images, Protestants were inspired by biblical prohibitions on idol worship and graven images, and Marian symbols of all kinds were a natural target for iconoclasm. So were images of saints, which had usually been drawn from the *Golden Legend*, and beyond that, from apocryphal books of Acts. Iconoclasm was a war against the material manifestations of Christian apocryphal literature.[17]

Outbreaks occurred in such early Reforming centers as Zurich, Basel, and Strasbourg. In Basel in 1529, the town council demanded absolute reliance on the Bible, strictly defined. It ordered every priest and preacher to "proclaim and preach nothing other than solely the pure, clear gospel, the holy divine word, comprehended in Biblical writ, along with whatever they might wish to protect and arm it, without recourse to other interpreters, human sentences." A month later, Basel witnessed widespread iconoclastic riots that destroyed virtually all the tokens of traditional Catholic worship and devotion in the cathedral and in the city's other leading churches. The image-breaking in John Calvin's Geneva was ferocious and comprehensive. Even these manifestations were dwarfed by the devastating Storm of Images (*Beeldenstorm*) that swept over the Netherlands in 1566. This movement was directed against any and all Catholic symbols—against stained-glass windows, statues of the Virgin and the saints, and holy medals and tokens. In words adapted from the Vulgate version of Job, the Calvinist motto proclaimed *Post Tenebras Lux*: After Darkness, Light (and that is still Geneva's motto).[18]

England suffered similar violence, although spread over several decades. If Fairford somehow, miraculously, preserved its stained-glass windows, the vast majority of other churches were not so fortunate. In eastern England's Fen country, Ely Cathedral once boasted a splendid Lady Chapel that contained a full set of sculptures depicting the cycle of stories from the Marian Gospels. Today, all that remains are the niches in which those figures once stood, before they fell to the hammers of enraged Puritans. Across Europe, we see similar evidence of Protestant fury. The Cathedral of Utrecht, for instance, was once blessed with a spectacular polychrome altarpiece. The faces of each individual character were carefully chiseled off in the 1560s, and the whole object was then concealed until rediscovery in modern times. What is unusual about such remains is that at least some traces survive to indicate the damage caused. More often, stone objects were smashed beyond recognition, and wooden items burned.[19]

A substantial modern literature suggests that the purge of alternative scriptures caused a catastrophic decline in the role of female imagery in Christianity, but again, this change occurred not in the fourth century, but in the sixteenth. In what became Protestant Christendom, it was the Reformation that suppressed the texts that justified the cult of Mary. In the ancient Gospel of the Egyptians, a notorious verse has Jesus proclaiming, "I am come to destroy the works of the female." Those words sound like the manifesto of the radical Reformers.[20]

As ROMAN CATHOLICS STRUGGLED to reform their own church to meet the new challenge, they, too, drew sharper lines between approved and unapproved scriptures. In the early decades of the Reformation, plenty of Catholic thinkers were sympathetic to Protestant demands about canon, scripture, and the quest to revive the authentic purity of the earliest church. At least some church leaders were willing to undertake quite sweeping reforms. Attitudes hardened over time as Protestant and Catholic realms plunged into prolonged warfare and waves of persecution. From the 1540s onward, Europe was swept by religious wars, which reached dreadful heights in France and the Netherlands in the 1560s. More important, a new generation of reforming Catholics vigorously defended many of the beliefs and practices that so alienated Protestants, including the traditions and scriptures on which they were based.

These divisions shaped Catholic attitudes toward scripture. After some debate, the church retained the Deuterocanonical books as fully accredited components of the Old Testament. But controversy continued. In 1592, the Sixto-Clementine Bible, produced at the command of Pope Clement VII, omitted Deuterocanonical books such as 1 and 2 Esdras and the Prayer of Manasseh, although they were printed in an appendix to prevent them from being lost altogether. If even these relatively respectable scriptures were so scorned, the apocrypha could expect little mercy. Catholics and Protestants alike debated taking their purges further, especially to eliminate Jewish postbiblical writings. Also in the 1590s, a much more critical attitude to fringe scriptures became evident when some sensational early Christian texts were allegedly uncovered in Granada, Spain, and enthusiasts even reported the finding of a supposed Arabic Gospel. After some early excitement, the Vatican recognized these Leaden Books as spurious and effectively suppressed them.[21]

Between 1545 and 1563, the church held its long promised reform council, which convened at Trent, Italy. (From the city's Latin name, we speak of Tridentine Catholicism.) Although the gathering disappointed many Catholic reformers, who wanted the council to go further, it did suppress some of the more extravagant cults and devotions to saints. The council limited the celebration of many events and individuals grounded only in the apocrypha, refusing, for instance, to devote a feast day for the Virgin's supposed father, Joachim.[22]

The visual arts show a major change in attitude toward apocryphal sources. The years between 1540 and 1680 were a glorious era for Catholic art and architecture, as thousands of new churches and religious houses were built or reconstructed. Each, also, was filled with newly commissioned works of painting or sculpture. Catholic painters now produced some of the greatest treasures of European art. Each depended on the patronage received from Catholic elites, whether lords or bishops, or else particular churches or religious houses. As we will see, some apocryphal stories retained a powerful hold on the Catholic imagination, above all those connected with the Virgin Mary; but other legends were winnowed ferociously.

Although it is difficult to generalize about the vast outpouring of religious art in this era, post-Tridentine artists did not address themes like the Infancy Gospels. Even more surprising is the disappearance, in the West at least, of the Harrowing of Hell. In the pre-Reformation years, between about 1360 and 1530, the Harrowing had attracted some of Europe's greatest artists. In 1568, Venetian artist Tintoretto painted an impressive example, focused on a memorably nude Eve, but that really marked the end of the tradition. The theme attracted none of the great artists of the succeeding eras of Mannerism and the Baroque. The Harrowing survived in occasional church murals, but it had definitely been confined to the plebeian depths, into which no savior ever descended to rescue it. The visual loss of the Harrowing was almost as thorough in Catholic Europe as in the Protestant world.[23]

Among both Protestants and Catholics, new technologies ensured the effectiveness of these stricter policies. In the Middle Ages, little prevented the copying of manuscripts, however incendiary their contents. In the new order, though, books were printed, and governments worked long and hard to regulate the output of printing presses. If an old manuscript account failed to make it into circulation as a printed book, its contents were unlikely to survive.

On both sides of the denominational divide, reforming Christians determined to downplay flagrantly noncanonical works, both in their own right and as part of collections like the *Golden Legend*. Reformers broadly defined—Catholic as well as Protestant—made that book the target of their zeal, using it as a symbol of everything wrong with the late medieval church. Gold, indeed! The Catholic rector of the Sorbonne mocked it as the *Iron Legend*, and Spanish theologian Melchior Cano said it must have been written by a man with an iron mouth and a heart of lead.[24]

Protestants were even harsher, and mocked the outrageous miracles attributed to saints. Denouncing the *Legend*, Luther complained that "'tis one of the devil's proper plagues that we have no good legends of the saints, pure and true. Those we have are stuffed so full of lies, that, without heavy labor, they cannot be corrected. . . . He that disturbed Christians with such lies was doubtless a desperate wretch, who surely has been plunged deep in hell." Beyond doubt, early modern states and churches were much more powerful than their medieval predecessors, with vastly more capacity to regulate thought and behavior. But repression alone did not explain the removal of older works like the *Legend* from the cultural mainstream. Across Europe, such books were not so much abolished as discarded: they had become unfashionable among respectable readers.[25]

Europe's Protestant and Catholic churches did not constitute the whole Christian world, however much their leaders might have acted as if that were the case. The Orthodox churches of the East maintained older attitudes about the biblical canon and continued to favor many apocryphal works. Their Old Testament still relies on the Septuagint. Even if they formally rejected the authenticity of works such as the Protevangelium, Orthodox churches cherished traditions derived from them. Still today, Joachim and Anna have their Orthodox feast day, and Orthodox icons depict Christ's birth in a cave. Under the title of the Anastasis, the Harrowing of Hell remained a favorite theme of icon painters.[26]

But the map of the Christian world was changing rapidly, making the opinions of Europe's churches—and specifically, Western Europe's—far more significant than they might have been centuries before. The Christian world of 1520 was far smaller in its geographical scope than it had been five hundred or a thousand years earlier. In 1000, the Roman church had had no say whatever in what Christians did in Egypt or Persia or India, and there were a great number of Christians in those parts of the world. During the fourteenth century, the number of non-European Christians shrank dramatically, and so did their political strength. The years between 1250 and 1500 were catastrophic for the Christian kingdoms that survived on the frontiers of Islam—for Armenia, Georgia, and Ethiopia, as well as the Byzantine realm itself. Some succumbed to Islamic rule, at least temporarily—permanently, in the Byzantine case—and Ottoman Muslim power stretched deep into Europe itself.[27]

Although Christianity survived in the Middle East, monasteries and churches lost much of their influence and power, and suffered disastrous losses in their artistic and cultural treasures. The region's greatest cities and cultural bastions were sacked, some repeatedly—by Christian Crusaders and Islamic jihadis, and later by Mongols. Baghdad was destroyed in 1258. Destruction was even worse along the old Silk Route territories of Central Asia, which from 1200 onward were successively devastated by Mongol and Tatar invaders. (In understanding these horrors, Christians turned naturally to a classic apocryphal apocalypse, the work of Pseudo-Methodius.) From the early fourteenth century, the marauders were not only Muslim but also aggressively intolerant of other faiths, including Christians and Manichaeans. The world of Late Antiquity, which had staggered on into the thirteenth century, now decisively ended. Cities like Merv in Central Asia, which in its day was one of the world's great cultural centers, perished in massacres with death tolls that contemporaries estimated in the hundreds of thousands. The era was cataclysmic for the survival of Christian libraries and for any alternative scriptures they held.

If it did not actually disappear in the later Middle Ages, "non-European Christianity" was a pale shadow of its former self. The remaining Christian world was much easier for the mainstream church to control. At least before the Protestant schism, the Roman pope was the sole independent church head remaining, as the Eastern patriarch had become a puppet of the Ottoman sultan. As Catholic powers began their march to global empire, they whipped into conformity many of the surviving remnants of those once-glorious non-European churches. In the process they destroyed any suspect scriptures they found. In retrospect, these actions look like egregious manifestations of European imperialism.

————————

INDIA WAS A BATTLEFRONT in this transcontinental struggle. The Christian presence in southern India dates back to very early times, at least to the second century. Claiming foundation by St. Thomas, the church there maintained its identity throughout the Middle Ages. It was firmly part of the Church of the East, the so-called Nestorian Church, which looked to the Iraq-based patriarch of Babylon. In the sixteenth century, new Christian adventurers appeared as Portuguese ships carved out their commercial empire in the Indian Ocean. Portuguese and Spanish Catholic clergy were intrigued but baffled by these Indian Christians, who claimed not even to have heard of the pope in Rome. Gradually, the Europeans expanded their power over the local churches.[28]

Matters came to a head in 1599 with the synod held at Diamper (Udayamperoor, in the modern Indian state of Kerala) under the Portuguese archbishop of Goa. The synod imposed Roman authority on the local church. It demanded that Indian believers renounce their Nestorian doctrines as well as any customs that could not be reconciled with European Catholic standards. This prohibition extended to Hindu-tinged practices that had crept in over the previous centuries.[29]

The synod's most significant act was its condemnation of many locally popular writings, including ancient apocryphal scriptures. Henceforward, on pain of excommunication, no person could "presume to keep, translate, read or hear read to others" any of the listed books. Thus condemned to the fire was a whole treasury of Syriac spiritual and theological writings. One was The Infancy of Our Savior (our Gospel of Pseudo-Matthew), which contained many ideas that had been the familiar fare of pseudo-gospels across the Christian world for centuries. Now, though, they were classified as damnable errors requiring the book's suppression and elimination. For instance, the book asserted

> that the Annunciation of the angel was made in the Temple of Jerusalem, where Our Lady was, which contradicts the Gospel of St. Luke, which says, it was made in Nazareth; as also that Joseph had actually another wife and children when he was betrothed to the holy Virgin; and that he often reproved the child Jesus for his naughty tricks; that the child Jesus went to school with the rabbis, and learned of them,

with a thousand other fables and blasphemies of the same nature . . . that St. Joseph, to be satisfied whether the Virgin had committed adultery, carried her before the priests who according to the law gave her the water of jealousy to drink; that Our Lady brought forth with pain, and parting from her company, not being able to go farther, she retired to a stable at Bethlehem.

An area once rich with ancient Christian scriptures was largely robbed of its heritage. Indian Syriac literature survived only as a ghost of its former self.[30]

Catholic authorities took it upon themselves to "correct" local versions of the scriptures and their deviant readings, many of which were authentically ancient. The easterners were not only ordered to purge and destroy apocryphal works, but also forced to add new texts that the Western Catholic Church considered canonical, including the Old Testament Deuterocanonical books of Esther, Tobit, and Wisdom. In the New Testament, the Indians had previously followed the Syriac *Peshitta* ("common" or "simple") translation, which dates from the fourth or fifth century. This version had omitted 2 John, 3 John, 2 Peter, Jude, and Revelation, the disputed books, *antilegomena*. Now, Indians were forced to conform to Western practice and had to adopt these texts.[31]

As MEDIEVAL HERESY-HUNTERS HAD LEARNED, though, a sizable gulf separates condemning a text from eliminating it altogether.

The Old Testament apocrypha proved surprisingly resilient. As we have seen, Catholics and Orthodox alike continue to treat the Deuterocanonical books as scriptural. Even Protestant Bibles like the Geneva and the King James continued to include those works, albeit segregating them into a special section labeled as apocrypha. Nevertheless, they were presented in the format of a biblical text with the same font as canonical books and the same division into chapters and verses. In the English-speaking world, they remained standard parts of the Bible through the eighteenth century. William Shakespeare named his two daughters Judith and Susanna, after Deuterocanonical heroines, and we have already noted John Milton's interest in Old Testament apocrypha, including quite marginal works. Only after 1800 did publishers begin excluding Deuterocanonical texts to create the slimmed-down text that modern Protestant readers have come to regard as the authentic Bible.

New Testament apocrypha also survived, even after forfeiting their near-scriptural status. Luther had described the Old Testament apocrypha as "not regarded as equal to the holy Scriptures, and yet profitable and good to read." Some of his followers were prepared to extend this tolerance still further. Lutherans read the Gospel of Nicodemus as improving literature and used apocryphal texts in their educational programs.[32]

Catholics were far more open to apocryphal stories, or at least to a narrowly selected range of motifs. After purging what it saw as vulgar superstitions, the post-Tridentine church emphasized devotion to the Virgin Mary and the saints. This devotion was reflected in literature but above all in the visual arts, which were at the heart of Tridentine piety. That Catholic artistic tradition represented the most powerful and widespread vehicle for apocryphal materials around the world.[33]

The new imagery stemmed from the Marian Gospels—both the infancy stories, derived from the Protevangelium, and the texts recording her passage from the world. In about 1517, Titian painted his celebrated image of the Assumption, which also became the subject of works by such distinguished artists as Tintoretto, Rubens, Guido Reni, Poussin, and Paolo Veronese. Among the paintings of El Greco (1541–1614), we find a *Dormition of the Virgin*, an *Assumption* (his first commission in Spain), the *Immaculate Conception*, and the *Holy Family with St. Anne*. His younger Italian contemporary Caravaggio also favored such "alternative" themes. In the years around 1600, he dealt with the *Rest on the Flight into Egypt* and the *Virgin with St. Anne* and also painted a controversial *Death of the Virgin*. Just to list a few major painters who treated the Coronation of the Virgin, the subject attracted El Greco, Rubens, Velázquez,

Veronese, Guido Reni, and Annibale Carracci (not to mention hundreds of smaller fry). Baroque painters of the seventeenth century were just as fond of the Marriage of the Virgin. Marian themes continued to flourish long afterward, especially with the new interest in the Immaculate Conception in the nineteenth century, and then the Assumption in the twentieth.[34]

Besides the great works of art, of course, humbler versions of such images appeared in thousands of Catholic churches in the form of paintings, mosaics, and sculptures, not to mention medals and holy cards. The themes even became proper names—cities were called Asunción, girls were christened Concepción. Californians know the names of Mary's alleged parents through such old established place names as San Joaquin and Santa Ana. So utterly familiar are these motifs that it seems bizarre to speak of them as in any sense apocryphal. For hundreds of millions of Christians worldwide, they are standard manifestations of faith.

Apocryphal stories of the saints also retained their influence. Patrons often wanted paintings of the great figures of the faith, together with the attributes and associations that allowed them to be identified, and that usually meant relying on apocryphal texts. Images of St. John the Evangelist, such as El Greco's from 1604, customarily depicted him with the poisoned cup with the snake, in the story taken from the Acts of John. Still in the seventeenth century, pious Catholics were encouraged to read the Litany of the Hours, where they found unreconstructed remnants of the old apocryphal Acts of the apostles, often tinged with ancient heresies. It was his shocked encounter with such volumes about 1600 that led one Dutch Jesuit, Héribert Rosweyde, to begin a critical historical analysis of saints' lives, using detailed manuscript scholarship to determine their origins and authorship. In seeking what authentic cores such works might contain, he was inventing the modern scholarly discipline of hagiography.[35]

THE OLD CHRISTIAN CULTURE, based on the alternative scriptures, now lost much of its appeal and influence. Oddly, though, a Europe seemingly pledged to reject those mythologies now found itself with much better access to those sources than ever before, and indeed, access to a dazzlingly wider range of texts. Just as ordinary people were losing their access to the old traditions, scholars and bibliographers were uncovering new treasure troves.

Partly through closer contacts with the Mediterranean world, scholars in western and northern Europe began to encounter texts and scriptures that had long circulated in the Greek and Syriac worlds. These works had vanished from the West, if they had ever penetrated there at all. Some of these finds attracted widespread interest, at least among scholars, but in a radically different way from what might have happened centuries earlier. Instead of being seen as remarkable fonts of spiritual truth, these texts were now studied as historical sources, the subject of elite scholarship rather than popular devotion. In the new European world, they were chiefly valued for their potential contributions to scholarship rather than faith.[36]

Over the previous millennium, Western scholars had known certain texts through brief summaries or from highly selective quotations in other works. The Sibylline Oracles, for instance, they mainly knew through quotations in Augustine, who gave them little sense of the size and diversity of the whole text. In 1540, a German scholar found and duly published a Greek manuscript of the complete Oracles. Around the same time, the French king sent an embassy to his Ottoman Turkish allies with polymath Guillaume Postel as interpreter. Postel brought back several important manuscripts, including the Protevangelium, which he suggested might be the lost introduction to the canonical gospel of Mark. (Only now did the text receive its potent "First Gospel" name.) By the 1560s, westerners had rediscovered the full Acts of John.[37]

Old Testament pseudepigrapha also came to light. Postel himself learned about 1 Enoch from a colony of Ethiopian clergy living in Rome, and he published some secondhand gleanings concerning the text. In 1606, a translation of the Byzantine writer Syncellus gave Western readers renewed access to large selections from 1 Enoch.

Meanwhile, European scholars were learning a much wider range of languages than hitherto, with some Arabic and Syriac as well as Greek.[38]

Scholars published substantial collections of alternative texts, partly from a genuine confusion about their authenticity. It was by no means obvious that some of the pseudo-gospels and apostolic Acts might not have been genuine patristic writings. One early and largely indiscriminate collection was the *Monumenta Sanctorum Patrum Orthodoxographa* (1569). This compilation was the work of Swiss Protestant scholar Johann Jakob Grynaeus, who sought to give Christians of different churches a common foundation from which to explore their shared origins.[39]

But the fact that works were available did not mean that they were treated uncritically, and scholars were cautious about what they recommended for wider reading. For one thing, they knew how thoroughly many of the alternative texts had been condemned in the early church, and they also applied their own excellent critical skills to assessing the works' credentials. By the end of the sixteenth century, critical readers such as Abraham Scultetus (Protestant) and Robert Bellarmine (Catholic) directed their skeptical analytical abilities to the newly available library of texts. The alternative scriptures found a definite niche, but in the academic library and lecture hall, rather than, as of old, in the parish church.[40]

This flood of critical scholarship permitted the first serious academic study of the alternative scriptures. The great pioneer was Leipzig polymath Johann Albert Fabricius, who well earned his title of Bibliographer of the Republic of Letters. He collected the New Testament apocrypha in his *Codex Apocryphus Novi Testamenti* (1703), which, among other books, included the Protevangelium, the Nativity of Mary, the Infancy Gospel of Thomas, the Arabic Infancy Gospel, the Gospel of Nicodemus, Christ's Letter to Abgar, and the Epistle to the Laodiceans. He then assembled the Old Testament texts in the *Codex Pseudepigraphus Veteris Testamenti* (1713), becoming the first to give these works the now standard name of "pseudepigrapha." Fabricius's works laid a foundation for all subsequent research.[41]

In these same years, John Toland's *Nazarenus* (1718) appeared, the first of what would in modern times become a very large literary genre. Through a scholarly critical analysis of an alternative gospel (in this case, Barnabas), an author tried to reconstruct what he believed to be the authentic history of the early Jesus movement in order to show the failings of orthodox Christian theology. For the first time, too, Toland was presenting an apocryphal gospel as the gold standard by which those flawed and partisan canonical texts must be judged. And however polemical his intent, Toland was representing his work as sober academic history.[42]

The canonical scriptures, too, would very shortly be subjected to a similar process of academic dissection. The modern historical-critical approach to the New Testament began with publications by German scholar Johann David Michaelis in the 1750s. Like his countless successors in the Republic of Letters, Michaelis dared treat scripture as just another text, amenable to analysis and criticism. By the end of the eighteenth century, some scholars were suggesting that the distinction between genuine and pseudo-scriptures was a matter of faith rather than history. The abundance of subsequent textual discoveries has only strengthened and popularized that conviction.[43]

NONCANONICAL SCRIPTURES WERE never wholly absent from church life. Christians at different times might have had better or worse access to these works, and reading them might have been viewed more favorably in some eras than in others, but believers never stopped having access to a wide range of pseudo-scriptural materials. That point needs to be stressed because it contradicts popular assumptions about the history of alternative scriptures. Contrary to myth, the modern-day discovery of ancient alternative works is nothing like as revolutionary as it is sometimes portrayed.

That myth-history is all the stranger when we realize how long the modern world has known about these alternative scriptures and how long we have had the resources to study them. Already from the start of the nineteenth century, popular English publishers were offering collections of noncanonical texts billed (then as now) as subversive works that had been deliberately excluded from the New Testament canon—suppressed voices of authentic early Christianity. Just how thoroughly acclimatized these ideas had become in American popular culture is evident from early Mormonism, with its deep interest in messianic figures like Enoch. From the middle of that century, the volume of alternative scriptures expanded massively as Western scholars of early Christianity and Judaism entered a thrilling age of discovery, or rather rediscovery. Largely, this resulted from expanded European contacts with the Middle East, Africa, and Asia, which unearthed new treasures in the Coptic, Syriac, and Ethiopian languages. As in so much else, Germany was the center of research on alternative scriptures, but the English-speaking world also entered a golden age of scholarship between about 1880 and 1930, when many treasures appeared in the vernacular.[44]

Apocryphal gospels and Acts became widely available. In 1930, scholar Edgar Goodspeed listed the texts that had come to light just since the 1870s: "the Teaching of the Twelve Apostles [Didache], the Gospel of Peter, the Revelation of Peter, the Apology of Aristides, the Acts of Paul, the Sayings of Jesus, the Odes of Solomon, and the Epistle of the Apostles—all from the second century." Meanwhile, the exploration of the Slavonic apocrypha was opening new vistas for Old Testament study.[45]

Any scholar with access to a major library could consult a massive array of alternative ancient scriptures, which became more generally available through the works of writers like M. R. James and R. H. Charles. Moreover, any interested reader could seek out an extensive library of Gnostic texts. This fact makes nonsense of any suggestion that the popular rediscovery of Gnosticism was a phenomenon of the 1970s. If that process had a single critical date, it was 1900, the year of G. R. S. Mead's mammoth and much-reprinted *Fragments of a Faith Forgotten*. *Fragments* presented extensive translations from the Gnostic writings themselves, including the *Pistis Sophia*, the Books of the Savior, and the Gospel of Mary. Mead consciously publicized these texts as hidden gospels, describing *Pistis Sophia* as "a sort of Gospel coming from some early Gnostic sect."[46]

Then as now, these ancient movements fascinated both sober scholars and activists of various stripes, including esoteric believers and feminists. In 1916, English composer Gustav Holst actually wrote a setting of the "Hymn of Jesus" from the Acts of John, the famous liturgical ring-dance song that so intrigued readers of Elaine Pagels's *Gnostic Gospels* in the 1970s. (Holst was undoubtedly inspired by Mead.) Also in 1916, George Moore published the bestselling novel *The Brook Kerith*, which in its themes suggests a thorough acquaintance with alternative approaches to early Christianity and with noncanonical scriptures. Jesus in Moore's depiction is an Essene who survives the crucifixion. He lives to confront the deluded Paul, who is spreading outrageous fantasies about the supposed Messiah from Nazareth. In disgust, Jesus flees to join a group of Buddhist monks who are evangelizing the Judean countryside.[47]

To see just how much general readers knew about alternative early gospels, we can turn to Robert Graves's bizarre popular novel *King Jesus*. The book appeared in 1946, just as the Nag Hammadi documents were being unearthed, and even before the finding of the Dead Sea Scrolls. Yet even at that date, Graves had full access to a panoply of lost gospels and Gnostic fragments, from which he concocted a mythology that includes virtually every radical view of Jesus that has surfaced in later years. We find Jesus as the secular revolutionary; the husband of the pagan goddess of the land; the expounder of Oriental wisdom; the secret heir to the secular kingdom of Israel; the master of Hellenistic mysteries; a participant in ancient tribal fertility rites; an esoteric teacher and numerologist; and—of course—the husband of Mary Magdalene.[48]

In light of all this, we must challenge some of the breathless claims made for recent finds, and especially the suggestion that such works were now being brought to light for the first time since the early church or the Second Temple era. In some cases, notably the Dead Sea Scrolls, such claims have been literally true. Other documents, though, such as 1 Enoch, were "discovered" in the sense of being brought to the attention of Western scholars, as against the Ethiopian churches for which they were canonical scripture. These texts were newly found in the sense that Columbus discovered America, which was already home to native peoples who had an excellent sense of where they were. The suggestion that some texts had simply disappeared since the fourth century was usually just wrong.

No less misleading was the suggestion that the "new" texts had been brought to light in a sudden moment of revelation. As we have seen, the process of restoring alternative scriptures to the West began with the Renaissance, and it was at floodtide in the nineteenth century. But the myth demanded a moment of dramatic discovery.

In virtually no case are the scholars who make the finds responsible for such excessive claims. Rather, the claims are the work of news media and publishers who want to make discoveries sound as sensational and epoch-making as possible, and tales of long-lost treasures and suppressed manuscripts naturally intrigue a general audience. Of necessity, each new find has to be portrayed as a stunning revelation, a wake-up call to a hidebound religious and academic establishment. The narrative must have its villains, in the form of a stubborn and repressive church hierarchy wedded absolutely to the Bible strictly defined, and to just four gospels. Daring scholars confront hidebound fogies.

———————

Such a mythological scheme is not hospitable to nuance. It is difficult to admit that different texts have not been lost as thoroughly as was asserted, and that a great many similar documents have always been known. If the texts are not in common view, then they are hiding in plain sight. Nor, crucially, should it be admitted that different Christian groups have over time used a wide variety of scriptures, many of them truly ancient. In consequence, the popular history of Christianity fails to notice some of the writings that have most profoundly shaped the religion's culture and beliefs.

10

Scriptures Unlimited?

The Place of Alternative
Scriptures in Christianity

*No man ought, for the confirmation of doctrines, to use books that
are not canonized Scriptures.*

Origen, c. AD 250

AFTER LONG TRAVELS SEEKING WISDOM, Jesus was received warmly
in Tibet:

> Now, after many days, and perils great, the guide and Jesus
> reached the Lassa temple in Tibet. And Meng-ste [Mencius]
> opened wide the temple doors, and all the priests and masters
> gave a welcome to the Hebrew sage. And Jesus had access to
> all the sacred manuscripts, and, with the help of Meng-ste,
> read them all.

You do not have to be a professional scholar to realize that this tale
is not part of a recognized Christian scripture. In fact, it is from *The
Aquarian Gospel of Jesus the Christ*, published in 1908 by Ohio-born
preacher Levi H. Dowling. Dowling believed that Christianity

should grow to incorporate the insights of spiritualism, Theosophy, and the world's other great religions. However, he did not write the *Aquarian Gospel* as imaginative fiction. Rather, he claimed to have received its words through mystical sessions in which he channeled the lost histories contained in the "akashic records." In Christian parlance, it was granted in heavenly visions.[1]

Like so many of his predecessors throughout history, Dowling presented the work as a fully inspired gospel that contained, corrected, and exceeded the canonical texts. As such, it has been widely popular over the past century. As a founding text of the New Age movement, it popularized the notion of a coming Age of Aquarius, and in the 1960s it found a sizable hippie readership. It is a canonical text of a tiny sect, the Aquarian Christine [*sic*] Church Universal.[2]

No mainstream church would consider admitting such a text into its biblical canon. But defining just why that is so unthinkable does raise questions about the nature of scripture and of canon. On what evidence might we accept claims of a work's inspired character? Put crudely, when did God decide to cease speaking through scriptures? If we agree that a given text is neither canonical nor inspired, then does it still have a place within the Christian scheme?

A fuller understanding of how churches have used a range of scriptures through the centuries raises significant questions for strictly contemporary debates: about the meanings and limitations of alternative gospels, about the role and definition of scripture, and about the possible use of "Other" scriptures today. However skeptical we might be of neo-gospels like Dowling's, the vast corpus of alternative scriptures clamors to be read as a source of inspiration and enlightenment over and above any historical or scholarly value individual works might have.

THE BEST ARGUMENT FOR READING the alternative texts of Late Antiquity and the Middle Ages is that they represent such a massive portion of the Christian spiritual heritage. Beyond that, they play a critical role in the artistic and cultural tradition that grew out of this faith. If we do not know these works, we are missing much of Christian history and literary output as well as the wider Western story. Many common assertions about what Christianity has or has not believed during its long history fall apart when we read the alternative scriptures, and even more when we acknowledge the central status they once held in popular belief and practice. As the phrase goes, if you don't know where you have come from, you can't know where you are going.

Such texts respond to familiar and enduring questions that have always intrigued Christians—or indeed, anyone interested in the faith. Today, if people want to explore issues of Christian theology or culture, they do so with specialized books that are so labeled. In earlier times, believers and teachers used narrative and storytelling, and arguably their explorations of vexed questions were at least as sophisticated as those found in modern works. Although it is not an apocryphal work, John Bunyan's *Pilgrim's Progress* (1678) has inspired and educated far more Christians through the centuries than all those learned theological texts combined. Only a very simplistic reader would critique such a work for its lack of historical content, or protest that the events portrayed in it never really happened. Instead, we admire the storytelling, which presents a complex message in accessible and memorable form. Wise readers are sensible enough to make allowances for the different literary assumptions prevailing in Bunyan's time. Similar remarks might apply to other profoundly influential fictional texts, from Charles Sheldon's *In His Steps* to C. S. Lewis's *Screwtape Letters*.

We can, and should, apply exactly the same principles to reading the alternative scriptures that come down to us from ancient and medieval times. Once we set aside crude ideas of historicity, we can understand the perplexing theological issues that those authors were contemplating, and appreciate the sophistication of the audiences that so loved the resulting stories.

Plenty of modern Christians agonize over the question of damnation and the existence of hell, which they can scarcely reconcile with the belief in a loving God. Yes, Christ offered the opportunity for human beings to gain salvation by accepting him, but where did that leave those whose date or place of birth seemingly excluded them from salvation? Christians wonder about the fate of those who never entered the faith, of the unbaptized, of members of other religions, and of those who died before Christ's coming. The Gospel of Nicodemus and its literary offspring tackled these questions boldly and comprehensively, showing how Mercy does indeed overcome Truth. A modern Christian reader might argue with the theologies offered in those works, but she or he has to take them seriously. The only danger those moderns face is that they will get carried away by the storytelling and the characters.

That is one example out of a great many that we have met in our quest for these enduring gospels. If modern believers think that historical Christianity is a patriarchal religion that has no room for exalted female characters, they have never read the elaborate cycles of stories in the Marian Gospels. A contemporary author who depicted Christ as a woman, and moreover as one who suffered through all the events of his Passion and Resurrection, would be seen as extremely bold, if not blasphemous. Yet, in a sense, such narratives did in effect circulate through the Middle Ages, in their portrayals of Mary's birth, life, and death, and these stories were immensely popular among the rigorously orthodox. Far from being superstitious medieval concoctions, these texts dated to the early and patristic Christian ages.

To take another thorny question for modern believers, how does the Old Testament narrative relate to the Christian story? In practice, many ordinary Christians today follow a kind of Marcionism, which demotes the Old Testament to the status of a primitive prehistory. In standard Christian theology, though, Christ existed from the beginning of time, and was the face that God the Father presented to the created world. From that perspective, Christ was, logically, present to some degree in the divine encounters reported in the Old Testament. When medieval artists painted God appearing to Moses in the Burning Bush, they usually gave him the face of Christ. Few ordinary believers today know that subtle theological approach, or would have much time for it. Many theologians likewise find this a deeply sensitive area, because the approach potentially relegates every word of the Old Testament to Christian prehistory. At its worst, it delegitimizes Judaism.

We have to draw a critical distinction in matters of historical intent. To declare that Moses or Isaiah literally prophesied Christ is one thing, and an argument that most biblical scholars of any faith tradition would reject. But that is quite different from exploring those long-term parallels and linkages symbolically and metaphorically, as is done so magnificently in the *Cave of Treasures* and the associated Adam literature that brings the Old Testament narrative wholly into the Christian story. Nor, crucially, does most of this literature seek to steal holy figures from Judaism. As we have seen, so much of the Old Testament pseudepigrapha concerns the pre-Flood generations, from Adam and Seth to Enoch and Noah, who, according to the Bible, are the common ancestors of all humanity, whether Christian, Jewish, or Muslim. Adam's story symbolizes the story of humanity itself, and as such, it is neither more nor less "historical" than Bunyan's account of Christian being imprisoned by Giant Despair in Doubting Castle.

While so many alternative texts repay reading, the largest gap in the modern Christian mind is these Old Testament–related works, which seem consigned to academic scholarship. How, after all, could they relate to Christian debates and thinking? As we have seen, their contribution to popular theology is in fact immense. A modern reader of the Adam literature, for instance, will experience a shock of recognition at the presence of so many characters and motifs that have entered the popular consciousness.

———————

THE OTHER MAJOR REASON FOR READING such works is that they help us understand how Christians—indeed, how followers of any tradition—make sense of their faith through storytelling. Christians have *always* produced and edited neo-gospels and pseudo-scriptures, because that is how literate people have so often chosen to explore their faith. People interested in Christianity, whether as friends or enemies, have done the same. In a faith based on "gospel truth," it has always been natural to build on or adapt the canonical text—to fill in holes, to make the scriptures more relevant to contemporary interests, or to explore what might have been if the words had been slightly different. In earlier generations, writers were happy to feature Christ, Mary, and the patriarchs as major characters for invented narratives, far more so than would later generations. That creative urge has been more in evidence in some historical periods than others, but at no point has it altogether dried up, and that is a critical fact in Christian history.

Those literary efforts continued into the Middle Ages, long after the end of Christian antiquity, and because of their relatively late date, we tend not to place such works in the same context as the ancient alternative gospels. About 1420, for instance, German mystic Thomas à Kempis wrote the *Imitation of Christ*, which has few peers in terms of its impact on Christian history. Apart from the Bible, no book has been translated into more languages. Yet as a spiritual dialogue between the disciple and the Risen Christ, it follows a format that would have been perfectly recognizable a thousand years before. Although it is quite orthodox in its content, it would have caused little surprise if such a text had been found together with a collection of Gnostic gospels from the fourth or fifth centuries.

Christians, in any and all eras, write neo-gospels, and in so doing they produce kaleidoscopically diverse images of Jesus, a figure with many faces. That was true in the early church, the era of the famous alternative gospels; it was true in the Middle Ages, when so many other gospels and anti-gospels circulated; and it is true today. Before remarking that a particular era had many massively diverse images of Jesus—a point often made about the early church—we should ask when that has *not* been true. When was the Christian world ever monolithic in such matters? No such historical moment ever existed. Jesuses abound, and always have. So do gospels.

Often, writers believe that a special revelation has authorized them to create such new contributions. In the nineteenth and twentieth centuries, Americans alone produced a whole library of new scriptures and gospels, including Dowling's *Aquarian Gospel*, the Book of Mormon, the *OAHSPE Bible*, and *The Occult Life of Jesus of Nazareth*. In the 1880s, the *Archko Volume* purported to reveal a trove of documents describing Christ's trial and death, including letters supposedly penned by Pontius Pilate himself. The urge to know how Pilate might have reported his encounter was far from new, and had in ancient times inspired the very influential Acts of Pilate. In 1931, Edgar Goodspeed published a collection of such strictly modern contributions—from the avowedly inspired to the grotesquely fraudulent.[3]

Just in the past decade, publishers have produced such updated literary and fictional treatments of the Jesus story as Colm Tóibín's novel (and play) *The Testament of Mary* (2012), Anne Rice's Jesus trilogy (2005, 2008, and still in progress), and Deepak Chopra's *Jesus: A Story of Enlightenment* (2008). Major films include Mel Gibson's *The Passion of the Christ* (2004) and, more recently, *Son of God* (2014). Although the motives for literary creativity might have been different in earlier ages—and the risks of deviations from orthodoxy more lethal—the impulse to adapt and expand was as common in 200 as in 600 or 1900, or as it is today.[4]

That fact puts into context the claims that regularly surface about newly discovered ancient pseudo-gospels. Every few years, the media are full of sensational claims concerning some early document, such as the Gospel of Judas in 2006–2007. The implication is that, because such texts date from the early Christian centuries, they must therefore contain authentic insights on the life and times of Jesus himself. Seemingly, both authenticity and significance are confirmed by the fact that the mainstream church thought fit to conceal their subversive truths.[5]

Conceivably, some document might someday come to light that could reveal new information about Jesus's life or teaching, which is the ultimate goal of such speculations. Perhaps we might indeed find a true alternative gospel, or an early draft of a gospel that we have in some other form. But however much this point contradicts common media assumptions, no such worthwhile historical evidence can possibly be found from works written in the third or fourth centuries, at least two hundred years after Jesus's death. Works like the Gospel of Judas have precisely no independent historical value for Jesus's time, and responsible scholars acknowledge this. Like Dowling's *Aquarian Gospel*, they tell us much about the times and circumstances in which they were written, but nothing about the era they are purporting to describe. No, Jesus did not share an esoteric Gnostic message with Judas, any more than he spent time with Mencius in Tibet. If in fact an early date implied a special link to Jesus's time, then scholars should be working to find a core of historical truth in mid-second-century works like the Protevangelium and the Infancy Gospel of Thomas, which they very sensibly are not.

This point about historical authenticity was well stated by Harvard scholar Karen King, who in 2012 drew attention to a supposedly ancient Coptic manuscript that referred to "Jesus's wife." In fact, this controversial fragment was almost certainly forged (of course, without King's knowledge), but even if it had been authentic, its historical significance would be minimal. As King herself noted, with exemplary caution, a text written in the late second or third century was much too far removed from Jesus's own time to tell us anything whatsoever about his marital status or personal life. If the fragment had been genuine, it could only have told us something about the attitudes held by particular Christian movements in later centuries. For many reasons, then, the waves of enthusiasm about successive alleged gospel finds are puzzling.[6]

Popular media tend to assume that there is an ancient era in which gospels were produced abundantly, presumably because the authors had some special knowledge or perception to share. In fact, such production carried on in high volume for much longer than this model suggests, at least through the sixth and seventh centuries, with many later contributions. At no point in history—say, around 400—did churches suddenly cease recording what they believed to be Christ's authentic message, and certainly they did not do so because of the edicts of some all-powerful hierarchy. The Christian story is one of organic growth and development, from early times, through medieval, to modern, and beyond.

FOR MANY REASONS, readers should discover the countless other works of fiction and fantasy, meditation and theologizing, speculation and dreaming, that sustained Christians both expert and ordinary in early and medieval times, and that called forth such stunning works of visual art. So influential were they, in fact, that they raise serious questions about our conventional definitions of canon and canonicity. In particular eras, the de facto Christian canon was much broader than the familiar one, and this informal "Bible" rarely receives the scholarly attention it deserves.

Christian definitions of scripture have varied a great deal according to time and place. We commonly hear assertions of the authority of scripture, but any kind of historical or comparative approach has to raise questions about how exactly that scripture is defined. It is hard to be a fundamentalist without first deciding precisely which scriptures are the foundation of belief. Startlingly, perhaps, for many American Christians, the familiar Bible that they know is quite a modern invention in terms of its precise contents and canon. The composition of that text is nothing like as obvious or inevitable as is often claimed. The process of making and defining scripture took many centuries, and we might ask whether it has fully ended.

If we just look at the largest churches existing today, all without exception admit four gospels to the canon, and no more, but beyond that, they differ greatly in their choice of approved works. Even if we dismiss the Ethiopian church as a distant outlier, substantial differences exist even between the Bibles used by mainstream Western churches. Catholic and Orthodox Bibles, for instance, include the Deuterocanonical books, which Protestant versions do not. In the English-speaking Protestant world, Old Testament apocrypha were still widely known and commonly printed in Bibles well into the nineteenth century. Distinctions between churches were still larger in earlier eras, when some of the world's then most thriving institutions disdained New Testament books like 1 John, Jude, and 2 Peter that are thoroughly accepted by most modern believers.

Such differences do not bother many Christians today, chiefly because they are not aware of them. But even if they were, it would take a very narrow-minded true-believer to reject the Christian credentials of another church solely on the grounds that its canon was not precisely correct, either too narrow or too wide. Such strict exclusionists certainly do exist, but in practice Christians grant each other some latitude in matters of canon. That is reasonable, because none of the disputed books really makes any great difference in guiding or defining doctrine. If, for instance, Protestants came to accept books like Maccabees or the Wisdom of Solomon, no theological revolution would result, any more than if they excluded Jude. Hard though it might be for fundamentalists to accept this principle, biblical books vary enormously in their significance for shaping the larger Christian worldview. Some are essential, some marginal. Some scriptures matter vastly more than others.

Today, churches differ in how they treat some Old Testament books, but only a few centuries ago, a flourishing New Testament apocrypha was just as esteemed, before it, too, fell into ignominy. Now, that analogy is not precise, in that no church ever granted formal canonical status to, say, the Gospel of Nicodemus—but that book did far more to shape Christianity over a millennium or so than perhaps any other biblical text outside the gospels and Revelation. At particular times and places, the same points have applied to the Marian Gospels. If we do not take full account of such books and their impact, we are missing a very large portion of the history of Christianity.

———————

To SAY, THOUGH, that works like the Gospel of Nicodemus were once regarded so highly does not mean that we should be thinking of expanding the Christian canon, as some recent writers have suggested. The fact that the canon has been wider and more open in the past does not mean it is infinitely flexible, or that it should in fact include something like Nicodemus, the *Cave of Treasures*, or, indeed, the *Aquarian Gospel*. That is not to denigrate the alternative scriptures or to underplay their significance, but rather to challenge popular ideas of history and historicity.

Under the influence of new discoveries and scholarship, some modern authors have advocated expanding the canon to include various alternative scriptures, with the Gospel of Thomas usually a prime candidate. In the 1990s, the group of critical thinkers who formed the Jesus Seminar published its wish-list of twenty works to be added to the familiar New Testament, optimistically billing their version as "The Complete Gospels." More recently, and growing directly out of that effort, scholar Hal Taussig has edited *A New New Testament: A Bible for the 21st Century Combining Traditional and Newly Discovered Texts*, which prints alternative apocryphal works interspersed with the canonical New Testament. Valuably, he aimed to include a wide range of texts going beyond the category of merely "Gnostic" writings. Suggesting a rather Marcionite approach, though, Taussig's complete "Bible" includes only an expanded *New* Testament, and the book's associated commentary has virtually nothing to say about the Old Testament or Hebrew Bible. It would, of course, be possible to incorporate a sizable number of pseudepigraphical works into the Old Testament as well, though the resulting volume would be gargantuan.[7]

Among the supplementary "New New" texts that Taussig includes are (inevitably) the Gospel of Thomas as well as the Odes of Solomon, the Gospel of Mary, the Gospel of Truth, the Acts of Paul and Thecla, and the Secret Revelation of John. Other presences and absences, however, indicate the highly subjective process that determined the selection. One weird addition is a Nag Hammadi text called "The Thunder: Perfect Mind," which is cryptic even by the standards of the Gnostic gospels, and which has no obvious relationship to Christianity of any kind. No less odd is the exclusion of indubitably early apocrypha like the Protevangelium. Whatever we may think of limiting or expanding the canon, though, all the texts presented in Taussig's version are useful resources for anyone interested in the diverse faces of early Christianity.

Obviously, any proposal for canon expansion is deeply sensitive. Not just among strict fundamentalists, the suggestion that a given denomination would admit scriptures over and above the agreed canon is enough to exile a sect to heretical status, or indeed to being placed altogether outside the Christian fold. This is a major reason for mainstream Christian suspicion of the Latter-day Saints church, or of Christian Science. But our historical survey also supplies plenty of practical reasons against any such opening of the canon. Particularly in the New Testament, it points to the sharp division between the canonical texts as we have them and any possible alternatives.

Contrary to what the scholars of the Jesus Seminar, and, more recently, Taussig's "Council for a New New Testament," might say, the alternative texts that they so esteem are significantly later than the canonical gospels, and almost entirely derivative from them. According to the overwhelming weight of scholarly opinion, none of the proposed "New New" scriptures dates from before 160 at the earliest, and some, like the Gospel of Mary, may be a century later. (The Gospel of Thomas might be somewhat earlier, say about 140.) In contrast, little of the canonical New Testament can plausibly be dated much later than 110 or so.

Whatever their possible spiritual or cultural value, those alternative works cannot begin to compete *as historical documents* with the canonical gospels and epistles. In many cases, the authors of those noncanonical texts would be startled at any suggestion that the spiritual and metaphorical accounts they were supplying should be confused with material realities. In that, such books contrast starkly with the canonical gospels. Of course, the canonical texts do not attempt to be sober academic history in any modern sense, and they have their theological agendas; but they really do take us directly to the world of Christ and his immediate followers in ways that no other candidate can or ever could. They represent the essential historical core.

Other works might be popular in particular times and places, but they cannot be placed in the same category of canon. They spoke beautifully at the time, but to a world that is now past, and it would be foolish to try to give them some perpetual status. Similarly, works that seem uniquely powerful or relevant to an early twenty-first-century audience might soon seem dated and even faddish. Texts that seem highly valuable in one era can make later generations shudder. Nothing dates worse than yesterday's modernity.

———————————

BUT TO EXCLUDE A TEXT from the canon obviously does not mean condemning or ignoring it, and we should take full advantage of whatever historical or religious merits it may have. Since the 1970s, many westerners have found real treasures in the Gnostic gospels, different and surprising sidelights on Christianity. But those texts are only part of a vastly wider literature that has its own nuggets, and often, its own creative solutions, to what different eras saw as gaps in the Christian message. Anyone interested in those rediscovered ancient gospels should be told the wonderful news—that a millennium of other writings awaits them, no less rich or provocative in their contents.

GLOSSARY

Adoptionism   The belief that Jesus was not fully equal to God. He
was born a human being, but then the divine nature descended
upon him at a specific moment, probably at his baptism.

agrapha   "Unwritten" or attributed sayings of Jesus recorded in
later writings.

Albigensian   A Dualistic sect that existed in Western Europe
between the eleventh and fourteenth centuries.

antilegomena   "Disputed" biblical books, which at least some
wished to exclude from fully canonical status.

apocrypha   "Hidden" works lacking fully canonical status.

apostolic fathers   A group of Christian writers, mainly from the
second century, whose works are revered, but not given the
same authoritative status as the canonical New Testament.

Bogomils   A Dualistic sect founded in tenth-century Bulgaria.

Deuterocanonical   Literally, from the "Second Canon." This
term refers to a group of biblical books that many churches
(including the Roman Catholic and Orthodox) include in
the canonical Old Testament, but that Protestants treat as
noncanonical and apocryphal.

Docetism   The idea that the Christ who appeared in the world
was a purely spiritual being, and that his earthly body was an
illusion rather than a material reality. (The name comes from
the Greek word for "to seem.")

Dualism   The theological belief in a cosmic conflict between the
worlds of matter and spirit, Light and Darkness.

Encratism   A theological view that the material world is an evil snare to be rejected by true believers. Followers condemned sexuality as well as the consumption of meat and wine.

Gnostic   A movement that held that the material world is ruled by a defective lower God, and that Christ is an emissary from the true higher forces of Light. Believers rise to higher spiritual realms through *gnosis*, knowledge.

Jesus movement   The movement of Jesus's followers in the first decades following his death, before we can reasonably speak of a Christian religion separated from Judaism.

Logia   Isolated sayings of Jesus recorded in various later sources.

Manichaean   Followers of the third-century Mesopotamian thinker Mani, who drew on Jewish, Christian, Buddhist, and Zoroastrian ideas, and who taught a radical Dualist message.

Marcionite   Followers of the second-century Christian leader Marcion, who taught that the good God of the New Testament had sent his Son, Jesus, to displace the Jewish God of the Old Testament.

midrash   A means of interpreting and expounding scripture developed by Jewish rabbinic scholars. It involves expanding and adapting texts in the light of later concerns, perhaps for legal or instructional ends. The word comes from a root implying study or inquiry.

Nag Hammadi   The Egyptian site where a very important collection of ancient gospels and other texts was discovered in 1945.

Nicene   Relating to the Council of Nicea called by the Emperor Constantine in AD 325. The event did much to shape and define Christian orthodoxy.

Paulician   A Christian theological movement that originated in seventh-century Armenia. Its views were Marcionite and Dualist.

Priscillianist   Followers of the fourth-century Spanish bishop Priscillian. The mainstream church condemned him as heretical because of his excessive asceticism and rejection of marriage.

pseudepigrapha   "Falsely titled" spiritual writings ascribed to a famous leader, often a patriarch or prophet.

ACKNOWLEDGMENTS

I have the great good fortune to be part of Baylor University's Institute for Studies of Religion, where I profit from the friendship and support of such colleagues as David Jeffrey, Byron Johnson, Jeff Levin, Gordon Melton, Tommy Kidd, and Rodney Stark. We are also blessed with superb administrative support from Cameron Andrews, Frances Malone, and Leone Moore.

My thanks also to such colleagues as Kathryn Hume, Gary Knoppers, Michael Legaspi, Mark Morrisson, Gregg Roeber, and Ralph Wood. I also record a debt of gratitude to my deceased friends and colleagues Bill Petersen and Paul Harvey.

Thanks to my excellent agent, Adam Eaglin, and to Lara Heimert, my editor at Basic.

As always, my greatest debt is to my wife, Liz Jenkins.

NOTES

CHAPTER ONE

1. Marvin Meyer and James M. Robinson, eds., *The Nag Hammadi Scriptures* (San Francisco: HarperOne, 2008).

2. John D. Turner and Anne McGuire, eds., *The Nag Hammadi Library After Fifty Years* (Leiden: Brill, 1997); Philip Jenkins, *Hidden Gospels* (New York: Oxford University Press, 2001); Philip Jenkins, "Shenoute and the Gnostics," August 12, 2013, www.patheos.com /blogs/anxiousbench/2013/08/shenoute-and-the-gnostics/. The use of the word "Gnostic" in this context is controversial in exaggerating the difference from "mainstream" Christianity: see Michael Allen Williams, *Rethinking "Gnosticism"* (Princeton, NJ: Princeton University Press, 1999); Karen King, *What Is Gnosticism?* (Cambridge, MA: Belknap Press of Harvard University Press, 2003).

3. The phrase is taken from G. R. S. Mead, *Fragments of a Faith Forgotten* (London: Theosophical Publishing Society, 1900). For the Christian gospel tradition, see Helmut Koester, *Ancient Christian Gospels* (London: SCM Press, 1990).

4. Elaine Pagels, *The Gnostic Gospels* (New York: Random House, 1979); Elaine H. Pagels, *Beyond Belief* (New York: Random House, 2003); Karen L. King, *The Gospel of Mary of Magdala* (Santa Rosa, CA: Polebridge Press, 2003); Willis Barnstone and Marvin Meyer, eds., *The Gnostic Bible* (Boston: Shambhala, 2003); Bart Ehrman, *Lost Christianities* (New York: Oxford University Press, 2003); Bart Ehrman, *Lost Scriptures* (New York: Oxford University Press, 2003); Marvin W. Meyer, *Secret Gospels* (Harrisburg, PA: Trinity Press International, 2003); Marvin W. Meyer and Esther A. de Boer, *The Gospels of Mary* (San Francisco: HarperCollins, 2004); Marvin W. Meyer, *The Gnostic Discoveries* (San Francisco: HarperOne, 2005); Marvin W. Meyer, ed., *The Gnostic Gospels of Jesus* (San Francisco: HarperOne,

2005); Rodolphe Kasser, Marvin Meyer, and Gregor Wurst, eds., *The Gospel of Judas* (Washington, DC: National Geographic Society, 2006); Karen L. King, *The Secret Revelation of John* (Cambridge, MA: Harvard University Press, 2006); Marvin W. Meyer, *Judas* (San Francisco: HarperOne, 2007); Elaine H. Pagels, *Reading Judas* (New York: Viking, 2007); Robert J. Miller, ed., *The Complete Gospels*, 4th ed. (Sonoma, CA: Polebridge Press, 2010); Tony Burke, *Secret Scriptures Revealed* (London: SPCK, 2013).

5. Early translations and selections from alternative scriptures include Montague Rhodes James, *The Apocryphal New Testament* (Oxford: Clarendon Press, 1924). Major modern works include Wilhelm Schneemelcher, ed., *New Testament Apocrypha*, trans. R. McL. Wilson, rev. ed., 2 vols. (London: James Clarke, 1991–1992); Bart Ehrman and Zlatko Pleše, *The Apocryphal Gospels* (Oxford: Oxford University Press, 2011); Bart Ehrman and Zlatko Pleše, eds., *The Other Gospels* (New York: Oxford University Press, 2013). J. K. Elliott, *The Apocryphal New Testament* (Oxford: Oxford University Press, 1993) updated the classic 1924 study by M. R. James. In the near future, we are promised a major collection of *More New Testament Apocrypha*, edited by Tony Burke and Brent Landau, to be published by William B. Eerdmans.

6. Schneemelcher, ed., *New Testament Apocrypha*, 1:38–41. The Gelasian Decree (*Decretum Gelasianum*) can also be found at The Tertullian Project, www.tertullian.org/decretum_eng.htm. The gospels condemned in that text are those named for Matthias, Barnabas, James the Younger, Peter, Bartholomew, and Andrew as well as "the Gospel in the name of Thomas that the Manichaeans use" and gospels forged by Lucianus and Hesychius. Throughout this book, I will myself refer to "heresies" or heretical movements, although a more appropriate and objective term would be "alternative forms of Christianity that are conventionally labeled as heresies."

7. Charlotte Allen, *The Human Christ* (New York: Free Press, 1998). For women in the early sects, see Madeleine Scopello, *Femme, gnose et manichéisme* (Leiden: Brill, 2005).

8. For the great diversity of political conditions under which Christians lived, see Philip Jenkins, *The Lost History of Christianity* (San Francisco: HarperOne, 2008); Diarmaid MacCulloch, *Christianity* (New York: Viking, 2010).

9. For alternative Jesus traditions, see Per Beskow, *Strange Tales About Jesus* (Philadelphia: Fortress Press, 1983); William D. Stroker,

Extracanonical Sayings of Jesus (Atlanta: Society of Biblical Literature 1989); J. K. Elliott, ed., *The Apocryphal Jesus* (New York: Oxford University Press, 1996).

10. L. Guerrier and S. Grébaut, *Le Testament en Galilée de Notre-Seigneur Jésus Christ* (Paris: Firmin-Didot, 1913); J. M. Harden, *An Introduction to Ethiopian Christian Literature* (London: SPCK, 1926). As I will explain, the Gospel of Barnabas cited here probably has no connection with the scripture of that name mentioned in the Gelasian Decree.

11. The bridge saying was inscribed on the entry gate to the mosque adjacent to the palace of Akbar at Fatehpur Sikri, Uttar Pradesh, India, c. 1570. Michael Meerson, Peter Schafer, and Yaacov Deutsch, eds., *Toledot Yeshu ("The Life Story of Jesus") Revisited* (Tübingen, Germany: Mohr Siebeck, 2011).

12. For Cyril, see Simon Gathercole, "Named Testimonia to the *Gospel of Thomas,*" *Harvard Theological Review* 105 (2012): 58. For the process of canon formation, see Michael W. Holmes, "The Biblical Canon," in Susan Ashbrook Harvey, ed., *The Oxford Handbook of Early Christian Studies* (New York: Oxford University Press, 2008); Lee M. McDonald, *The Biblical Canon*, 3rd ed. (Peabody, MA: Hendrickson Publishers, 2007); Lee M. McDonald, *Forgotten Scriptures* (Louisville, KY: Westminster John Knox Press, 2009); Lee M. McDonald, *Formation of the Bible* (Peabody, MA: Hendrickson Publishers, 2012).

13. Schneemelcher, ed., *New Testament Apocrypha*; François Bovon, Ann Graham Brock, and Christopher R. Matthews, eds., *The Apocryphal Acts of the Apostles* (Cambridge, MA: Center for the Study of World Religions, 1999); Amy-Jill Levine with Maria Mayo Robbins, eds., *A Feminist Companion to the New Testament Apocrypha* (New York: T&T Clark, 2006); H.-J. Klauck, *The Apocryphal Acts of the Apostles*, trans. B. McNeil (Waco, TX: Baylor University Press, 2008); Lee M. McDonald and James H. Charlesworth, eds., *"Non-Canonical" Religious Texts in Early Judaism and Early Christianity* (London: T&T Clark, 2012).

14. James H. Charlesworth, *Authentic Apocrypha* (North Richland Hills, TX: D&F Scott, 1998). For Abgar, see Elliott, *Apocryphal New Testament*, 541–542; Hans J. W. Drijvers, "The Abgar Legend," in Schneemelcher, ed., *New Testament Apocrypha*, 1:492–500.

15. William Granger Ryan, ed., *The Golden Legend*, 2 vols. (Princeton, NJ: Princeton University Press, 1993); Richard Hamer, ed., *Gilte*

Legende, 3 vols. (Oxford: Early English Text Society / Oxford University Press, 2006–2012).

16. Antti Marjanen and Petri Luomanen, eds., *A Companion to Second-Century Christian "Heretics"* (Leiden: Brill, 2008).

17. R. N. Swanson, *Religion and Devotion in Europe, c. 1215–c. 1515* (Cambridge, UK: Cambridge University Press, 1995); Katherine Breen, *Imagining an English Reading Public, 1150–1400* (Cambridge, UK: Cambridge University Press, 2010).

18. David R. Cartlidge and J. Keith Elliott, *Art and the Christian Apocrypha* (London: Routledge, 2001).

19. Elliott, *Apocryphal New Testament*, 46–99.

20. For the impact of the Protevangelium, see Ehrman and Pleše, *Apocryphal Gospels*, 422. Zbigniew S. Izydorczyk, ed., *The Medieval Gospel of Nicodemus* (Tempe: Arizona Center for Medieval and Renaissance Studies, 1997); Hans-Joachim Klimkeit, "Apocryphal Gospels in Central and East Asia," in Manfred Heuser and Hans-Joachim Klimkeit, *Studies in Manichaean Literature and Art* (Leiden: Brill, 1998), 189–211.

21. "The Gospel of Pseudo-Matthew," in Alexander Roberts, ed., *The Ante-Nicene Fathers* (1896), 8:374.

22. "Vita Adae et Evae," Christian Classics Ethereal Library, www.ccel.org/c/charles/otpseudepig/adamnev.htm; Gary A. Anderson, "Life of Adam and Eve," in Louis H. Feldman, James L. Kugel, and Lawrence H. Schiffman, eds., *Outside the Bible* (Philadelphia: Jewish Publication Society, 2013), 2:1331–1358.

23. Jeffrey B. Russell, ed., *Religious Dissent in the Middle Ages* (New York: Wiley, 1971); Malcolm Lambert, *Medieval Heresy* (Oxford: Blackwell, 2002 [1976]).

24. For the Bogomils, see Walter L. Wakefield and Austin P. Evans, *Heresies of the High Middle Ages* (New York: Columbia University Press, 1969); Yuri Stoyanov, *The Other God* (New Haven, CT: Yale Nota Bene, 2000).

25. James Brashler and Roger A. Bullard, eds., "The Apocalypse of Peter," in James M. Robinson, ed., *The Nag Hammadi Library in English*, 4th rev. ed. (Leiden: Brill, 1996), 372–378; Andreas Werner, "The Coptic Gnostic Apocalypse of Peter," in Schneemelcher, ed., *New Testament Apocrypha*, 2:700–712; Marvin Meyer, "The Revelation of Peter," in Marvin Meyer and James M. Robinson, eds., *The Nag Hammadi Scriptures* (San Francisco: HarperOne, 2008), 487–498; John Dart, *The Laughing Savior* (New York: Harper and Row, 1976).

26. Janet Hamilton and Bernard Hamilton, eds., with Yuri Stoyanov, *Christian Dualist Heresies in the Byzantine World, c. 650–c. 1450* (Manchester, UK: Manchester University Press, 1998), 157. The editors suggest (p. 147) that the "Peter" referred to here might be the fifth-century Monophysite Peter the Iberian, but it is difficult to see why that work would so appeal to Dualists. My identification with the Gnostic Apocalypse of Peter is all the more likely, as Euthymius then proceeds to condemn another Gnostic-tainted work, namely, the Gospel of Thomas, which he credits to Manichaeans. Simon Gathercole, "Named Testimonia to the *Gospel of Thomas*," *Harvard Theological Review* 105 (2012): 72.

27. Gathercole, "Named Testimonia," 73.

28. I disagree here with the views of Elaine Pagels, as expressed in her *Beyond Belief* (New York: Random House, 2003).

29. The use of alternative scriptures in the Middle Ages is quite familiar in works such as James, *Apocryphal New Testament*; Elliott, *Apocryphal New Testament*; or Joseph Gaer, *The Lore of the New Testament* (Boston: Little Brown, 1952). The problem is that the implications of the abundant materials offered here have not penetrated the literature on the early church and its texts.

30. For the history of the idea of gospels, see Koester, *Ancient Christian Gospels*; and Wilhelm Schneemelcher, "Introduction," in Schneemelcher, ed., *New Testament Apocrypha*, 1:9–34.

31. Gelasian Decree (*Decretum Gelasianum*), The Tertullian Project, www.tertullian.org/decretum_eng.htm.

32. Schneemelcher, ed., *New Testament Apocrypha*, vol. 1; Marvin Meyer and James M. Robinson, eds., *The Nag Hammadi Scriptures* (San Francisco: HarperOne, 2008). I will discuss Sethians below (Chapter 5).

33. Els Rose summarizes this view of "the false, naive, phantasy version of the 'real' New Testament of canonical truth" in Els Rose, *Ritual Memory* (Leiden: Brill, 2009).

34. S. J. Shoemaker, "Early Christian Apocryphal Literature," in Susan Ashbrook Harvey, ed., *The Oxford Handbook of Early Christian Studies* (New York: Oxford University Press, 2008).

35. I draw here on the idea of the "Whole Gospel" formulated by David R. Cartlidge and J. Keith Elliott, *Art and the Christian Apocrypha*, 18–20, also 77. Brian Murdoch has studied the very wide range of texts that constituted what he aptly terms *The Medieval Popular Bible* (Cambridge, UK: D. S. Brewer, 2003).

36. "Stories People Want" is a chapter title in Averil Cameron, *Christianity and the Rhetoric of Empire* (Berkeley: University of California Press, 1994). For modern alternative gospels, see, for instance, Levi H. Dowling, *The Aquarian Gospel of Jesus the Christ* (Los Angeles: Royal, 1908); Edgar J. Goodspeed, *Strange New Gospels* (Chicago: University of Chicago Press, 1931); Edgar J. Goodspeed, *Modern Apocrypha* (Boston: Beacon Press, 1956); Elizabeth Clare Prophet, *The Lost Years of Jesus* (Malibu, CA: Summit University Press, 1984); Laurie F. Maffly-Kipp, *American Scriptures* (New York: Penguin Classics, 2010); Philip Jenkins, "Of Scriptures and Superheroes," October 12, 2014, www.patheos.com/blogs/anxiousbench/2014/10/of-sscriptures-and-superheroes/.

37. Wallis Budge, ed., *The Book of the Cave of Treasures*, 224–225, Internet Sacred Text Archive, www.sacred-texts.com/chr/bct/bct09.htm; Alexander Toepel, "The Cave of Treasures," in Richard Bauckham, James R. Davila, and Alex Panayotov, eds., *Old Testament Pseudepigrapha: More Noncanonical Scriptures*, 2 vols. (Grand Rapids, MI: Wm. B. Eerdmans, 2013–?), 1:531–584.

38. S. J. Shoemaker, *Ancient Traditions of the Virgin Mary's Dormition and Assumption* (Oxford: Oxford University Press, 2002). Jesus's postmortem teachings are described in Acts 1.3.

39. For Terah and the idols, see O. S. Wintermute, "Jubilees," in James H. Charlesworth, ed., *The Old Testament Pseudepigrapha*, 2 vols. (Garden City, NY: Doubleday, 1983–1985), 2:79–80. For the close relationship between Jewish and early Christian approaches to scripture, see Dan Jaffé, ed., *Studies in Rabbinic Judaism and Early Christianity* (Leiden: Brill, 2010); Amy-Jill Levine and Marc Zvi Brettler, eds., *The Jewish Annotated New Testament* (New York: Oxford University Press, 2011).

CHAPTER TWO

1. Henri-Charles Puech, "Other Gnostic Gospels and Related Literature," in Wilhelm Schneemelcher, ed., *New Testament Apocrypha*, trans. R. McL. Wilson, rev. ed., 2 vols. (London: James Clarke, 1991–1992), 1:380–381, 406; Han J. W. Drijvers, *East of Antioch* (London: Variorum Reprints, 1984); Antti Marjanen and Petri Luomanen, eds., *A Companion to Second-Century Christian "Heretics"* (Leiden: Brill, 2008); Sebastian Moll, *The Arch-Heretic Marcion* (Tübingen, Germany: Mohr Siebeck, 2010); Jason D. BeDuhn, *The First New Testament* (Salem, OR: Polebridge, 2013); "Bardesanes

and Bardesanites," New Advent, www.newadvent.org/cathen/02293a .htm; Bayard Dodge, ed., *The Fihrist of al-Nadīm* (New York: Columbia University Press, 1970), 2:806–807, 814–816.

2. A. F. J. Klijn and G. J. Reinink, eds., *Patristic Evidence for Jewish-Christian Sects* (Leiden: Brill, 1973), 216; A. F. J. Klijn, *Jewish-Christian Gospel Tradition* (Leiden: Brill, 1992); Oskar Skarsaune and Reidar Hvalvik, eds., *Jewish Believers in Jesus* (Peabody, MA: Hendrickson Publishers, 2007); Petri Luomanen, *Recovering Jewish-Christian Sects and Gospels* (Leiden: Brill, 2012); Philipp Vielhauer, "Jewish-Christian Gospels," in Schneemelcher, ed., *New Testament Apocrypha*, 1:134–178. For the prolonged Jewish-Christian interactions from which such texts emerged, see David Frankfurter, "Beyond Jewish Christianity," in Adam H. Becker and Annette Yoshiko Reed, eds., *The Ways That Never Parted* (Tübingen, Germany: Mohr Siebeck, 2003).

3. Yuri Stoyanov, *The Other God* (New Haven, CT: Yale Nota Bene, 2000).

4. Alister McGrath, *Heresy* (New York: HarperOne, 2009).

5. 2 John 1.7–11; 2 Timothy 2.17–18. Faustus is quoted from Augustine's *Contra Faustum*, Book II, no. 1, The Gnosis Archive, http://gnosis.org/library/contf1.htm; Bart D. Ehrman, *The Orthodox Corruption of Scripture* (New York: Oxford University Press, 2011).

6. For Serapion, see Eusebius, *Ecclesiastical History*, Book VI, chap. 12, New Advent, www.newadvent.org/fathers/250106.htm. One version of Athanasius's letter can be found at Christian Classics Ethereal Library, www.ccel.org/ccel/schaff/npnf204.xxv.iii.iii.xxv.html. John Barton, *Holy Writings, Sacred Text* (Louisville, KY: Westminster John Knox Press, 1998).

7. Elaine H. Pagels, *Beyond Belief* (New York: Random House, 2003), 97. Pagels cites as her source the work of David Brakke, including his *Athanasius and the Politics of Asceticism* (Oxford: Clarendon, 1995). Brakke includes a scholarly translation of the various fragments of the Festal Letter (326–332), in which Athanasius says believers should "decline" apocryphal scriptures, "reject" them, and "not . . . proclaim anything in them, nor . . . speak anything in them, with those who want to be instructed." There is no suggestion of suppression or destruction. I do not know the source of Pagels's statement, unless it is a mistaken recollection of a later writing by the monastic founder Shenoute.

8. Hugo Lundhaug, "Mystery and Authority in the Writings of Shenoute," in Christian H. Bull, Liv Lied, and John D. Turner,

Mystery and Secrecy in the Nag Hammadi Collection and Other Ancient Literature (Leiden: Brill, 2011), 262; compare Philip Jenkins, "Shenoute's Wars," August 11, 2013, www.patheos.com/blogs/anxious bench/2013/08/shenoutes-wars/.

9. Philip Jenkins, "Shenoute and the Gnostics," August 12, 2013, www.patheos.com/blogs/anxiousbench/2013/08/shenoute-and-the -gnostics/; Johannes Hahn, Stephen Emmel, and Ulrich Gotter, eds., *From Temple to Church* (Leiden: Brill, 2008).

10. Pope Leo I, Letter XV to Bishop Turribius, xvi, New Advent, www.newadvent.org/fathers/3604015.htm.

11. Beate Blatz, "The Coptic Gospel of Thomas," in Schneemelcher, ed., *New Testament Apocrypha*, 1:110–133; Marvin Meyer, *The Gospel of Thomas* (San Francisco: Harper, 1992); Mark Goodacre, *Thomas and the Gospels* (Grand Rapids, MI: Wm. B. Eerdmans, 2012); Stephen J. Patterson, *The Gospel of Thomas and Christian Origins* (Leiden: Brill, 2013); Simon Gathercole, *The Gospel of Thomas* (Leiden: Brill, 2014); Stephen J. Patterson, *The Lost Way* (San Francisco: HarperOne, 2014).

12. Bart D. Ehrman, ed., *The Apostolic Fathers*, 2 vols. (Cambridge, MA: Harvard University Press, 2003); Brakke, *Athanasius and the Politics of Asceticism*, 326–332; Michael J. Kok, *The Gospel on the Margins: The Reception of Mark in the Second Century* (Minneapolis: Fortress Press, 2015).

13. David Bundy, "Pseudepigrapha in Syriac Literature," *SBL Seminar Papers* (Atlanta: Scholars Press, 1991), 745–765; M. Debié, A. Desreumaux, C. Jullien, and F. Jullien, eds., *Les apocryphes syriaques* (Paris: Geuthner, 2005).

14. Schneemelcher, ed., *New Testament Apocrypha*, 1:41–42.

15. Simon Gathercole, "Named Testimonia to the *Gospel of Thomas*," *Harvard Theological Review* 105 (2012): 53–89; Michael E. Stone, "Armenian Canon Lists VI," *Harvard Theological Review* 94 (2001): 477–491.

16. Gathercole, "Named Testimonia," 61.

17. J. K. Elliott, *The Apocryphal New Testament* (Oxford: Oxford University Press, 1993), 46–122; Agnes Smith Lewis, ed., *Apocrypha Syriaca* (Cambridge, UK: Cambridge University Press, 2012).

18. Wilhelm Schneemelcher and Knut Schäferdiek, "Second and Third Century Acts of Apostles," in Schneemelcher, ed., *New Testament Apocrypha*, 2:75–100. Many other Acts circulated: see, for instance, Francois Bovon and Christopher Matthews, *The Acts of Philip* (Waco, TX: Baylor University Press, 2012). For Augustine, see *Contra*

Faustum, Book XXII, no. 79, New Advent, www.newadvent.org/fa thers/140622.htm.

19. "The Hymn of the Lord Which He Sang in Secret to the Holy Apostles, His Disciple," The Gnosis Archive, http://gnosis.org/hymn jesu.html; Montague Rhodes James, *The Apocryphal New Testament* (Oxford: Clarendon Press, 1924), 253. See also Pagels, *Beyond Belief.*

20. Knut Schäferdiek, "The Acts of John," in Schneemelcher, ed., *New Testament Apocrypha*, 2:152–212.

21. J. N. Bremmer, ed., *The Apocryphal Acts of Thomas* (Leuven, Belgium: Peeters, 2002); A. F. J. Klijn, ed., *The Acts of Thomas*, 2nd ed. (Leiden: Brill, 2003); Hans J. W. Drijvers, "The Acts of Thomas," in Schneemelcher, ed., *New Testament Apocrypha*, 2:322–411.

22. Elliott, *Apocryphal New Testament*, 439–512; William Granger Ryan, ed., *The Golden Legend*, 2 vols. (Princeton, NJ: Princeton University Press, 1993), 1:29.

23. Anthony Ashley Bevan, *The Hymn of the Soul Contained in the Syriac Acts of St. Thomas* (Cambridge, UK: Cambridge University Press, 1897). A translation can be found at The Gnosis Archive, www .gnosis.org/library/hymnpearl.htm; see also "The Hymn of the Pearl," translated by Brian Colless, https://sites.google.com/site/collesseum /pearlhymn.

24. Vincent's original formulation was *"Quod ubique, quod semper, quod ab omnibus creditum est."* "St. Vincent of Lérins," New Advent, www.newadvent.org/cathen/15439b.htm; Hilaire Belloc, *Europe and the Faith* (New York: Paulist Press, 1920).

25. Belloc, *Europe and the Faith.*

26. Philip Jenkins, *The Lost History of Christianity* (San Francisco: HarperOne, 2008).

27. For the political background to these splits, see Philip Jenkins, *Jesus Wars* (San Francisco: HarperOne, 2010); Michael Angold, ed., *Cambridge History of Christianity: Eastern Christianity* (Cambridge, UK: Cambridge University Press, 2006).

28. Timothy Michael Law, *When God Spoke Greek* (New York: Oxford University Press, 2013); Michael L. Satlow, *How the Bible Became Holy* (New Haven, CT: Yale University Press, 2014).

29. Edmon L. Gallagher, *Hebrew Scripture in Patristic Biblical Theory* (Leiden: Brill, 2012); Eugen J. Pentiuc, *The Old Testament in Eastern Orthodox Tradition* (New York: Oxford University Press, 2014).

30. For Psalm 151, see Henry B. Swete, *An Introduction to the Old Testament in Greek* (Cambridge, UK: Cambridge University Press,

1914); Emanuel Tov, *Textual Criticism of the Hebrew Bible*, 3rd rev. and expanded ed. (Minneapolis: Fortress, 2012).

31. Wilhelm Schneemelcher, "The Epistle to the Laodiceans," in Schneemelcher, ed., *New Testament Apocrypha*, 2:42–45. Lightfoot is quoted from Bruce M. Metzger, *The Canon of the New Testament* (New York: Oxford University Press, 1997).

32. J. R. W. Cowley, "The Biblical Canon of the Ethiopian Orthodox Church Today," *Ostkirchliche Studien* 23(1974): 318–323; James L. Kugel, "Jubilees," in Louis H. Feldman, James L. Kugel, and Lawrence H. Schiffman, eds., *Outside the Bible* (Philadelphia: Jewish Publication Society, 2013), 1:272–466.

33. J. M. Harden, *An Introduction to Ethiopian Christian Literature* (London: SPCK, 1926).

34. L. Guerrier and S. Grébaut, *Le Testament en Galilée de Notre-Seigneur Jésus Christ* (Paris: Firmin-Didot, 1913), 57–58, my translation from the French; Antti Marjanen and Petri Luomanen, eds., *A Companion to Second-Century Christian "Heretics"* (Leiden: Brill, 2008).

35. Jorunn J. Buckley, *The Mandaeans* (New York: Oxford University Press, 2002); Birger A. Pearson, *Ancient Gnosticism* (Minneapolis: Fortress Press, 2007); Gerard Russell, *Heirs to Forgotten Kingdoms* (New York: Basic Books, 2014).

36. Jenkins, *Jesus Wars*; M. E. Stone, *Selected Studies in Pseudepigrapha and Apocrypha* (Leiden: Brill, 1991); Michael E. Stone, *Apocrypha, Pseudepigrapha and Armenian Studies* (Leuven, Belgium: Peeters, 2006); Michael E. Stone, *Adam and Eve in the Armenian Traditions* (Atlanta: Society of Biblical Literature, 2013).

37. Jenkins, *Lost History of Christianity*; Valerie Hansen, *The Silk Road* (New York: Oxford University Press, 2012); Nicholas Sims-Williams, *The Christian Sogdian Manuscript C2* (Berlin: Akademie-Verlag, 1985); Nicholas Sims-Williams, "Sogdian and Turkish Christians in the Turfan and Tun-Huang Manuscripts," in Alfredo Cannona, ed., *Turfan and Tun-Huang* (Florence, Italy: Leo S. Olschki Editore, 1992), 43–61.

38. "From aeon to aeon" is quoted from Hans Jonas, *The Gnostic Religion*, 2nd ed. (Boston: Beacon Press, 1963), 230. For Manichaeans, see Dodge, ed., *The Fihrist of al-Nadīm*, 2:775–803; Samuel N. C. Lieu, *Manichaeism in Mesopotamia and the Roman East* (Leiden: Brill, 1994); John C. Reeves, *Heralds of That Good Realm* (Leiden: Brill, 1996); Andrew Welburn, ed., *Mani, the Angel and the Column of Glory* (Edinburgh: Floris Books, 1998); Paul Mirecki and Jason BeDuhn,

eds., *The Light and the Darkness* (Leiden: Brill, 2001); Jason David BeDuhn, *New Light on Manichaeism* (Leiden: Brill, 2009); J. Kevin Coyle, *Manichaeism and Its Legacy* (Leiden: Brill, 2009); Nicholas J. Baker-Brian, *An Ancient Faith Rediscovered* (London: T&T Clark, 2011); Iain Gardner, Jason BeDuhn, and Paul Dilley, *Mani at the Court of the Persian Kings* (Leiden: Brill, 2015).

39. For the eastward expansion of the Manichaean faith, see Hans-Joachim Klimkeit, *Gnosis on the Silk Road* (San Francisco: Harper, 1993); Paul Mirecki and Jason BeDuhn, eds., *Emerging from Darkness* (Leiden: Brill, 1997); Samuel N. C. Lieu, *Manichaeism in Central Asia and China* (Leiden: Brill, 1998).

40. Leo the Great, Sermon 34, New Advent, www.newadvent.org/fathers/360334.htm.

41. Gelasian Decree (*Decretum Gelasianum*), The Tertullian Project, www.tertullian.org/decretum_eng.htm; Simon Gathercole, "Named Testimonia to the *Gospel of Thomas*," *Harvard Theological Review* 105 (2012): 58, 69; F. Forrester Church and Gedaliahu G. Stroumsa, "Mani's Disciple Thomas and the Psalms of Thomas," *Vigiliae Christianae* 34(1980): 47–55.

42. Hans-Joachim Klimkeit, "Apocryphal Gospels in Central and East Asia," in Manfred Heuser and Hans-Joachim Klimkeit, *Studies in Manichaean Literature and Art* (Leiden: Brill, 1998), 189–211.

43. "You must attach yourself to the true Christians" is quoted from Klimkeit, "Apocryphal Gospels in Central and East Asia."

44. Henri-Charles Puech, "Other Gnostic Gospels and Related Literature," in Schneemelcher, ed., *New Testament Apocrypha*, 1:404–409; Loren Theo Stuckenbruck, "The Book of Giants," in Louis H. Feldman, James L. Kugel, and Lawrence H. Schiffman, eds., *Outside the Bible* (Philadelphia: Jewish Publication Society, 2013), 1:221–236. The Book of Giants is the subject of a chapter in Richard Bauckham, James R. Davila, and Alex Panayotov, eds., *Old Testament Pseudepigrapha: More Noncanonical Scriptures*, 2 vols. (Grand Rapids, MI: Wm. B. Eerdmans, 2013–?), vol. 2, forthcoming.

45. Puech, "Other Gnostic Gospels and Related Literature," 1:380.

46. Klimkeit, "Apocryphal Gospels in Central and East Asia." For the texts known to Manichaeans, see J. Kevin Coyle, *Manichaeism and Its Legacy* (Leiden: Brill, 2009), 125.

47. Jenkins, *Lost History of Christianity*.

48. Klimkeit, *Gnosis on the Silk Road*; Klimkeit, "Apocryphal Gospels in Central and East Asia."

49. "The essence of the Buddha Vairocana" is from Klimkeit, *Gnosis on the Silk Road*, 326.

50. "The jewel of the law" is from Klimkeit, "Apocryphal Gospels in Central and East Asia," 199; D. Durkin-Meisterernst, Y. Kasai, and A. Yakup, eds., *Die Erforschung des Tocharischen und die alttürkische Maitrisimit* (Turnhout, Belgium: Brepols, 2013).

51. C. Detlef G. Müller, "Apocalypse of Peter," in Schneemelcher, ed., *New Testament Apocrypha*, 2:620–639; Elliott, *Apocryphal New Testament*, 593–613.

52. Both quotations are from James, *Apocryphal New Testament*, 508–509.

53. The Muratori Canon is quoted from Schneemelcher, ed., *New Testament Apocrypha*, 1:34–36. Sozomen is quoted from his *Ecclesiastical History*, Book VII, chap. 19, New Advent, www.newadvent.org /fathers/26027.htm. For Mechitar, see Stone, "Armenian Canon Lists VI," 485.

54. Martha Himmelfarb, *Tours of Hell* (Philadelphia: University of Pennsylvania Press, 1983); Hugo Duensing and Aurelio de Santos Otero, "Apocalypse of Paul," in Schneemelcher, ed., *New Testament Apocrypha*, 2:712–747; Elliott, *Apocryphal New Testament*, 616–644; Jan Nicolaas Bremmer and István Czachesz, eds., *The Visio Pauli and the Gnostic Apocalypse of Saint Paul* (Leuven, Belgium: Peeters, 2007). Compare Richard Bauckham, "The Latin Vision of Ezra," in Richard Bauckham, James R. Davila, and Alex Panayotov, eds., *Old Testament Pseudepigrapha: More Noncanonical Scriptures*, 2 vols. (Grand Rapids, MI: Wm. B. Eerdmans, 2013–?), 1:498–528.

CHAPTER THREE

1. Henry M. Bannister, "Liturgical Fragments," *Journal of Theological Studies* 9 (1908): 398–427.

2. Wilhelm Schneemelcher, ed., *New Testament Apocrypha*, trans. R. McL. Wilson, rev. ed., 2 vols. (London: James Clarke, 1991–1992), 1:38.

3. One of the great scholars of apocryphal texts was M. R. James, who a century ago remarked that "the Anglo-Saxon and Irish scholars seem to have been in possession of a good deal of rather rare apocryphal literature." See M. R. James, "A Fragment of the *Penitence of Jannes and Jambres*," *Journal of Theological Studies* 2(1901): 577.

4. Kathleen Hughes, *The Church in Early Irish Society* (Ithaca, NY: Cornell University Press, 1966); Dáibhí Ó Cróinín, *Early Medieval Ireland, 400–1200* (New York: Longman, 1995). For modern myths

about the Celtic church, see Ian Bradley, *Celtic Christianity* (Edinburgh: Edinburgh University Press, 1999).

5. J. N. Hillgarth, *Visigothic Spain, Byzantium and the Irish* (London: Variorum Reprints, 1985); David Dumville, "Biblical Apocrypha and the Early Irish," *Proceedings of the Royal Irish Academy* 73 (1973): 299–338; Peter Brown, *The Rise of Western Christendom*, rev. ed. (Malden, MA: Wiley-Blackwell, 2013).

6. William Dalrymple, "The Egyptian Connection," *New York Review of Books*, October 23, 2008; Éamonn Ó. Carragáin, *Ritual and the Rood*, British Library Studies in Medieval Culture (Toronto: University of Toronto Press, 2005).

7. "The Faddan More Psalter," National Museum of Ireland, www .museum.ie/en/list/projects.aspx?article=27229a4b-9f2f-42ba-869 3-4b00bcf1cddd.

8. Denis Meehan, ed., *Adomnan's De Locis Sanctis* (Dublin: Institute for Advanced Studies, 1958); Thomas O'Loughlin, *Adomnán and the Holy Places* (London: T&T Clark, 2007). For Dicuil, see James J. Tierney, *Liber de Mensura Orbis Terrae* (Dublin: Institute for Advanced Studies, 1967).

9. Martin McNamara, *The Apocrypha in the Irish Church* (Dublin: Institute for Advanced Studies, 1975); Máire Herbert and Martin McNamara, eds. and trans., *Irish Biblical Apocrypha* (Edinburgh: Continuum, 1989); Martin McNamara, ed., *Apocalyptic and Eschatological Heritage: The Middle East and Celtic Realms* (Dublin: Four Courts, 2003).

10. M. R. James, *Latin Infancy Gospels* (Cambridge, UK: Cambridge University Press, 1927); Fergus Kelly and Brian Murdoch, *The Irish Adam and Eve Story from Saltair na Rann*, 2 vols. (Dublin: Institute for Advanced Studies, 1976).

11. McNamara, *Apocrypha in the Irish Church*, 36–39, 46–47; Herbert and McNamara, eds. and trans., *Irish Biblical Apocrypha*, 48.

12. "What James of the Knees says" is quoted from Herbert and McNamara, eds. and trans., *Irish Biblical Apocrypha*, 42.

13. McNamara, *Apocrypha in the Irish Church*, 43–44.

14. Mary Clayton, *The Apocryphal Gospels of Mary in Anglo-Saxon England* (New York: Cambridge University Press, 1998); Kathryn Powell and Donald Scragg, eds., *Apocryphal Texts and Traditions in Anglo-Saxon England* (Cambridge, UK: D. S. Brewer, 2003); Frederick M. Biggs, *Sources of Anglo-Saxon Literary Culture: The Apocrypha* (Kalamazoo, MI: Medieval Institute Publications, 2007).

15. Richard Gameson, ed., *The Cambridge History of the Book in Britain*, vol. 1, *c. 400–1100* (Cambridge, UK: Cambridge University Press, 2012); Clare A. Lees, ed., *The Cambridge History of Early Medieval English Literature* (Cambridge, UK: Cambridge University Press, 2013).

16. John Blair, *The Church in Anglo-Saxon Society* (New York: Oxford University Press, 2005).

17. Michelle P. Brown and Carol A. Farr, eds., *Mercia* (London: Leicester University Press, 2001).

18. "Well read both in sacred and in secular literature" is quoted from Bede, *Ecclesiastical History of the English Nation*, Book IV, chap. 2.

19. Powell and Scragg, eds., *Apocryphal Texts and Traditions*.

20. Biggs, *Sources of Anglo-Saxon Literary Culture*; Bernhard Bischoff and Michael Lapidge, *Biblical Commentaries from the Canterbury School of Theodore and Hadrian* (Cambridge, UK: Cambridge University Press, 1994).

21. Michael Lapidge, *The Anglo-Saxon Library* (Oxford: Oxford University Press, 2006), 42; Patrizia Lendinara, "The *Versus Sibyllae de die iudicii* in Anglo-Saxon England," in Powell and Scragg, eds., *Apocryphal Texts and Traditions*; J. E. Cross, ed., *Two Old English Apocrypha and Their Manuscript Source* (Cambridge, UK: Cambridge University Press 1996); Clayton, *Apocryphal Gospels of Mary*.

22. Clare A. Lees, "The 'Sunday Letter' and the 'Sunday Lists,'" *Anglo-Saxon England* 14 (1985): 129–151; Dorothy Haines, *Sunday Observance and the Sunday Letter in Anglo-Saxon England* (Woodbridge, UK: Boydell and Brewer, 2010). Compare *Our Saviour's Letter!* (Dudley, UK: M. Shaw, c. 1890).

23. Frederick M. Biggs, "An Introduction and Overview of Recent Work," in Powell and Scragg, eds., *Apocryphal Texts and Traditions*, 12–15.

24. Thomas N. Hall, "Æelfric and the Epistle to the Laodiceans," in Powell and Scragg, eds., *Apocryphal Texts and Traditions*; Philip L. Tite, *The Apocryphal Epistle to the Laodiceans* (Leiden: Brill, 2012).

25. Samantha Zacher, *Rewriting the Old Testament in Anglo-Saxon Verse* (London: Bloomsbury, 2013).

26. George W. E. Nickelsburg and James C. VanderKam, *1 Enoch* (Minneapolis: Fortress Press, 2004); Annette Yoshiko Reed, *Fallen Angels and the History of Judaism and Christianity* (Cambridge, UK: Cambridge University Press, 2005); Miryam T. Brand, "1 Enoch," in

Louis H. Feldman, James L. Kugel, and Lawrence H. Schiffman, eds., *Outside the Bible* (Philadelphia: Jewish Publication Society, 2013), 2:1359–1452; Angela Kim Harkins, Kelley Coblentz Bautch, and John C. Endres, eds., *The Watchers in Jewish and Christian Traditions* (Minneapolis: Augsburg Fortress, 2014); John C. Reeves, "Jewish Pseudepigrapha in Manichaean Literature," in John C. Reeves, ed., *Tracing the Threads* (Atlanta: Society of Biblical Literature, 1994), 173–203.

27. R. E. Kaske, "Beowulf and the Book of Enoch," *Speculum* 46, no. 3 (1971): 421–431; Ruth Mellinkoff, "Cain's Monstrous Progeny in Beowulf," *Anglo-Saxon England* 8 (1979): 143–162; 9 (1981): 183–197.

28. For the process of making Bibles, see Susan Boynton and Diane J. Reilly, eds., *The Practice of the Bible in the Middle Ages* (New York: Columbia University Press, 2011).

29. Brown, *Rise of Western Christendom*.

30. Douglas Dales, *Alcuin* (Cambridge, UK: James Clarke, 2012).

31. A. F. J. Klijn, *Jewish-Christian Gospel Tradition* (Leiden: Brill, 1992); Antti Marjanen and Petri Luomanen, eds., *A Companion to Second-Century Christian "Heretics"* (Leiden: Brill, 2008); Bart Ehrman and Zlatko Pleše, eds., *The Other Gospels* (New York: Oxford University Press, 2013), 99–114; Petri Luomanen, *Recovering Jewish-Christian Sects and Gospels* (Leiden: Brill, 2012); Adam H. Becker and Annette Yoshiko Reed, eds., *The Ways That Never Parted* (Tübingen, Germany: Mohr Siebeck, 2003).

32. According to James Edwards, "the Hebrew Gospel was the most highly esteemed non-canonical document in the early church." Quoted from James R. Edwards, "The Hebrew Gospel in Early Christianity," in Lee M. McDonald and James H. Charlesworth, eds., *'Non-Canonical' Religious Texts in Early Judaism and Early Christianity* (London: T&T Clark, 2012), 151. James Edwards, *The Hebrew Gospel and the Development of the Synoptic Tradition* (Grand Rapids, MI: Wm. B. Eerdmans, 2009); Schneemelcher, ed., *New Testament Apocrypha*, 1:41–42. Bede is quoted from Biggs, "An Introduction and Overview of Recent Work," 16.

33. J. K. Elliott, *The Apocryphal New Testament* (Oxford: Oxford University Press, 1993), 3–16; Montague Rhodes James, *A Descriptive Catalogue of the McClean Collection of Manuscripts in the Fitzwilliam Museum* (Cambridge, UK: Cambridge University Press, 1912), 64.

34. McNamara, *Apocrypha in the Irish Church*, 37–42; Klijn, *Jewish-Christian Gospel Tradition*, 22–25, 81–88.

35. This section draws heavily on William L. Petersen, *Tatian's Diatessaron* (Leiden: Brill, 1994).

36. For executing the Law, see Petersen, *Tatian's Diatessaron*, 22–24.

CHAPTER FOUR

1. William Granger Ryan, ed., *The Golden Legend*, 2 vols. (Princeton, NJ: Princeton University Press, 1993); Richard Hamer, ed., *Gilte Legende*, 3 vols. (Oxford: Oxford University Press, 2006–2012).

2. For the work's popularity, see Eamon Duffy, "The Intense Afterlife of the Saints," *New York Review of Books*, June 19, 2014. Caxton's Prologue can be found at Fordham University, Medieval History, www.fordham.edu/halsall/basis/goldenlegend/GoldenLegend-Volume 1.asp#PROLOGUE.

3. Ryan, ed., *Golden Legend*, 1:27–29, for Lucy; and 2:343–346, for St. James the Dismembered.

4. Emma Gatland, *Women from the Golden Legend* (Woodbridge, UK: Tamesis, 2011).

5. The reference to Nicodemus is from the account of the Resurrection at Fordham University, Medieval History, www.fordham.edu/halsall/basis/goldenlegend/GL-vol1-resurrection.asp. The John the Evangelist reference is from the *Legend's* account of Mary's Assumption.

6. For Jerome, see Els Rose, *Ritual Memory* (Leiden: Brill, 2009), 49–52, 56; Frederick M. Biggs, "An Introduction and Overview of Recent Work," in Kathryn Powell and Donald Scragg, eds., *Apocryphal Texts and Traditions in Anglo-Saxon England* (Cambridge, UK: D. S. Brewer, 2003), 11n.

7. Isidore of Seville is quoted from Biggs, "An Introduction and Overview of Recent Work," 12.

8. Agobard is quoted from Rose, *Ritual Memory*, 76, and see p. 27 for Notker.

9. J. K. Elliott, *The Apocryphal New Testament* (Oxford: Oxford University Press, 1993).

10. Oscar Cullman, "Infancy Gospels," in Wilhelm Schneemelcher, ed., *New Testament Apocrypha*, trans. R. McL. Wilson, rev. ed., 2 vols. (London: James Clarke, 1991–1992), 1:414–469; Claire Clivaz, ed., *Infancy Gospels* (Tübingen, Germany: Mohr Siebeck, 2011).

11. Irenaeus, *Against Heresies*, 1:xx, New Advent, www.newadvent. org/fathers/0103120.htm. For the Marcosian story in the gospel, chap. 14, see "The Infancy Gospel of Thomas," New Advent, www .newadvent.org/fathers/0846.htm. E. A. Wallis Budge, *The History of the Blessed Virgin Mary and the History of the Likeness of Christ*, 2 vols. (London: Luzac, 1899); M. R. James, *Latin Infancy Gospels* (Cambridge, UK: Cambridge University Press, 1927); Elliott, *Apocryphal New Testament*, 46–122; J. K. Elliott, *A Synopsis of the Apocryphal Nativity and Infancy Narratives* (Leiden: Brill, 2006); C. Dimier-Paupert, *Livre de l'Enfance du Sauveur* (Paris: CERF, 2006); Abraham Terian, ed., *The Armenian Gospel of the Infancy* (New York: Oxford University Press, 2008); Claire Clivaz, Andreas Dettwiler, Luc Devillers, and Enrico Norelli, eds., *Infancy Gospels* (Tübingen, Germany: Mohr Siebeck, 2011).

12. Bart Ehrman and Zlatko Pleše, *The Apocryphal Gospels* (Oxford: Oxford University Press, 2011), 3; Stephen Gero, "The Infancy Gospel of Thomas," *Novum Testamentum* 13 (1971): 46–80.

13. "After that He was again passing through the village" is from the Infancy Gospel of Thomas, the First Greek Form, New Advent, www .newadvent.org/fathers/0846.htm.

14. Ibid.

15. Tony Burke, "The Infancy Gospel of Thomas: Irish," www.tony burke.ca/infancy-gospel-of-thomas/the-infancy-gospel-of-thomas-irish/.

16. Catherine Ella Laufer, *Hell's Destruction* (Farnham, UK: Ashgate, 2013).

17. Elliott, *Apocryphal New Testament*, 164–225; Bart Ehrman and Zlatko Pleše, eds., *The Other Gospels* (New York: Oxford University Press, 2013), 231–312.

18. Felix Scheidweiler, "The Gospel of Nicodemus, Acts of Pilate and Christ's Descent into Hell," in Schneemelcher, ed., *New Testament Apocrypha*, 1:501–536.

19. Montague Rhodes James, *The Apocryphal New Testament* (Oxford: Clarendon Press, 1924), 167; Schneemelcher, ed., *New Testament Apocrypha*, 1:540–542.

20. Matthew 27.51–53; 1 Peter 3.19; Ephesians 4.8–10; Karl Tamburr, *The Harrowing of Hell in Medieval England* (Woodbridge, UK: D. S. Brewer, 2007), 15.

21. David Dumville, "Biblical Apocrypha and the Early Irish," *Proceedings of the Royal Irish Academy* 73 (1973): 302; Sven Meeder,

"Boniface and the Irish Heresy of Clemens," *Church History* 80 (2011): 251–280.

22. Eamon Duffy, *The Stripping of the Altars*, rev. ed. (New Haven, CT: Yale University Press, 2005).

23. "Then Karinus and Leucius signed to them" is from Gospel of Nicodemus, Part II, Second Latin Form, New Advent, www.newadvent.org/fathers/08072c.htm.

24. "Lift up your heads" is from Psalm 24.7–10 (NIV). "Then Hades thus replied" is from Gospel of Nicodemus, Part II, Second Latin Form), New Advent, www.newadvent.org/fathers/08072c.htm.

25. "And again there came" is from Gospel of Nicodemus, Part II, Second Latin Form, New Advent, www.newadvent.org/fathers/08072c.htm.

26. R. N. Swanson, *Religion and Devotion in Europe, c. 1215–c. 1515* (Cambridge, UK: Cambridge University Press, 1995).

27. "Asked the Lord to leave as a sign of victory" is from Gospel of Nicodemus, Part II, Second Latin Form, New Advent, www.newadvent.org/fathers/08072c.htm.

28. Zbigniew S. Izydorczyk, ed., *The Medieval Gospel of Nicodemus* (Arizona State University, Arizona Center for Medieval and Renaissance Studies, 1997); David R. Cartlidge and J. Keith Elliott, *Art and the Christian Apocrypha* (London: Routledge, 2001).

29. Elliott, *Apocryphal New Testament*; Kirsten Wolf, "The Influence of the Evangelium Nicodemi on Norse literature," in Izydorczyk, ed., *Medieval Gospel of Nicodemus*, 269.

30. Izydorczyk, ed., *Medieval Gospel of Nicodemus*, passim; Dante, *Inferno*, Canto 4, http://genius.com/Dante-alighieri-inferno-canto-4-annotated. For Dis, see Cantos 8–9.

31. This is the *Golden Legend* account of the Resurrection, from Fordham University, Medieval History, www.fordham.edu/halsall/basis/goldenlegend/GL-vol1-resurrection.asp; compare Ryan, ed., *Golden Legend*, 1:221–224.

32. A. B. Kuypers, *The Prayer Book of Aedeluald the Bishop* (Cambridge, UK: Cambridge University Press, 1902).

33. Izydorczyk, ed., *Medieval Gospel of Nicodemus*; William Tydeman, *The Medieval European Stage, 500–1550* (Cambridge, UK: Cambridge University Press, 2001).

34. See, for instance, Richard Beadle and Pamela M. King, *York Mystery Plays* (Oxford: Oxford University Press, 1984); William Hone, *Ancient Mysteries Described* (Detroit: Singing Tree Press, 1969 [1823]).

35. From the *Saddlers Play*, www.rhaworth.myby.co.uk/pofstp /REED/York37.html. A modern version of the Latin would be: *"Attollite portas, principes, vestras, et elevamini, portæ æternales, et introibit rex gloriæ."*

36. Emily Steiner, *Reading* Piers Plowman (New York: Cambridge University Press, 2013); William Langland, *Piers Plowman*, ed. Derek Pearsall (Exeter, UK: University of Exeter Press, 2008).

37. George Economou, ed. and trans., *William Langland's* Piers Plowman: *The C Version* (Philadelphia: University of Pennsylvania Press, 1996). The poem can be found in full Middle English text at University of Michigan, Corpus of Middle English Prose and Verse, http://quod.lib.umich.edu/c/cme/PPlLan/1:19?rgn=div1;view=fulltext.

38. Passus 18, Harvard University, Geoffrey Chaucer Page, http://sites.fas.harvard.edu/~chaucer/special/authors/langland/pp-pas18.html.

39. Wikisource, http://en.wikisource.org/wiki/Piers_Plough |man_%28Wright%29/Passus_18, lines 12734–12764.

40. Robert Lutton, *Lollardy and Orthodox Religion in Pre-Reformation England* (Woodbridge, UK: Royal Historical Society / Boydell Press, 2006); Andrew Cole, *Literature and Heresy in the Age of Chaucer* (Cambridge, UK: Cambridge University Press, 2008).

41. Rose, *Ritual Memory*, 26–27.

42. Tamburr, *Harrowing of Hell in Medieval England*, 4.

43. John Skinner, *The Book of Margery Kempe* (New York: Random House, 2011); John C. Hirsh, *The Revelations of Margery Kempe* (Leiden: Brill, 1989).

44. Joseph Ernest Renan, *History of the Origins of Christianity*, chap. 26, Christian Classics Ethereal Library, www.ccel.org/ccel/renan /hadrian_pius.xxviii.html.

45. Ibid.

46. Shannon McSheffrey, *Gender and Heresy* (Philadelphia: University of Pennsylvania Press, 1995); Peter Biller and Anne Hudson, *Heresy and Literacy, 1000–1530* (Cambridge, UK: Cambridge University Press, 1996); Euan Cameron, *Waldenses* (New York: Wiley, 2000); Gabriel Audisio, *Preachers by Night* (Leiden: Brill, 2007). For the Waldensians, see also Reinarius Saccho, *Of the Sects of the Modern Heretics*, Fordham University, Medieval History, www.fordham.edu /Halsall/source/waldo2.asp.

47. Renan, *History of the Origins of Christianity*, chap. 26.

CHAPTER FIVE

1. Epiphanius, *The Panarion of Epiphanius of Salamis*, trans. Frank Williams, 2nd ed., rev. and expanded (Leiden: Brill, 2009).

2. Stephen J. Shoemaker, "Epiphanius of Salamis, the Kollyridians, and the Early Dormition Narratives," *Journal of Early Christian Studies* 16, no. 3 (2008): 371–401.

3. G. R. S. Mead, ed., *Pistis Sophia* (London: J. M. Watkins, 1921 [1896]); Carl Schmidt and Viola MacDermot, eds., *Pistis Sophia* (Leiden: Brill, 1978); Karen L. King, ed., *Images of the Feminine in Gnosticism* (Harrisburg, PA: Trinity Press International, 2000); Karen L. King, *The Gospel of Mary of Magdala* (Santa Rosa, CA: Polebridge Press, 2003).

4. For veneration of the Virgin in one region, see Andrew Breeze, *The Mary of the Celts* (Leominster, UK: Gracewing, 2008); Stephen J. Shoemaker, ed., *The Life of the Virgin by Maximus the Confessor* (New Haven, CT: Yale University Press, 2012).

5. Susan Haskins, *Mary Magdalen* (New York: Harcourt, Brace, 1993); Marvin Meyer with Esther A. de Boer, *The Gospels of Mary* (San Francisco: HarperCollins, 2004); Bart D. Ehrman, *Peter, Paul, and Mary Magdalene* (New York: Oxford University Press, 2006); Esther de Boer, *The Mary Magdalene Cover-Up* (London: T&T Clark, 2007); Robin Griffith-Jones, *Beloved Disciple* (New York: HarperOne, 2008).

6. Henri-Charles Puech, "Other Gnostic Gospels and Related Literature," in Wilhelm Schneemelcher, ed., *New Testament Apocrypha*, trans. R. McL. Wilson, rev. ed., 2 vols. (London: James Clarke, 1991–1992), 1:361–369, 390–396.

7. Karen L. King, "The Gospel of Mary," in Marvin Meyer and James M. Robinson, eds., *The Nag Hammadi Scriptures* (San Francisco: HarperOne, 2008), 755–770 (see also "Gospel of Mary of Magdela," Polebridge Press, www.maryofmagdala.com/GMary_Text/gmary_text.html); Hans-Martin Schenke, "The Gospel of Philip," in Schneemelcher, ed., *New Testament Apocrypha*, 1:179–208; Madeleine Scopello and Marvin W. Meyer, "The Gospel of Philip," in Marvin Meyer and James M. Robinson, eds., *The Nag Hammadi Scriptures* (San Francisco: HarperOne, 2008), 157–186; Deirdre Good, ed., *Mariam, the Magdalen, and the Mother* (Bloomington: Indiana University Press, 2005).

8. Birger Pearson, *Ancient Gnosticism* (Minneapolis: Fortress Press, 2007); Richard Bauckham, *Studies of the Named Women in the Gospels* (Grand Rapids, MI: Wm. B. Eerdmans, 2002).

9. Ariel Sabar, "The Inside Story of a Controversial New Text About Jesus," *Smithsonian*, September 18, 2012, www.smithsonianmag.com /history/the-inside-story-of-a-controversial-new-text-about-jesus -41078791/; Charlotte Allen, "Jesus's Ex-Wife," *Weekly Standard*, October 8, 2012. The idea of the "fall into patriarchy" is critiqued in Kathleen L. Corley, "Feminist Myths of Christian Origins," in Elizabeth A. Castelli and Hal Taussig, eds., *Reimagining Christian Origins* (Valley Forge, PA: Trinity Press International, 1996), 51–67.

10. William Granger Ryan, ed., *The Golden Legend*, 2 vols. (Princeton, NJ: Princeton University Press, 1993); 1:374–382; Helen M. Garth, *Saint Mary Magdalene in Mediaeval Literature* (Baltimore: Johns Hopkins University Press, 1950); Katherine Ludwig Jansen, *The Making of the Magdalen* (Princeton, NJ: Princeton University Press, 2000); Michelle A. Erhardt and Amy M. Morris, eds., *Mary Magdalene* (Leiden: Brill, 2012).

11. "The Life of S. Mary Magdalene," *Golden Legend*, Fordham University, Medieval History, www.fordham.edu/halsall/basis/golden legend/GoldenLegend-Volume4.asp; compare at Christian Classics Ethereal Library, www.ccel.org/ccel/voragine/goldleg4.xv.html.

12. Medieval European mystics also had a lively tradition of feminine imagery, which they applied to Jesus himself; see Caroline Walker Bynum, *Jesus as Mother* (Berkeley: University of California Press, 1982).

13. Marina Warner, *Alone of All Her Sex* (New York: Knopf, 1976); R. N. Swanson, *Religion and Devotion in Europe, c. 1215–c. 1515* (Cambridge, UK: Cambridge University Press, 1995); R. N. Swanson, ed., *The Church and Mary* (Woodbridge, UK: Boydell Press, 2004); Good, ed., *Mariam, the Magdalen*; Miri Rubin, *Mother of God* (New Haven, CT: Yale University Press, 2009).

14. Revelation 12.1–6.

15. Justin Martyr, *Dialogue with Trypho*, chap. 100, Christian Classics Ethereal Library, www.ccel.org/ccel/schaff/anf01.viii.iv.c.html; Averil Cameron, "The Cult of the Virgin in Late Antiquity," in Swanson, ed., *The Church and Mary*.

16. Irenaeus, "Against Heresies," 5.19, New Advent, www.newadvent.org/fathers/0103519.htm; John Flood, *Representations of Eve in Antiquity and the English Middle Ages* (New York: Routledge, 2011).

17. For the modern discovery of various supposedly "lost" gospels of Mary, see Forbes Robinson, ed., *Coptic Apocryphal Gospels* (Cambridge, UK: Cambridge University Press, 1896).

18. Mary Clayton, *The Cult of the Virgin Mary in Anglo-Saxon England* (New York: Cambridge University Press, 1990), 55–56; Brian K. Reynolds, *Gateway to Heaven* (Hyde Park, NY: New City Press, 2012).

19. Lily C. Vuong, *Gender and Purity in the Protevangelium of James* (Tübingen, Germany: Mohr Siebeck, 2013); Oscar Cullman, "Infancy Gospels," in Wilhelm Schneemelcher, ed., *New Testament Apocrypha*, trans. R. McL. Wilson, rev. ed., 2 vols. (London: James Clarke, 1991–1992), 1:414–469; J. K. Elliott, *The Apocryphal New Testament* (Oxford: Oxford University Press, 1993), 48–67; Stephen J. Shoemaker, "Between Scripture and Tradition," in Lorenzo DiTommaso and Lucian Turcesu, eds., *The Reception and Interpretation of the Bible in Late Antiquity* (Leiden: Brill, 2008), 491–510; Bart Ehrman and Zlatko Pleše, eds., *The Other Gospels* (New York: Oxford University Press, 2013), 18–36.

20. Henry Chadwick, ed., *Contra Celsum* (Cambridge, UK: Cambridge University Press, 1953).

21. Lily C. Vuong, *Gender and Purity in the Protevangelium of James* (Tübingen, Germany: Mohr Siebeck, 2013).

22. Quoted from the Protevangelium, in Elliott, *Apocryphal New Testament*, 58; E. A. Wallis Budge, *The History of the Blessed Virgin Mary and the History of the Likeness of Christ*, 2 vols. (London: Luzac, 1899).

23. "Nurtured" is from the Protevangelium, in Montague Rhodes James, *The Apocryphal New Testament* (Oxford: Clarendon Press, 1924), 45.

24. "I have sons" is from the Protevangelium, in James, *Apocryphal New Testament*, 42.

25. William L. Petersen, "John 8:11, the Protevangelium Iacobi, and the History of the *Pericope Adulterae*," in Jan Krans and Joseph Verheyden, eds., *Patristic and Text-Critical Studies* (Leiden: Brill, 2012). For the complex figure of Salome in early Christian literature, see Silke Petersen, *Zerstört die Werke der Weiblichkeit!* (Leiden: Brill, 1999).

26. Elliott, *Apocryphal New Testament*, 48; E. A. Wallis Budge, ed., *Legends of Our Lady Mary, the Perpetual Virgin and Her Mother Hanna* (London: Oxford University Press, 1933); Frederica Mathewes-Green, *The Lost Gospel of Mary* (Brewster, MA: Paraclete Press, 2007).

27. Elliott, *Apocryphal New Testament*, 84–99; J. K. Elliott, *A Synopsis of the Apocryphal Nativity and Infancy Narratives* (Leiden: Brill, 2006); Ehrman and Pleše, eds., *The Other Gospels*, 37–57.

28. Ryan, *Golden Legend*, 1:38, 2:149–158.

29. "A community of virgins" is from "The Gospel of Pseudo-Matthew," Internet Sacred Text Archive, www.sacred-texts.com/chr/ecf/008/0081182.htm.

30. Quoted from James, *Apocryphal New Testament*, 171–172.

31. Rubin, *Mother of God*.

32."Betook himself into the wilderness" is from James, *Apocryphal New Testament*, 39.

33. "Immaculate Conception," New Advent, www.newadvent.org/cathen/07674d.htm.

34. "Ineffabilis Deus," Papal Encyclicals Online, www.papalencyclicals.net/Pius09/p9ineff.htm.

35. Walter Burghardt, *The Testimony of the Patristic Age Concerning Mary's Death* (Westminster, MD: Newman Press, 1957), 6.

36. Philip Jenkins, *Jesus Wars* (San Francisco: HarperOne, 2010).

37. Stephen J. Shoemaker, *Ancient Traditions of the Virgin Mary's Dormition and Assumption* (Oxford: Oxford University Press, 2002). Shoemaker has compiled several key texts at University of Oregon, "Early Traditions of the Virgin Mary's Dormition (*Dormitio Mariae*)," http://pages.uoregon.edu/sshoemak/texts/dormindex.htm.

38. Shoemaker, *Ancient Traditions*; Stephen J. Shoemaker, "Apocrypha and Liturgy in the Fourth Century," in James H. Charlesworth and Lee M. McDonald, eds., *Jewish and Christian Scriptures* (London: T&T Clark, 2010), 153–163.

39. W. Wright, "The Departure of My Lady Mary from this World," *Journal of Sacred Literature and Biblical Record* 7 (1865), 129–160.

40. "The apostles carried the couch" is from "The Account of St. John the Theologian of the Falling Asleep of the Holy Mother of God," New Advent, www.newadvent.org/fathers/0832.htm; compare Stephen J. Shoemaker, University of Oregon, Early Traditions of the Virgin Mary's Dormition, "(Ps.-) John the Theologian, *The Dormition of the Holy Theotokos*," http://pages.uoregon.edu/sshoemak/texts/dormitionG2/dormitionG2.htm. Simon Claude Mimouni, *Les traditions anciennes sur la Dormition et l'Assomption de Marie* (Leiden: Brill, 2011).

41. Stephen J. Shoemaker, University of Oregon, Early Traditions of the Virgin Mary's Dormition, "(Ps.-) Melito of Sardis, *The Passing of Blessed Mary*," http://pages.uoregon.edu/sshoemak/texts/dormitionL/dormitionL1.htm.

42. "And when they had sat down in a circle consoling her" is from ibid.

43. "And when the Lord had thus spoken" is from ibid.

44. Ibid. The story also appears in the *Golden Legend*, for which see Ryan, ed., *Golden Legend*, 2:77–97.

45. "And He ordered the archangel Michael" is from Shoemaker, "(Ps.-) Melito of Sardis."

46. The Assumption is described at great length in Ryan, ed., *Golden Legend*, 2:77–97; the girdle story occurs at p. 82. The story of Thomas at Mary's death also features in one of the York Mystery Plays, *The Assumption of the Virgin (Thomas Apostolus)*, University of Rochester, Middle English Texts Series, http://d.lib.rochester.edu/teams/text /davidson-play-45-the-assumption-of-the-virgin-thomas-apostolus. Elliott, *Apocryphal New Testament*, 691–723.

47. Qur'an 5.116.

48. Gelasian Decree, from Schneemelcher, ed., *New Testament Apocrypha*, 1:38–40.

49. Bede is quoted from Clayton, *Cult of the Virgin Mary*, 16n; see 20n for Ambrosius Autpertus, 246n for Aelfric.

50. Gregory of Tours is quoted from Rod Bennett, *Four Witnesses* (San Francisco: Ignatius Press, 2002), 334–335. Mimouni, *Les traditions anciennes sur la Dormition*; "The Feast of the Assumption," New Advent, www.newadvent.org/cathen/02006b.htm. For John of Damascus, see "The Feast of the Assumption," New Advent, www .newadvent.org/cathen/02006b.htm.

51. Henry Mayr-Harting, "The Idea of the Assumption of Mary in the West, 800–1200," in R. N. Swanson, ed., *The Church and Mary* (Woodbridge, UK: Boydell Press, 2004); Mimouni, *Les traditions anciennes sur la Dormition*; Forbes Robinson, ed., *Coptic Apocryphal Gospels* (Cambridge, UK: Cambridge University Press, 1896). For visual art, see Philip Jenkins, "The Child Mary," September 1, 2013, www .patheos.com/blogs/anxiousbench/2013/09/the-child-mary/.

52. Mimouni, *Les traditions anciennes sur la Dormition*; "The Feast of the Assumption," New Advent, www.newadvent.org/cathen/02006b .htm. For the 1950 statement, see Pope Pius XII, Munificentissimus Deus, November 1, 1950, http://w2.vatican.va/content/pius-xii/en/apost _constitutions/documents/hf_p-xii_apc_19501101_munificentissimus -deus.html.

53. Wright, "Departure of My Lady Mary," 152–153.

54. "Devotion to the Blessed Virgin Mary," New Advent, www .newadvent.org/cathen/15459a.htm; "Feast of the Presentation of the Blessed Virgin Mary," New Advent, www.newadvent.org

/cathen/12400a.htm; "Feast of the Nativity of the Blessed Virgin Mary," New Advent, www.newadvent.org/cathen/10712b.htm; Clayton, *Cult of the Virgin Mary*, 25–51.

55. *Golden Legend*, vol. 4, Christian Classics Ethereal Library, www.ccel.org/ccel/voragine/goldleg4.xxxviii.html.

56. Clifford Davidson, ed., *The York Corpus Christi Plays* (Kalamazoo, MI: Medieval Institute Publications, 2011), 371; also available at University of Rochester, Camelot Project, www.lib.rochester.edu/camelot/teams//dcyp45f.htm. This chant is adapted from the Song of Solomon 4.8.

57. Davidson, ed., *York Corpus Christi Plays*.

58. "The Cherry-Tree Carol," Internet Sacred Text Archive, www.sacred-texts.com/neu/eng/child/ch054.htm.

59. "It would be difficult to find any image of the Virgin which has not been affected by the iconic version of the Protevangelium and its sister documents," according to David R. Cartlidge and J. Keith Elliott, *Art and the Christian Apocrypha* (London: Routledge, 2001), 41.

60. Cartlidge and Elliott, *Art and the Christian Apocrypha*.

61. Ibid., 78–88.

62. Ibid.; Jacqueline Lafontaine-Dosogne, *Iconographie de l'enfance de la Vierge dans l'Empire byzantin et en Occident* (Brussels: Academie royale de Belgique, 1992).

63. Giuseppe Basile, ed., *Giotto* (London: Thames & Hudson, 2002). For the extensive use of apocryphal themes in popular visual culture, including prints, see William Hone, Jeremiah Jones, and William Wake, eds., *The Lost Books of the Bible* (New York: World, 1926).

64. Sarah Brown, "Repackaging the Past," in Virginia Chieffo Raguin, ed., *Art, Piety and Destruction in the Christian West, 1500–1700* (Farnham, UK: Ashgate, 2010); Gary Waller, *The Virgin Mary in Late Medieval and Early Modern English Literature and Popular Culture* (Cambridge, UK: Cambridge University Press, 2011).

65. For the Purification of Mary in the *Golden Legend*, see Ryan, ed., *Golden Legend*, 1:143. See 2:149 for the Virgin's birth, and 2:77–97 for the Assumption. Eamon Duffy, *The Stripping of the Altars*, rev. ed. (New Haven, CT: Yale University Press, 2005).

Chapter Six

1. Testament of Levi, The Tertullian Project, www.tertullian.org/fathers2/ANF-08/anf08-07.htm; H. C. Kee, "Testaments of the Twelve Patriarchs," in James H. Charlesworth, ed., *The Old Testament*

Pseudepigrapha, 2 vols. (Garden City, NY: Doubleday, 1983–1985), 1:775–828; James L. Kugel, "Testaments of the Twelve Patriarchs," in Louis H. Feldman, James L. Kugel, and Lawrence H. Schiffman, eds., *Outside the Bible* (Philadelphia: Jewish Publication Society, 2013), 2:1697–1856; Annette Yoshiko Reed, "The Modern Invention of Old Testament Pseudepigrapha," *Journal of Theological Studies* 60 (2009): 403–436.

2. M. De Jonge, ed., *Outside the Old Testament* (New York: Cambridge University Press, 1985); James R. Davila, *The Provenance of the Pseudepigrapha* (Leiden: Brill, 2005).

3. Edward Earle Ellis, *The Old Testament in Early Christianity* (Tübingen, Germany: Mohr Siebeck, 1991).

4. M. De Jonge, *Pseudepigrapha of the Old Testament as Part of Christian Literature* (Leiden: Brill, 2003); Alexander Toepel, "The Cave of Treasures," in Richard Bauckham, James R. Davila, and Alex Panayotov, eds., *Old Testament Pseudepigrapha: More Noncanonical Scriptures*, 2 vols. (Grand Rapids, MI: Wm. B. Eerdmans, 2013–?), 1:531–584.

5. Louis H. Feldman, James L. Kugel, and Lawrence H. Schiffman, *Outside the Bible*, 3 vols. (Philadelphia: Jewish Publication Society 2013).

6. William L. Petersen, *Tatian's Diatessaron* (Leiden: Brill, 1994), 409–411.

7. Richard N. Longenecker, *Biblical Exegesis in the Apostolic Period* (Grand Rapids, MI: Wm. B. Eerdmans, 1999); Emmanouela Grypeou and Helen Spurling, *The Book of Genesis in Late Antiquity* (Leiden: Brill, 2013).

8. Psalm 96.10 (KJV); Quentin F. Wesselschmidt and Thomas C. Oden, eds., *Psalms 51–150* (Downer's Grove, IL: InterVarsity Press, 2007), 195. For the Enochic context, see Margaret Barker, *Great High Priest* (London: A&C Black, 2003), 243–246.

9. A. F. J. Klijn and G. J. Reinink, eds., *Patristic Evidence for Jewish-Christian Sects* (Leiden: Brill, 1973), 216.

10. 2 Esdras 14.45; P. R. Ackroyd and C. F. Evans, eds., *The Cambridge History of the Bible*, vol. 1 (Cambridge, UK: Cambridge University Press, 1970); James L. Kugel, *Traditions of the Bible* (Cambridge, MA: Harvard University Press, 1998).

11. Armin Daniel Baum, *Pseudepigraphie und literarische Fälschung im frühen Christentum* (Tübingen, Germany: Mohr-Paul Siebeck, 2001); Bart Ehrman, *Forgery and Counter-Forgery* (New York: Oxford University Press, 2013). I am speaking here of modern usage. In

antiquity, the term "pseudepigrapha" did have a negative sense, and such works were contrasted with the "true" gospels; see Simon Gathercole, "Named Testimonia to the *Gospel of Thomas*," *Harvard Theological Review* 105 (2012): 58.

12. James H. Charlesworth, ed., *The Old Testament Pseudepigrapha*, 2 vols. (Garden City, NY: Doubleday, 1983–1985); Richard Bauckham, James R. Davila, and Alex Panayotov, eds., *Old Testament Pseudepigrapha: More Noncanonical Scriptures*, 2 vols. (Grand Rapids, MI: Wm. B. Eerdmans, 2013–?). For earlier collections of these documents, see E. A. Wallis Budge, *The Book of the Bee* (Oxford: Clarendon Press, 1886); R. H. Charles, *The Apocrypha and Pseudepigrapha of the Old Testament* (Oxford: Clarendon Press, 1913); M. R. James: *The Lost Apocrypha of the Old Testament* (London: Society for Promoting Christian Knowledge, 1920); E. A. Wallis Budge, ed., *The Book of the Cave of Treasures* (London: Religious Tract Society, 1927). For the impact of this literature, see James H. Charlesworth, *The Old Testament Pseudepigrapha and the New Testament* (Cambridge, UK: Cambridge University Press, 1985); Robert Kraft, "The Pseudepigrapha in Christianity," in John C. Reeves, ed., *Tracing the Threads* (Atlanta: Society of Biblical Literature, 1994), 55–86; Gerbern S. Oegema and James H. Charlesworth, eds., *The Pseudepigrapha and Christian Origins* (New York: T&T Clark, 2008).

13. Annette Yoshiko Reed, "Apocrypha, 'Outside Books,' and Pseudepigrapha: Ancient Categories and Modern Perceptions of Parabiblical Literature," Handout from 40th Philadelphia Seminar on Christian Origins: Parabiblical Literature, October 10, 2002, http://ccat.sas.upenn.edu/psco/year40/areed2.html.

14. For the Jewish context, see Alan Segal, *Two Powers in Heaven* (Leiden: Brill, 1977); Jaan Lahe, *Gnosis und Judentum* (Leiden: Brill, 2012).

15. Birger A. Pearson and Soren Giversen, "Melchizedek," in James M. Robinson, ed., *The Nag Hammadi Library in English*, 4th rev. ed. (Leiden: Brill, 1996), 438–444. In Marvin Meyer and James M. Robinson, eds., *The Nag Hammadi Scriptures* (San Francisco: HarperOne, 2008), see Madeleine Scopello and Marvin W. Meyer, "The Revelation of Adam," 343–356; Marvin Meyer, "The Second Discourse of Great Seth," 473–486; John D. Turner, "The Three Steles of Seth," 523–536; and John D. Turner, "The Sethian School of Gnostic Thought," 784–789. Esther Quinn, *The Quest of Seth for the Oil of Life* (Chicago: University of Chicago Press, 1973); A. F. J. Klijn, *Seth in*

Jewish, Christian and Gnostic Literature (Leiden: Brill, 1977); Alexander Toepel, "The Apocryphon of Seth," in Bauckham et al., eds., *Old Testament Pseudepigrapha*, 1:33–39; Dylan M. Burns, *Apocalypse of the Alien God* (Philadelphia: University of Pennsylvania Press, 2014).

16. James H. Charlesworth, ed., *The Odes of Solomon* (Oxford: Clarendon, 1973); James H. Charlesworth, "Odes of Solomon," in Charlesworth, ed., *Old Testament Pseudepigrapha*, 2:725–774.

17. Yoshiko Reed, "Modern Invention of Old Testament Pseudepigrapha." For the rediscovery of these texts, see Bauckham et al., eds., *Old Testament Pseudepigrapha*, 1:xvii–xxxviii.

18. Wilhelm Schneemelcher, ed., *New Testament Apocrypha*, trans. R. McL. Wilson, rev. ed., 2 vols. (London: James Clarke, 1991–1992), 1:41–42.

19. Lorenzo DiTommaso and Christfried Böttrich, eds., *The Old Testament Apocrypha in the Slavonic Tradition* (Tübingen, Germany: Mohr Siebeck, 2011).

20. Otto Wahl, ed., *Apocalypsis Esdrae; Apocalypsis Sedrach; Visio Beati Esdrae* (Leiden: Brill, 1977); Bruce M. Metzger, "The Fourth Book of Ezra," in Charlesworth, ed., *Old Testament Pseudepigrapha*, 1:517–560; Michael E. Stone, "Greek Apocalypse of Ezra," in ibid., 1:561–580; Michael E. Stone, "Questions of Ezra," ibid, 1:591–600.

21. The Book of 2 Esdras as we have it today includes several components that were once separate. Alastair Hamilton, *The Apocryphal Apocalypse* (New York: Oxford University Press, 1999); Gabriele Boccaccini and Jason M. Zurawski, *Interpreting 4 Ezra and 2 Baruch* (London: T&T Clark, 2014). For 5 and 6 Ezra, see Theodore A. Bergren, "Fifth Ezra" and "Sixth Ezra," in Bauckham et al., eds., *Old Testament Pseudepigrapha*, 1:467–482, 483–497; Hugo Duensing and Aurelio de Santos Otero, "The Fifth and Sixth Books of Ezra," in Schneemelcher, ed., *New Testament Apocrypha*, 2:641–652; Richard Bauckham, "The Latin Vision of Ezra," in Bauckham et al., eds., *Old Testament Pseudepigrapha*, 1:498–528.

22. Hamilton, *Apocryphal Apocalypse*.

23. Philip Jenkins, *The Lost History of Christianity* (San Francisco: HarperOne, 2008); M. Debié, A. Desreumaux, C. Jullien, and F. Jullien, eds., *Les apocryphes syriaques* (Paris: Geuthner, 2005).

24. "The Odes of Solomon," The Gnosis Archive, http://gnosis.org/library/odes.htm; Charlesworth, "Odes of Solomon," 725–734.

25. Kenneth R. Jones, *Jewish Reactions to the Destruction of Jerusalem in A.D. 70* (Leiden: Brill, 2011); Matthias Henze, *Jewish*

Apocalypticism in Late First Century Israel (Tübingen, Germany: Mohr Siebeck, 2011); Gerbern S. Oegema, *Apocalyptic Interpretation of the Bible* (London: T&T Clark, 2012); Michael E. Stone and Matthias Henze, *4 Ezra and 2 Baruch* (Minneapolis: Fortress, 2013); Matthias Henze, Gabriele Boccaccini, and Jason M. Zurawski, eds., *Fourth Ezra and Second Baruch* (Leiden: Brill, 2013). For Baruch's links with the *Visio Pauli*, see Philip Jenkins, "Papias and the Miraculous Vines," September 9, 2013, www.patheos.com/blogs/anxiousbench/2013/09 /papias-and-the-ten-thousand-branches/.

26. David Bundy, "Pseudepigrapha in Syriac Literature," SBL Seminar Papers (Atlanta: Scholars Press, 1991), 745–765; Liv Ingeborg Lied, "The Reception of the Pseudepigrapha in Syriac Traditions," in Lee M. McDonald and James H. Charlesworth, eds., *Jewish and Christian Scriptures* (London: T&T Clark, 2010), 52–60.

27. O. S. Wintermute, "Jubilees," in Charlesworth, ed., *Old Testament Pseudepigrapha*, 2:35–142; Michael Segal, *The Book of Jubilees* (Leiden: Brill, 2007); Gabriele Boccaccini and Giovanni Ibba, eds., *Enoch and the Mosaic Torah* (Grand Rapids, MI: Wm. B. Eerdmans, 2009); James L. Kugel, "Jubilees," in Louis H. Feldman, James L. Kugel, and Lawrence H. Schiffman, eds., *Outside the Bible* (Philadelphia: Jewish Publication Society, 2013), 1:272–466; Lied, "Reception of the Pseudepigrapha."

28. Genesis 5.22–29; James C. VanderKam, *Enoch: A Man for All Generations* (Columbia: University of South Carolina Press, 1995).

29. F. I. Anderson, "2 (Slavonic Apocalypse of) Enoch," in James H. Charlesworth, ed., *Old Testament Pseudepigrapha*, 2 vols. (Garden City, NY: Doubleday, 1983–1985), 1:91–221; Gabriele Boccaccini, ed., *Enoch and Qumran Origins* (Grand Rapids, MI: Wm. B. Eerdmans, 2005); Gabriele Boccaccini and John J. Collins, eds., *The Early Enoch Literature* (Leiden: Brill, 2007); Gabriele Boccaccini and Giovanni Ibba, eds., *Enoch and the Mosaic Torah* (Grand Rapids, MI: Wm. B. Eerdmans, 2009); Michael A. Knibb, *Essays on the Book of Enoch and Other Early Jewish Texts and Traditions* (Leiden: Brill, 2009); Andrei A. Orlov and Gabriele Boccaccini, eds., *New Perspectives on 2 Enoch* (Leiden: Brill, 2012).

30. Annette Yoshiko Reed, *Fallen Angels and the History of Judaism and Christianity* (Cambridge, UK: Cambridge University Press, 2005).

31. For Tertullian, see James D. G. Dunn, ed., *Jews and Christians* (Grand Rapids, MI: Wm. B. Eerdmans, 1992), 81; Charlesworth,

The Old Testament Pseudepigrapha and the New Testament; David A. DeSilva, *The Jewish Teachers of Jesus, James, and Jude* (New York: Oxford University Press, 2012).

32. David Brakke, *Athanasius and the Politics of Asceticism* (Oxford: Clarendon, 1995), 326–332. For Augustine, see Christian Classics Ethereal Library, www.ccel.org/ccel/schaff/npnf102.iv.XV.23.html.

33. Robert Henry Charles, *The Ethiopic Version of the Book of Enoch* (Oxford: Clarendon, 1906).

34. R. E. Kaske, "Beowulf and the Book of Enoch," *Speculum* 46, no. 3 (1971): 421–431.

35. Still much debated, for instance, is the so-called testimony of the historian Josephus to Christ's divine status; see "Josephus and Jesus: The Testimonium Flavianum Question," Early Christian Writings, www.earlychristianwritings.com/testimonium.html.

36. Paul J. Alexander, ed., *The Byzantine Apocalyptic Tradition* (Berkeley: University of California Press, 1985); Andrew Palmer, ed., *The Seventh Century in the West-Syrian Chronicles* (Liverpool: Liverpool University Press, 1993); W. J. van Bekkum, Jan Willem Drijvers, and Alexander Cornelis Klugkist, eds., *Syriac Polemics* (Leuven, Belgium: Peeters, 2007); Sidney H. Griffith, *The Church in the Shadow of the Mosque* (Princeton, NJ: Princeton University Press, 2008); Benjamin Garstad, ed., *Apocalypse—Pseudo-Methodius* (Cambridge, MA: Harvard University Press, 2012); Michael Philip Penn, "God's War and His Warriors," in Sohail H. Hashmi, ed., *Just Wars, Holy Wars, and Jihads* (New York: Oxford University Press, 2012), 75–78.

37. For newer works attributed to Ezra and Enoch, see Robert A Kraft, *Exploring the Scripturesque* (Leiden: Brill, 2009), 129–172; John C. Reeves, *Trajectories in Near Eastern Apocalyptic* (Leiden: Brill, 2006); Griffith, *The Church in the Shadow of the Mosque*. For Daniel, see G. T. Zervos, "Apocalypse of Daniel," in Charlesworth, ed., *Old Testament Pseudepigrapha*, 1:755–756; Matthias Henze, *The Syriac Apocalypse of Daniel* (Tübingen, Germany: Mohr Siebeck, 2001); Lorenzo DiTommaso, *The Book of Daniel and the Apocryphal Daniel Literature* (Leiden: Brill, 2005). For a fifth-century text, see Sergio LaPorta, "The Seventh Vision of Daniel," in Bauckham et al., eds., *Old Testament Pseudepigrapha*, 1:410–434.

38. John J. Collins, "Sibylline Oracles," in Charlesworth, ed., *Old Testament Pseudepigrapha*, 1:317–472; Ursula Treu, "Christian Sibyllines," in Schneemelcher, ed., *New Testament Apocrypha*, 2:652–684;

Rieuwerd Buitenwerf, "The Tiburtine Sibyl," in Bauckham et al., eds., *Old Testament Pseudepigrapha*, 1:176–188.

39. John J. Collins, *Seers, Sybils and Sages in Hellenistic-Roman Judaism* (Leiden: Brill, 1997); Kenneth R. Jones, *Jewish Reactions to the Destruction of Jerusalem in A.D. 70* (Leiden: Brill, 2011).

40. "Sibylline Oracles," Internet Sacred Text Archive, www.sacred-texts.com/chr/ecf/102/1020541.htm; Aloisius Rzach, *The Sibylline Oracles* (New York: Eaton and Mains, 1899), 275; Patrizia Lendinara, "The Versus Sibyllae de die iudicii in Anglo-Saxon England," in Kathryn Powell and Donald Scragg, eds., *Apocryphal Texts and Traditions in Anglo-Saxon England* (Cambridge, UK: D. S. Brewer, 2003).

41. Milton S Terry, *The Sibylline Oracles* (New York: Eaton and Mains, 1899), Early Christian Writings, www.earlychristianwritings.com/sibylline.html; "Sibylline Oracles" Early Christian Writings, www.earlychristianwritings.com/info/sibylline-cathen.html; Bernard McGinn, *Visions of the End* (New York: Columbia University Press, 1998).

42. Judith E. Kalb, *Russia's Rome* (Madison: University of Wisconsin Press, 2010); Michael Pesenson, "The Sibylline Tradition in Medieval and Early Modern Slavic Culture," in Lorenzo DiTommaso and Christfried Böttrich, eds., *The Old Testament Apocrypha in the Slavonic Tradition* (Tübingen, Germany: Mohr Siebeck, 2011), 353–356.

43. Andrew Graham-Dixon, *Michelangelo and the Sistine Chapel* (New York: Skyhorse, 2009).

44. Lutz Röhrich, *Adam und Eva* (Stuttgart: Verlag Muller und Schindler , 1968); Debié et al., eds., *Les apocryphes syriaques*, 22; Brian Murdoch, *The Apocryphal Adam and Eve in Medieval Europe* (Oxford: Oxford University Press, 2009); Orlov and Boccaccini, eds., *New Perspectives on 2 Enoch*.

45. I make great use here of the work of polymath scholar Michael E. Stone. Michael E. Stone, *A History of the Literature of Adam and Eve* (Atlanta: Scholars Press, 1992); Michael E. Stone, *Apocryphal Adam Books* (Leiden: Brill, 1996); Gary A. Anderson, Michael Stone, and Johannes Tromp, *Literature on Adam and Eve* (Leiden: Brill, 2000); Gary A. Anderson and Michael E. Stone, *A Synopsis of the Books of Adam and Eve*, 2nd rev. ed. (Atlanta: Society of Biblical Literature, 2001); Michael E. Stone, *Adam and Eve in the Armenian Traditions* (Atlanta: Society of Biblical Literature, 2013). See also Johannes Bartholdy Glenthøj, *Cain and Abel in Syriac and Greek Writers*

(Leuven, Belgium: Peeters, 1997); James L. Kugel, *Traditions of the Bible* (Cambridge, MA: Harvard University Press, 1998); Gerard P. Luitikhuizen, ed., *Eve's Children* (Leiden: Brill, 2003); Charlesworth, ed., *Old Testament Pseudepigrapha*, vol. 1, contains G. MacRae, "Apocalypse of Adam" (707–720) and S. E. Robinson, "Testament of Adam" (989–995). Volume 2 includes M. D. Johnson, "Life of Adam and Eve" (249–296).

46. Robinson, "Testament of Adam," 994.

47. "And God said that He should go about" is from Testamentum Adami, Internet Sacred Text Archive, www.sacred-texts.com/chr/bct /bct10.htm. "Do not fear." is from Robinson, "Testament of Adam," 994.

48. "Conflict of Adam and Eve," Internet Sacred Text Archive, www.sacred-texts.com/bib/fbe/fbe005.htm.

49. Toepel, "Cave of Treasures"; Budge, ed., *Book of the Cave of Treasures*. Besides the 1927 version published by the Religious Tract Society in London, the book can be found online at Internet Sacred Text Archive, www.sacred-texts.com/chr/bct/.

50. Budge, *Book of the Cave of Treasures*, 37, 62–63; Serge Ruzer and Aryeh Kofsky, *Syriac Idiosyncrasies* (Leiden: Brill, 2010), 87–120.

51. Budge, *Book of the Cave of Treasures*, 126–127.

52. Genesis 14.18–20; Psalms 110.4; Hebrews 7.4. For Melchizedek in the Islamic tradition, see Philip Jenkins, "The Green Man and the King of Salem," October 7, 2013, www.patheos.com/blogs/anx iousbench/2013/10/the-green-man/. Pierluigi Piovanelli, "The Story of Melchizedek," in Bauckham et al., eds., *Old Testament Pseudepigrapha*, 1:64–84.

53. Budge, *Book of the Cave of Treasures*, 224–225.

54. Ibid., 222–224.

55. Brent Landau, *Revelation of the Magi* (San Francisco: HarperCollins, 2010).

56. Robinson, "Testament of Adam" 994; S. C. Malan, ed., *The Book of Adam and Eve Also Called the Conflict of Adam and Eve with Satan* (London: G. Norman, 1882), Internet Archive, https://archive .org/stream/bookofadamandeve00malauoft/bookofadamandeve 00malauoft_djvu.txt. For the influence of these stories in the wider Christian world, see, for instance, Witold Witakowski, "The Magi in Ethiopic Tradition," *Aethiopica* 2 (1999): 69–89.

57. Michael E. Stone, *Adam's Contract with Satan* (Bloomington: Indiana University Press, 2002).

58. E. A. Wallis Budge, *The Book of the Bee* (Oxford: Clarendon Press, 1886), available at Internet Sacred Text Archive, www.sacred-texts.com/chr/bb/bbpref.htm.

59. Ibid., 50.

60. Ibid., 94–95.

61. Abraham Terian, ed., *The Armenian Gospel of the Infancy* (New York: Oxford University Press, 2008), 44–47.

62. J. K. Elliott, *The Apocryphal New Testament* (Oxford: Oxford University Press, 1993), 192.

63. Richard Morris, ed., *Legends of the Holy Rood* (London: Early English Text Society / N. Trübner, 1871). The poem is the "Dispute Between Mary and the Cross." William Granger Ryan, ed., *The Golden Legend*, 2 vols. (Princeton, NJ: Princeton University Press, 1993), 1:277.

64. Barbara Baert, *A Heritage of Holy Wood* (Leiden: Brill, 2004), 289–349.

65. Fergus Kelly and Brian Murdoch, *The Irish Adam and Eve Story from Saltair na Rann*, 2 vols. (Dublin: Institute for Advanced Studies, 1976); Brian Murdoch, *The Apocryphal Adam and Eve in Medieval Europe* (Oxford: Oxford University Press, 2009); Stone, *History of the Literature of Adam and Eve*, 20–22.

CHAPTER SEVEN

1. Throughout this chapter I will be drawing on Jeffrey B. Russell, ed., *Religious Dissent in the Middle Ages* (New York: Wiley, 1971); Malcolm Lambert, *Medieval Heresy* (Oxford: Blackwell, 2002 [1976]); Sean Martin, *The Cathars* (London: Pocket Essentials, 2004); Malcolm Barber, *The Cathars* (New York: Longman, 2000); Stephen O'Shea, *The Perfect Heresy* (London: Profile Books, 2001); Michael Frassetto, ed., *Heresy and the Persecuting Society in the Middle Ages* (Leiden: Brill, 2006); Michael Frassetto, *The Great Medieval Heretics* (New York: BlueBridge, 2008); Jennifer Kolpacoff Deane, *A History of Medieval Heresy and Inquisition* (Lanham, MD: Rowman and Littlefield, 2011).

2. "Cathar Gospel," Fordham University, Medieval History, www.fordham.edu/halsall/source/cathar-gospel.asp.

3. Edina Bozóky, *Interrogatio Iohannis* (Paris: Editions Beauchesne, 1980); Bernard Hamilton, "Wisdom from the East," in Peter Biller and Anne Hudson, *Heresy and Literacy, 1000–1530* (Cambridge, UK: Cambridge University Press, 1996), 38–60; Bernard Hamilton,

"Bogomil Influences on Western Heresy," in Frassetto, ed., *Heresy and the Persecuting Society*, 93–111.

4. Barber, *The Cathars*.

5. For the Inquisition, see Bernard Gui, *The Inquisitor's Guide*, ed. Janet Shirley (Welwyn Garden City, UK: Ravenhall Books, 2006). For the long historical continuities of Gnosticism and Dualism, see Richard Smoley, *Forbidden Faith* (San Francisco: HarperOne, 2006).

6. Walter L. Wakefield and Austin P. Evans, *Heresies of the High Middle Ages* (New York: Columbia University Press, 1969); Hamilton, "Wisdom from the East"; Janet Hamilton and Bernard Hamilton, eds., with Yuri Stoyanov, *Christian Dualist Heresies in the Byzantine World, c. 650–c. 1450* (Manchester, UK: Manchester University Press, 1998); Yuri Stoyanov, *The Other God* (New Haven, CT: Yale Nota Bene, 2000).

7. Hamilton, "Wisdom from the East," 42–43; Walter Simons, *Cities of Ladies* (Philadelphia: University of Pennsylvania Press, 2001), 16–18.

8. For the Paulicians, see Hamilton and Hamilton, eds., *Christian Dualist Heresies*, 1–92. For the transformation of Paulicianism into Bogomilism, see Lambert, *Medieval Heresy*, 10–16. Frederick C. Conybeare, *The Key of Truth* (Oxford: Clarendon Press, 1898), was presented as "A Manual of the Paulician Church of Armenia," but that attribution is controversial. Dimitri Obolensky, *The Bogomils* (Cambridge, UK: Cambridge University Press, 1948); Nina G. Garsoïan, *The Paulician Heresy* (Paris: Mouton, 1967); Émile Turdeanu, *Apocryphes Slaves et Roumains de l'Ancien Testament* (Leiden: Brill, 1981); Stoyanov, *The Other God*; Frassetto, *Great Medieval Heretics*.

9. Hamilton and Hamilton, eds., *Christian Dualist Heresies*, 114–134.

10. Émile Turdeanu, "Apocryphes bogomiles et apocryphes pseudo -bogomiles," *Revue de l'histoire des religions* 138 (1950): 38–42; Andrei Orlov, *Selected Studies in the Slavonic Pseudepigrapha* (Leiden: Brill, 2009), 133–164.

11. For the Synodikon, see Kiril Petkov, *The Voices of Medieval Bulgaria* (Leiden: Brill, 2008), 249–254.

12. "And how can they call themselves Christians" is quoted from "The Presbyter Cosmas's Sermon Regarding the Newly-Appeared Bogomil Heresy," www.bogomilism.eu/Other%20authors/Cosma .html; "called our sacred churches" is quoted from Anna Comnena, *The Alexiad*, from Fordham University, Medieval History, www.ford ham.edu/halsall/source/comnena-bogomils.asp.

13. Hamilton, "Wisdom from the East," 38–60. Heretical expansion in the West is the theme of several important essays in Michael Frassetto, ed., *Heresy and the Persecuting Society in the Middle Ages*; see, for example, Daniel F. Callahan, "Ademar of Chabannes and the Bogomils." Claire Taylor, *Heresy in Medieval France* (Woodbridge, UK: Royal Historical Society / Boydell Press, 2005).

14. Wakefield and Evans, *Heresies of the High Middle Ages*, 168–170.

15. Raynaldus, "On the Accusations Against the Albigensians," in S. R. Maitland, ed., *History of the Albigenses and Waldenses* (London: C. J. G. and F. Rivington, 1832), 392–394.

16. Lambert, *Medieval Heresy*; Janet Shirley, ed., *The Song of the Cathar Wars* (Aldershot, UK: Ashgate, 2000); Mark G. Pegg, *The Corruption of Angels* (Princeton, NJ: Princeton University Press, 2005); Mark G. Pegg, *A Most Holy War* (New York: Oxford University Press, 2008); L. J. Sackville, *Heresy and Heretics in the Thirteenth Century* (Woodbridge, UK: Boydell and Brewer, 2011); Peter Biller, *Inquisitors and Heretics in Thirteenth-Century Languedoc* (Leiden: Brill, 2011); Catherine Léglu, Rebecca Rist, and Claire Taylor, eds., *The Cathars and the Albigensian Crusade* (London: Routledge, 2014). "Cathar Heresy" was the subject of a special issue of the *Journal of Religious History*; see vol. 35, no. 4 (2011): 469–626.

17. Sir Steven Runciman, *The Medieval Manichee* (Cambridge, UK: Cambridge University Press, 1947); Stoyanov, *The Other God*; Obolensky, *The Bogomils*, bore the subtitle *A Study in Balkan Neo-Manichaeism*. For a contemporary Inquisitorial account of Dualist views, see "Raynaldus: On the Accusations Against the Albigensians," Fordham University, Medieval History, www.fordham.edu/Halsall /source/heresy1.asp.

18. The most influential scholars in this critical school are R. I. Moore and Mark Gregory Pegg. R. I. Moore's books include *The Birth of Popular Heresy* (New York: St. Martin's Press, 1975); *The Origins of European Dissent* (New York: St. Martin's Press, 1977); *The Formation of a Persecuting Society* (New York: Blackwell, 1987); and *The War on Heresy* (London: Profile Books, 2012). Gregory Pegg's include *The Corruption of Angels* and *A Most Holy War*, both cited above. Compare Monique Zerner, ed., *L'histoire du catharisme en discussion* (Nice, France: Centre d'Études Medievales, Université de Nice Sophia-Antipolis, 2001).

19. Compare Jochen Burgtorf, Paul Crawford, and Helen Nicholson, *The Debate on the Trial of the Templars, 1307–1314* (Farnham,

UK: Ashgate, 2010). Undoubtedly, some non-Dualist dissidents did get caught up in the church's movement to suppress the Albigensians. See, for instance, Louisa A. Burnham, *So Great a Light, So Great a Smoke* (Ithaca, NY: Cornell University Press, 2008).

20. Even when the views fall short of true Dualism, the rejection of the Old Testament is explicit, for instance, in the debates at the Council of Lombers in 1165: Edward Peters, ed., *Heresy and Authority in Medieval Europe* (Philadelphia: University of Pennsylvania Press, 1980), 117–121; Lambert, *Medieval Heresy*, 29. An extensive collection of Catharist literature can be found in Wakefield and Evans, *Heresies of the High Middle Ages*, 447–630.

21. For *affitilhas*, see Emmanuel LeRoy Ladurie, *Montaillou* (New York: G. Braziller, 1978); René Weis, *The Yellow Cross* (New York: Knopf, 2001); Wakefield and Evans, *Heresies of the High Middle Ages*. For visions of the fall, see Lambert, *Medieval Heresy*, 133–137.

22. Richard Smoley, *Forbidden Faith* (San Francisco: Harper, 2006).

23. Gary K. Waite, *Eradicating the Devil's Minions* (Toronto: University of Toronto Press, 2007); Kathrin Utz Tremp, *Von der Häresie zur Hexerei* (Hannover: Hahnsche Buchhandlung, 2008). For Catharism as an authentic church, see Caterina Bruschi, *The Wandering Heretics of Languedoc* (Cambridge, UK: Cambridge University Press, 2009).

24. Irenaeus, "Against Heresies," New Advent, www.newadvent .org/fathers/0103108.htm. For some Gnostic uses of New Testament passages, see Philip Jenkins, "Heracleon," August 4, 2013, www.pa theos.com/blogs/anxiousbench/2013/08/heracleon/.

25. For the Devil's power over the world, see Matthew 4.8–9 and John 14.30. The story of the wheat and the tares is found in Matthew 13.24–30.

26. The Prodigal Son story is from Luke 15.11–32. Cosmas is quoted from Hamilton and Hamilton, eds., *Christian Dualist Heresies*, 114–134; "Presbyter Cosmas's Sermon," www.bogomilism.eu /Other%20authors/Cosma.html. Frassetto, *Great Medieval Heretics*; Turdeanu, "Apocryphes bogomiles."

27. The story of the unjust steward is from Luke 16.1–13. Hamilton and Hamilton, eds., *Christian Dualist Heresies*, 183. For the Good Samaritan, see Stoyanov, *The Other God*, 285.

28. Turdeanu, "Apocryphes bogomiles."

29. Raynaldus, "On the Accusations Against the Albigensians," in Maitland, ed., *History of the Albigenses and Waldenses*, 392–394;

Edward Peters, ed., *Heresy and Authority in Medieval Europe* (Philadelphia: University of Pennsylvania Press, 1980), 123–124.

30. Hamilton and Hamilton, eds., *Christian Dualist Heresies*, 289–291.

31. "Cathar Ritual," The Gnosis Archive, http://gnosis.org/library /Cathar_Ritual-full_text.html; "Cathar Rites: The Apparelhamentum, from the *Lyons Ritual*," Fordham University, Medieval History, www.fordham.edu/Halsall/source/cathar-appara.asp.

32. This point about the ancient character is strongly made by Zoe Oldenbourg, *Massacre at Montségur* (New York: Minerva, 1968), 42–43.

33. Émile Turdeanu, *Apocryphes Slaves et Roumains de l'Ancien Testament* (Leiden: Brill, 1981); Andrei Orlov, *From Apocalypticism to Merkabah Mysticism* (Leiden: Brill, 2007); Andrei Orlov, *Selected Studies in the Slavonic Pseudepigrapha* (Leiden: Brill, 2009); Lorenzo DiTommaso and Christfried Böttrich, eds., *The Old Testament Apocrypha in the Slavonic Tradition* (Tübingen, Germany: Mohr Siebeck, 2011); Yuri Stoyanov, "Medieval Christian Dualist Perceptions and Conceptions of Biblical Paradise," *Studia Ceranea* 3 (2013): 149–166.

34. F. I. Anderson, "2 (Slavonic Apocalypse of) Enoch," in James H. Charlesworth, ed., *The Old Testament Pseudepigrapha*, 2 vols. (Garden City, NY: Doubleday, 1983–1985), 1:91–221; Andrei A. Orlov and Gabriele Boccaccini, eds., *New Perspectives on 2 Enoch* (Leiden: Brill, 2012).

35. For Leon Mung, see R. Rubinkiewicz, "Apocalypse of Abraham," in Charlesworth, ed., *Old Testament Pseudepigrapha*, 1:682–683; Kiril Petkov, *The Voices of Medieval Bulgaria* (Leiden: Brill, 2008). For other possible Jewish influences, see G. Macaskill, "The Slavonic Pseudepigrapha," 2007, University of St. Andrews, School of Divinity, www.st-andrews.ac.uk/divinity/rt/otp/abstracts/slavonic_intro/.

36. Stoyanov, *The Other God*, 265. For the Apocalypse of Abraham, see Alexander Kulik, *Retroverting Slavonic Pseudepigrapha* (Leiden: Brill, 2005). Jordan Ivanov, *Livres et Légendes Bogomiles* (Paris: Maisonneuve et Larose, 1976).

37. C. Detlef G. Müller, "The Ascension of Isaiah," in Wilhelm Schneemelcher, ed., *New Testament Apocrypha*, trans. R. McL. Wilson, rev. ed., 2 vols. (London: James Clarke, 1991–1992), 2:603–619; M. A. Knibb, "Martyrdom and Ascension of Isaiah," in Charlesworth, ed., *Old Testament Pseudepigrapha*, 2:143–176. "[Gabriel] the angel of the Holy Spirit" is quoted from Ascension of Isaiah 3.16–20, Early

Christian Writings, www.earlychristianwritings.com/text/ascension .html.

38. According to David Frankfurter, "The Ascension of Isaiah itself seems to have functioned centrally in Bogomil ideology." David Frankfurter, "The Legacy of Jewish Apocalypses in Early Christianity," in James C. VanderKam and William Adler, eds., *The Jewish Apocalyptic Heritage in Early Christianity* (Minneapolis: Fortress, 1996), 140. Wakefield and Evans, *Heresies of the High Middle Ages*, 449–456. "A certain book" is quoted from Hamilton, "Wisdom from the East," 52–53. Hamilton, "Bogomil Influences on Western Heresy," 107; Stoyanov, *The Other God*, 260–286.

39. These quotations are taken from the Vision of Isaiah, in Wakefield and Evans, *Heresies of the High Middle Ages*, 449–456.

40. This and the following quotations from the Secret Supper are from Wakefield and Evans, *Heresies of the High Middle Ages*, 458–463. See also "Cathar Gospel," www.fordham.edu/halsall/source/cathar -gospel.asp.

41. For the text's use of 2 Enoch, see Florentina Badalanova Geller, *2 (Slavonic Apocalypse of) Enoch* (Berlin: Max-Planck-Institut für Wissenschaftsgeschichte, 2010), www.mpiwg-berlin.mpg.de/Preprints /P410.PDF.

42. Sarah Hamilton, "The Virgin Mary in Cathar Thought," *Journal of Ecclesiastical History* 56 (2005): 24–49.

43. "Cathar Gospel," www.fordham.edu/halsall/source/cathar-gospel.asp.

44. "Said in my presence" is from Wakefield and Evans, *Heresies of the High Middle Ages*, 344, and also 362 for the account of Nazarius; Moore, *Birth of Popular Heresy*, 147; Sackville, *Heresy and Heretics*, 47; Hamilton, "Wisdom from the East"; Hamilton and Hamilton, *Christian Dualist Heresies*, 250.

45. Anselm of Alessandria is quoted in Wakefield and Evans, *Heresies of the High Middle Ages*, 361–372; and for Nazarius, see also 167.

46. Wakefield and Evans, *Heresies of the High Middle Ages*, 344. For Italian Catharism, see Carol Lansing, *Power and Purity* (New York: Oxford University Press, 1998).

47. Wakefield and Evans, *Heresies of the High Middle Ages*, 362–370. "That Christ brought His body down from heaven" is quoted from Sarah Hamilton, "The Virgin Mary in Cathar Thought," *Journal of Ecclesiastical History* 56 (2005): 24–49.

48. Wakefield and Evans, *Heresies of the High Middle Ages*, 363–364.

49. "When Satan saw Adam seated" is from "The Cave of Treasures," Internet Sacred Text Archive, www.sacred-texts.com/chr/bct/bct04.htm. For other crown imagery, see Dylan M. Burns, "Sethian Crowns, Sethian Martyrs?" *Numen* 6, no. 04 (2014): 55–68.

50. For the *Apocalypse of Moses*, see Charles F. Horne, ed., *The Sacred Books and Early Literature of the East* (New York: Parke, Austin and Lipscomb, 1917), 38, Internet Archive, http://archive.org/stream/The BooksOfAdamAndEve/the-books-of-adam-and-eve_djvu.txt.

51. "Adam Kadmon," Jewish Encyclopedia, www.jewishencyclopedia.com/articles/761-adam-kadmon.

52. Arthur Green, *A Guide to the Zohar* (Redwood City, CA: Stanford University Press, 2003). For clerical converts to Judaism, see Christoph Ochs, *Matthaeus Adversus Christianos* (Tübingen, Germany: Mohr Siebeck, 2013), 29–37. For Judaizing sects in the thirteenth century, see Louis I. Newman, *Jewish Influence on Christian Reform Movements* (New York: Columbia University Press, 1925), 240–302; Newman also discusses overlaps between Cathar and Qabalistic ideas (173–176).

53. Abolqasen Esmailpour, "Manichaean Gnosis and Creation Myth," in Victor H. Mair, ed., *Sino-Platonic Papers 156* (2005); Bayard Dodge, ed., *The Fihrist of al-Nadīm* (New York: Columbia University Press, 1970), 2:782, and 785–786 for the crown episode.

54. Robert E. Lerner, *The Heresy of the Free Spirit in the Later Middle Ages* (Berkeley: University of California Press, 1972); Raoul Vaneigem, *The Movement of the Free Spirit* (New York: Zone Books; Cambridge, MA: MIT Press, 1994); Frassetto, *Great Medieval Heretics*.

55. Wakefield and Evans, *Heresies of the High Middle Ages*, 81.

56. Norman Cohn, *The Pursuit of the Millennium*, rev. ed. (New York: Oxford University Press, 1970); Christopher W. Marsh, *The Family of Love in English Society, 1550–1630* (New York: Cambridge University Press, 1994); David R. Como, *Blown by the Spirit* (Redwood City, CA: Stanford University Press, 2004).

57. Lerner, *Heresy of the Free Spirit*; Lambert, *Medieval Heresy*, 199–207; Irene Leicht, *Marguerite Porete* (Freiburg im Breisgau, Germany: Herder, 1999).

58. Lerner, *Heresy of the Free Spirit*, 136–138; Vaneigem, *Movement of the Free Spirit*, 184–185; Gordon Leff, *Heresy in the Later Middle Ages* (Manchester, UK: Manchester University Press, 1999), 378–379.

59. Lerner, *Heresy of the Free Spirit*, 136–138.

CHAPTER EIGHT

1. "Then Jesus said" is from Lonsdale Ragg and Laura Ragg, eds., *Gospel of Barnabas*, 6th rev. ed. (Houston: M.B.I., 1991 [1907]), Internet Sacred Text Archive, www.sacred-texts.com/isl/gbar/gbar043 .htm. "O blessed time" is from the Gospel of Barnabas, chap. 44, Internet Sacred Text Archive, www.sacred-texts.com/isl/gbar/gbar044 .htm. For the whole text of the Gospel of Barnabas, see Internet Sacred Text Archive, www.sacred-texts.com/isl/gbar/.

2. Annette Yoshiko Reed, "Muslim Gospel Revealing the 'Christian Truth' Excites the *Da Vinci Code* Set," *Religion Dispatches*, May 22, 2014, www.religiondispatches.org/archive/atheologies/7888/_mus lim_gospel__revealing_the_christian_truth_excites_the_da_vinci _code_set/.

3. Philip Jenkins, *The Lost History of Christianity* (San Francisco: HarperOne, 2008).

4. See, especially, the work of Irfan Shahîd, whose books include *Byzantium and the Semitic Orient Before the Rise of Islam* (London: Variorum Reprints, 1988); *Byzantium and the Arabs in the Sixth Century*, 2 vols. (Washington, DC: Dumbarton Oaks Research Library and Collection, 1995–2002). François Nau, *Les Arabes Chrétiens de Mésopotamie et de Syrie du VIIe au VIIIe Siècle* (Paris: Imprimerie Nationale, 1933); Walter D. Ward, *Mirage of the Saracen* (Berkeley: University of California Press, 2015). For the religious background of these regions, see Philip Jenkins, "By the Rivers of Babylon," December 1, 2014, www.patheos.com/blogs/anxiousbench/2014/12/by -the-rivers-of-babylon/, and Philip Jenkins, "Christians in Babylon," December 5, 2014, www.patheos.com/blogs/anxiousbench/2014/12 /the-lords-family/.

5. Barbara Roggema, *The Legend of Sergius Baḥīrā* (Leiden: Brill, 2009).

6. G. W. Bowersock, *The Throne of Adulis* (New York: Oxford University Press, 2013).

7. *Arabia haeresium ferax* is quoted from Irfan Shahid, *Byzantium and the Arabs in the Fourth Century* (Washington DC: Dumbarton Oaks Library, 1984), 278.

8. P. L. Cheikho, SJ, "Quelques légendes islamiques apocryphes," *Mélanges de la Faculté Orientale, Université Saint-Joseph* 4 (1910): 33– 56; David Thomas, ed., *The Bible in Arab Christianity* (Leiden: Brill, 2007); Ibn Warraq, ed., *Koranic Allusions* (Amherst, NY: Prometheus Books, 2013).

9. James R. Edwards, "The Hebrew Gospel in Early Christianity," in Lee M. McDonald and James H. Charlesworth, eds., *"Non-Canonical" Religious Texts in Early Judaism and Early Christianity* (London: T&T Clark, 2012). For Aramaic sources, see Emran I. El-Badawi, *The Qur'ān and the Aramaic Gospel Traditions* (New York: Routledge, 2014). For the possible survival of Jewish-Christian gospel materials into tenth-century Islam, see John G. Gager, "Did Jewish Christians See the Rise of Islam?" in Adam H. Becker and Annette Yoshiko Reed, eds., *The Ways That Never Parted* (Tübingen, Germany: Mohr Siebeck, 2003), 361–372.

10. Christoph Luxenberg, *The Syro-Aramaic Reading of the Koran* (Berlin: Hans Schiler, 2007); Christoph Burgmer, *Streit um den Koran* (Berlin: Schiler Verlag, 2004).

11. For this dating of *Cave of Treasures*, see Alexander Toepel, "The Cave of Treasures," in Richard Bauckham, James R. Davila, and Alex Panayotov, eds., *Old Testament Pseudepigrapha: More Noncanonical Scriptures*, 2 vols. (Grand Rapids, MI: Wm. B. Eerdmans, 2013–?). For al-Khidr, see Qur'an 18.50; Philip Jenkins, "The Green Man and the King of Salem," October 7, 2013, www.patheos.com/blogs/anxiousbench/2013/10/the-green-man/.

12. See, especially, Qur'an 5, "The Table." Geoffrey Parrinder, *Jesus in the Qur'an* (Oxford: Oneworld, 1996).

13. Qur'an 3, *Imran*.

14. The Qur'an's reliance on apocryphal gospels is the subject of a sizable polemical literature. See, for instance, Ibn Warraq, *The Origins of the Koran* (Amherst, NY: Prometheus Books, 1998).

15. Qur'an 5.110. Compare "The Arabic Gospel of the Infancy of the Savior," New Advent, www.newadvent.org/fathers/0806.htm; see also Tony Burke, "The Arabic Infancy Gospel of Thomas," www.tonyburke.ca/infancy-gospel-of-thomas/the-arabic-infancy-gospel-of-thomas/.

16. Qur'an 18.9–26; Sebastian P. Brock, "Jacob of Serugh's Poem on the Sleepers of Ephesus," in Pauline Allen, Majella Franzmann, and Rick Strelan, eds., *I Sowed Fruits into Hearts* (Strathfield, Australia: St. Paul's, 2007), 13–30.

17. Qur'an 4.157–158; Mona Siddiqui, *Christians, Muslims, and Jesus* (New Haven, CT: Yale University Press, 2014).

18. Quran 4.171, translated by Yusuf Ali and Marmaduke Pickthall, respectively. For the possible Jewish-Christian presence in the world of early Islam, see Gager, "Did Jewish Christians See the Rise of Islam?" I mention the Ebionites here with some caution, as modern

Muslim controversialists argue for a major connection between that group and early Islam. Rhetorically, that serves to link Islam to the authentic and strictly monotheist roots of Christianity rather than with later Trinitarian distortions.

19. Emmanouela Grypeou, Mark Swanson, and David Thomas, eds., *The Encounter of Eastern Christianity with Early Islam* (Leiden: Brill, 2006); Sidney H. Griffith, *The Church in the Shadow of the Mosque* (Princeton, NJ: Princeton University Press, 2008); Samuel Noble and Alexander Treiger, eds., *The Orthodox Church in the Arab World, 700–1700* (DeKalb: Northern Illinois Press, 2014).

20. Siddiqui, *Christians, Muslims, and Jesus*; Tarif Khalidi, ed., *The Muslim Jesus* (Cambridge, MA: Harvard University Press, 2001).

21. Khalidi, ed., *Muslim Jesus*, 86.

22. Ibid., 53, 60, 71, 73, 201.

23. Bart Ehrman and Zlatko Pleše, *The Apocryphal Gospels* (Oxford: Oxford University Press, 2011), 351–367.

24. Khalidi, ed., *Muslim Jesus*, 75, 97. "Jesus meets a man" is from Tarif Khalidi, "Jesus Through Muslim Eyes," BBC, www.bbc.co.uk /religion/religions/islam/beliefs/isa.shtml; F. F. Bruce, *Jesus and Christian Origins Outside the New Testament* (Grand Rapids, MI: Wm. B. Eerdmans, 1974).

25. "Be in the middle" is from Khalidi, ed., *Muslim Jesus*, 107. "Become passers by" is from Gospel of Thomas 42, Early Christian Writings, www.earlychristianwritings.com/thomas/gospelthomas42.html. "Those who are with me "is from Wilhelm Schneemelcher, "Acts of Peter," in Wilhelm Schneemelcher, ed., *New Testament Apocrypha*, trans. R. McL. Wilson, rev. ed., 2 vols. (London: James Clarke, 1991– 1992), 2:297. "Blessed is he who sees" is from Khalidi, ed., *Muslim Jesus*, 106. "Do not own any wealth" is from ibid., 74. "I am near you" is from Ehrman and Pleše, *Apocryphal Gospels*, 367. "Satan accompanies the world" is from Khalidi, ed., *Muslim Jesus*, 91. "Why do you marvel at my signs?" is from Ehrman and Pleše, *Apocryphal Gospels*, 367. "Be skillful moneychangers" is from ibid., 363. "If people appoint you as their heads" is from Khalidi, ed., *Muslim Jesus*, 101.

26. Khalidi, *Muslim Jesus*, 31.

27. Ibid., 83, 117. For the Dialogue of the Savior, see Beate Blatz, "The Dialogue of the Saviour," in Schneemelcher, ed., *New Testament Apocrypha*, 1:300–312.

28. Quran 5.82. For monks' liking the Apocalypse of Paul, see Sozomen, *Ecclesiastical History*, Book VII, chap. 19, Christian Classics

Ethereal Library, www.ccel.org/ccel/schaff/npnf202.iii.xii.xix.html. For Jesus as an apocalyptic figure in Islam, see Zeki Saritoprak, *Islam's Jesus* (Gainesville: University Press of Florida, 2014).

29. For esoteric (*batiniya*) movements, see Malise Ruthven, *Islam in the World*, 3rd ed. (New York: Oxford University Press, 2006).

30. John V. Fine, *The Bosnian Church* (London: SAQI, Bosnian Institute, 2007 [1875]). For Bosnian Dualists, see Janet Hamilton and Bernard Hamilton, eds., with Yuri Stoyanov, *Christian Dualist Heresies in the Byzantine World, c. 650–c. 1450* (Manchester, UK: Manchester University Press, 1998), 254–259, 265–266, 276–277.

31. Krisztina Kehl-Bodrogi, Barbara Kellner Heinkele, and Anke Otter Beaujean, eds., *Syncretistic Religious Communities in the Near East* (Leiden: Brill, 1997); Gilles Veinstein, ed., *Syncretismes et Heresies dans l'orient Seldjoukide et Ottoman* (Leuven, Belgium: Peeters, 2005); Noel Malcolm, "Crypto-Christianity and Religious Amphibianism in the Ottoman Balkans," in Celia Hawkesworth, Muriel Heppell, and Harry Norris, eds., *Religious Quest and National Identity in the Balkans* (Basingstoke, UK: Palgrave Macmillan, 2001), 91–109.

32. John Toland, *Nazarenus, or Jewish, Gentile and Mahometan Christianity* (London: J. Brown, 1718). For good measure, Toland's volume also included evidence from a medieval Irish gospel manuscript, in which he claimed to find the traces of the authentic lost early faith. Alan Harrison, "John Toland and the Discovery of an Irish Manuscript in Holland," *Irish University Review* 22 (1992): 33–39; F. Stanley Jones, ed., *The Rediscovery of Jewish Christianity* (Atlanta: Society of Biblical Literature, 2012).

33. Ragg and Ragg, eds., *Gospel of Barnabas*.

34. Jan Joosten, "The Gospel of Barnabas and the Diatessaron," *Harvard Theological Review* 95 (2002): 73–96; Jan Joosten, "The Date and Provenance of the Gospel of Barnabas," *Journal of Theological Studies* 61 (2010): 200–215; Gerald Wiegers, "Gospel of Barnabas," Encyclopedia of Islam, http://referenceworks.brillonline.com/entries/encyclopaedia-of-islam-3/gospel-of-barnabas-COM_27509; Theodore Pulcini, "In the Shadow of Mount Carmel," *Islam and Christian-Muslim Relations* 12, no. 2 (2001): 191–209. For the extensive Muslim knowledge of Christian scripture in the later Middle Ages, see Lejla Demiri, ed., *Muslim Exegesis of the Bible in Medieval Cairo* (Leiden: Brill, 2013).

35. For possible Ebionite / Jewish-Christian survivals in the Gospel of Barnabas, see R. Blackhirst, "*Barnabas* and the Gospels," *Journal of Higher Criticism* 7 (2000): 1–22.

36. "1,500-Year-Old Handwritten Bible Kept in Ankara, Ministry Confirms," *Today's Zaman*, February 23, 2012, www.todayszaman.com/news-272334-1500-year-old-handwritten-bible-kept-in-ankara-ministry-confirms.html; Yoshiko Reed, "Muslim Gospel Revealing the 'Christian Truth.'"

37. Joosten, "The Gospel of Barnabas and the Diatessaron."

38. "The soldiers took Judas" is from Ragg and Ragg, eds., Gospel of Barnabas, chap. 217; "Then God, seeing," is from chap. 215.

39. "After Jesus had departed" is from ibid., chap. 222.

40. The story of Simon of Cyrene is reported in Irenaeus, *Against Heresies*, 24.4, The Gnosis Archive, http://gnosis.org/library/advh1.htm. Joseph A. Gibbons and Roger A. Bullard, "The Second Treatise of the Great Seth," in James M. Robinson, ed., *The Nag Hammadi Library in English*, 4th rev. ed. (Leiden: Brill, 1996), 332, 362–371, 332, The Gnosis Archive, http://gnosis.org/naghamm/2seth.html. Mani is quoted from Bayard Dodge, ed., *The Fihrist of al-Nadīm* (New York: Columbia University Press, 1970), 2:798.

41. Roelof van den Broek, ed., *Pseudo-Cyril of Jerusalem on the Life and the Passion of Christ* (Leiden: Brill, 2013).

42. "Christ our God was born" is from "The Synodicon," www.bogomilism.eu/Other%20authors/Butler-synodicon.html.

43. For conversions in this era, see Steven A. Epstein, *Purity Lost* (Baltimore: Johns Hopkins University Press, 2006). For debates over the Bible, see Sidney H. Griffith, "Arguing from Scripture," in Thomas J. Heffernan and Thomas E. Burman, eds., *Scripture and Pluralism* (Leiden: Brill, 2005).

44. A. F. J. Klijn, *Jewish-Christian Gospel Tradition* (Leiden: Brill, 1992).

45. For Talmudic references to Hebrew gospels circulating in Jewish circles, see James R. Edwards, "The Hebrew Gospel in Early Christianity," in Lee M. McDonald and James H. Charlesworth, eds., *"Non-Canonical" Religious Texts in Early Judaism and Early Christianity* (New York: T&T Clark, 2012), 134–135. Peter J. Tomson and Doris Lambers-Petry, eds., *The Image of the Judaeo-Christians in Ancient Jewish and Christian Literature* (Tübingen, Germany: Mohr Siebeck, 2003).

46. Christoph Ochs, *Matthaeus Adversus Christianos* (Tübingen, Germany: Mohr Siebeck, 2013); George Howard, *Hebrew Gospel of Matthew* (Macon, GA: Mercer University Press, 1995).

47. Compare Peter Schäfer, *Jesus in the Talmud* (Princeton, NJ: Princeton University Press, 2007). For earlier polemics, see Ruth Langer, *Cursing the Christians?* (New York: Oxford University Press, 2012). A classic work on the theme is R. Travers Herford, *Christianity in Talmud and Midrash* (London: Williams and Northgate, 1903).

48. Peter Schäfer, Michael Meerson, and Yaacov Deutsch, eds., *Toledot Yeshu ("The Life Story of Jesus") Revisited* (Tübingen, Germany: Mohr Siebeck, 2011); Morris Goldstein, *Jesus in the Jewish Tradition* (London: Macmillan, 1950), 148–154.

49. The *Toledot Yeshu* can also be found online; see Jewish and Christian Literature website, http://jewishchristianlit.com/Topics/Jewish Jesus/toledoth.html.

50. *Toledot Yeshu*, Jewish and Christian Literature, http://jewish christianlit.com/Topics/JewishJesus/toledoth.html.

51. James Carleton Paget, *Jews, Christians and Jewish Christians in Antiquity* (Tübingen, Germany: Mohr Siebeck, 2010).

52. Henry Chadwick, ed., *Contra Celsum* (Cambridge, UK: Cambridge University Press, 1953).

CHAPTER NINE

1. Virginia Nixon, *Mary's Mother* (University Park: Pennsylvania State University Press, 2004).

2. Diarmaid MacCulloch, *Reformation* (London: Allen Lane, 2003); Euan Cameron, *The European Reformation*, 2nd ed. (Oxford: Oxford University Press, 2012).

3. Brad S. Gregory, *The Unintended Reformation* (Cambridge, MA: Harvard University Press, 2012).

4. Irena Backus, *Historical Method and Confessional Identity in the Era of the Reformation (1378–1615)* (Leiden: Brill, 2003); R. Po-chia Hsia, ed., *A Companion to the Reformation World* (Oxford: Blackwell, 2004); R. Po-chia Hsia, ed., *Cambridge History of Christianity*, vol. 6 (Cambridge, UK: Cambridge University Press, 2006).

5. From a vast literature, there are concise accounts of this story in the venerable *Cambridge Modern History* (Cambridge, UK: Cambridge University Press, 1902–1903), especially the chapters by Richard C. Jebb and M. R. James on the classical Renaissance and the Christian Renaissance, respectively, pp. 532–619.

6. "Donation of Constantine," New Advent, www.newadvent.org /cathen/05118a.htm.

7. "St. Ignatius of Antioch," New Advent, www.newadvent.org/ca then/07644a.htm; Allen Brent, *Ignatius of Antioch* (London: Bloomsbury / T&T Clark, 2007).

8. For the growth of lay reading publics, see, for instance, Eamon Duffy, *The Stripping of the Altars*, rev. ed. (New Haven, CT: Yale University Press, 2005); MacCulloch, *Reformation*.

9. For issues of censorship and control, Kathryn Kerby-Fulton, *Books Under Suspicion* (Notre Dame, IN: University of Notre Dame Press, 2007).

10. Sheila M. Porrer, ed., *Jacques Lefèvre d'Étaples and the Three Maries Debates* (Geneva: Droz, 2009).

11. "Canon of the Old Testament," New Advent, www.newadvent .org/cathen/03267a.htm; Lee M. McDonald, *The Biblical Canon*, 3rd ed. (Peabody, MA: Hendrickson Publishers, 2007).

12. A. Wikgren, "Luther and 'New Testament Apocrypha,'" in R. H. Fischer, ed., *A Tribute to Arthur Vööbus* (Chicago: Lutheran School of Theology, 1977), 379–390.

13. Duffy, *Stripping of the Altars*.

14. "Concerning the Worship of the Church," Book of Common Prayer.

15. MacCulloch, *Reformation*.

16. Gary Waller, *The Virgin Mary in Late Medieval and Early Modern English Literature and Popular Culture* (Cambridge, UK: Cambridge University Press, 2011). For new forms of religious art and publishing, see David J. Davis, *Seeing Faith, Printing Pictures* (Leiden: Brill, 2013).

17. Tabitha Barber and Stacy Boldrick, eds., *Art Under Attack* (London: Tate, 2013).

18. Carlos M. N. Eire, *War Against the Idols* (Cambridge, UK: Cambridge University Press, 1989). "Proclaim and preach" is quoted from Lee Palmer Wanderl, *Voracious Idols and Violent Hands* (New York: Cambridge University Press, 1995), 166. For Geneva, see James Noyes, *The Politics of Iconoclasm* (London: I. B. Tauris, 2013), 23–58. Virginia Chieffo Raguin, ed., *Art, Piety and Destruction in the Christian West, 1500–1700* (Farnham, UK: Ashgate, 2010).

19. Sarah Brown, "Repackaging the Past," in Chieffo Raguin, ed., *Art, Piety and Destruction in the Christian West, 1500–1700*; Julie Spraggon, *Puritan Iconoclasm During the English Civil War* (Woodbridge, UK: Boydell Press, 2003); John Phillips, *The Reformation of Images* (Berkeley: University of California Press, 1973); Gary Waller, *The Virgin Mary in Late Medieval and Early Modern English Literature*

and Popular Culture (Cambridge, UK: Cambridge University Press, 2011).

20. For the Gospel of the Egyptians, see Early Christian Writings, www.earlychristianwritings.com/text/gospelegyptians.html.

21. "Canon of the Old Testament," New Advent, www.newadvent .org/cathen/03267a.htm; Bruce M. Metzger, *The Canon of the New Testament* (Oxford: Oxford University Press, 1997). For Christian debates over Jewish texts, see Avner Shamir, *Christian Conceptions of Jewish Books* (Copenhagen: Museum Tusculanum, 2009). The Granada affair is described in Mercedes García-Arenal and Fernando Rodríguez Mediano, *The Orient in Spain* (Leiden: Brill, 2013). For a similar controversy in seventeenth-century Italy, see Ingrid D. Rowland, *The Scarith of Scornello* (Chicago: University of Chicago Press, 2004).

22. John W. O'Malley, *Trent* (Cambridge, MA: Harvard University Press, 2013).

23. David R. Cartlidge and J. Keith Elliott, *Art and the Christian Apocrypha* (London: Routledge, 2001). In 1708, though, Handel did include the Harrowing of Hell in his oratorio *La Resurrezione*.

24. James Townley, *Illustrations of Biblical Literature Exhibiting the History and Fate of the Sacred Writings* (New York: Carlton and Porter, 1856), 2:235.

25. "'Tis one of the devil's proper plagues" is from Martin Luther, *Table Talk* (Boston: Mobile Reference, 2010), 771.

26. Magne Sæbø, ed., *Hebrew Bible, Old Testament* (Göttingen: Vandenhoeck and Ruprecht, 2008); Eugen J. Pentiuc, *The Old Testament in Eastern Orthodox Tradition* (New York: Oxford University Press, 2014).

27. Philip Jenkins, *The Lost History of Christianity* (San Francisco: HarperOne, 2008).

28. Hsia, ed., *Cambridge History of Christianity*, vol. 6. Compare John M. Flannery, *The Mission of the Portuguese Augustinians to Persia and Beyond* (Leiden: Brill, 2013).

29. Scaria Zacharia, *The Acts and Decrees of the Synod of Diamper 1599* (Edamattom, India: Indian Institute of Christian Studies, 1994); James Hough, *The History of Christianity in India* (London: R. B. Seeley and W. Burnside, 1839), 2:543–544.

30. William Wright, *A Catalogue of the Syriac Manuscripts Preserved in the Library of the University of Cambridge* (Cambridge, UK: Cambridge University Press, 1901), xxi.

31. Vahan S. Hovhanessian, ed., *The Canon of the Bible and the Apocrypha in the Churches of the East* (New York: Peter Lang, 2012).

32. Backus, *Historical Method and Confessional Identity*, 253–325.

33. For continuing post-Reformation interest in Mary Magdalene, see Bridget Heal, *The Cult of the Virgin Mary in Early Modern Germany* (Cambridge, UK: Cambridge University Press, 2007); Patricia Badir, *The Maudlin Impression* (Notre Dame, IN: University of Notre Dame Press, 2009).

34. Caroline H. Ebertshauser, Herbert Haag, Joe H. Kirchberger, and Dorothee Solle, *Mary: Art, Culture, and Religion Through the Ages*, trans. Peter Heinegg (New York: Crossroad, 1998).

35. Els Rose, *Ritual Memory* (Leiden: Brill, 2009).

36. I draw heavily here on the work of Annette Yoshiko Reed, for instance, in "The Modern Invention of Old Testament Pseudepigrapha," *Journal of Theological Studies* 60 (2009): 403–436.

37. Ibid.

38. Ibid. For Postel, see also Ariel Hessayon, "Og King of Bashan, Enoch and the Books of Enoch," in Ariel Hessayon and Nicholas Keene, eds., *Scripture and Scholarship in Early Modern England* (Farnham, UK: Ashgate, 2006), 1–40.

39. Backus, *Historical Method and Confessional Identity*, 253–262.

40. Ibid., 201–208, 218–229.

41. Yoshiko Reed, "Modern Invention of Old Testament Pseudepigrapha"; J. A. Fabricius, *Codex apocryphus Novi Testamenti* (1703); J. A. Fabricius, *Codex pseudepigraphus Veteris Testamenti* (1713); J. A. Fabricius, *Codicis pseudepigraphi Veteris Testamenti Volumen alterum* (1723).

42. John Toland, *Nazarenus, or Jewish, Gentile and Mahometan Christianity* (London: J. Brown, 1718).

43. Albert Schweitzer, *The Quest of the Historical Jesus* (Minneapolis: Fortress Press, 2001); Michael C. Legaspi, *The Death of Scripture and the Rise of Biblical Studies* (New York: Oxford University Press, 2010).

44. From many examples, see Alexander Walker, trans., *Apocryphal Gospels, Acts, and Revelations*, Ante-Nicene Christian Library 16 (Edinburgh, 1873); J. Rendel Harris, *The Newly-Recovered Gospel of St. Peter* (New York: James Pott, 1893); Bernard P. Grenfell and Arthur S. Hunt, eds., *New Sayings of Jesus and a Fragment of a Lost Gospel from Oxyrhynchus* (London: H. Frowde, 1904); R. H. Charles, *The Apocrypha and Pseudepigrapha of the Old Testament* (Oxford: Clarendon Press, 1913); Montague Rhodes James, *The Apocryphal New Testament* (Oxford: Clarendon Press, 1924).

45. Edgar J. Goodspeed, *Strange New Gospels* (Chicago: University of Chicago Press, 1931); Philip Jenkins, *Hidden Gospels* (New York: Oxford University Press, 2001).

46. For the rediscovery of Gnosticism, see Charles William King, *The Gnostics and Their Remains* (London: Bell and Dalby, 1864); G. R. S. Mead, ed., *Pistis Sophia* (London: J. M. Watkins, 1921 [1896]); G. R. S. Mead, *Fragments of a Faith Forgotten* (London: Theosophical Publishing Society, 1900); Clare Goodrick-Clarke and Nicholas Goodrick-Clarke, eds., *G. R. S. Mead and the Gnostic Quest* (Berkeley, CA: North Atlantic Books, 2005).

47. For feminist approaches, see Frances Swiney, *The Esoteric Teachings of the Gnostics* (London: Yellon, Williams, 1909). For *The Brook Kerith*, see Harold Orel, *Popular Fiction in England, 1914–1918* (Lexington: University Press of Kentucky, 1992); Jennifer Stevens, *The Historical Jesus and the Literary Imagination, 1860–1920* (Liverpool: Liverpool University Press, 2010).

48. Robert Graves, *King Jesus* (New York: Farrar, Straus and Cudahy, 1946).

CHAPTER TEN

1. The gospel's text can be found online at "The Aquarian Gospel of Jesus the Christ," Internet Sacred Text Archive, www.sacred-texts .com/chr/agjc/. Joseph Gaer, *The Lore of the New Testament* (Boston: Little, Brown, 1952).

2. "The Aquarian Gospel of Jesus the Christ."

3. Edgar J. Goodspeed, *Strange New Gospels* (Chicago: University of Chicago Press, 1931); Laurie F. Maffly-Kipp, *American Scriptures* (New York: Penguin Classics, 2010).

4. For Jesus in the cinema, see Peter Malone, *Screen Jesus* (Lanham, MD: Scarecrow, 2012).

5. Philip Jenkins, *Hidden Gospels* (New York: Oxford University Press, 2001).

6. Charlotte Allen, "The Wife of Jesus Tale," *Weekly Standard*, May 5, 2014, www.weeklystandard.com/articles/wife-jesus-tale_787360 .html. For the relative value of the canonical and noncanonical New Testament texts, see Jenkins, *Hidden Gospels*.

7. Robert Miller, *The Complete Gospels*, 4th ed. (Salem, OR: Polebridge, 2010); Hal Taussig, ed., *A New New Testament: A Bible for the 21st Century Combining Traditional and Newly Discovered Texts* (New York: Houghton Mifflin Harcourt, 2013). Compare Willis Barnstone, ed., *The Restored New Testament* (New York: W. W. Norton, 2009).

INDEX